NO SMALL MIRACLES

Testimonials Collected by a
Christian Writers Group

Photo by R.T. Byrum
Cover layout by Jeff Reeves

R.T. Byrum
www.rtbwriter.com
2005

NO SMALL MIRACLES

Stories of Faith
Collected by the
Christian Authors Guild

R. T. Byrum
Contributing Editor

CONTENTS

Foreword

The Christian Authors Guild was founded in 2000 as *The Cherokee Christian Writers Group*. The original name was a combination of founder Cheryl Norwood's faith and the Georgia county in which she lived. As our membership grew we expanded beyond the county, and even beyond the borders of our state. Our new name reflects that growth in size, area, and purpose. It was Cheryl's dream to create an organization to help her and others improve their writing skills, while sharing their Christian faith with each other and with readers of their works. She believed that her writing was a gift to be used in a ministry that could wash like a Christian Wave over the secular world she lived in.

The Apostle Matthew recorded Jesus' parable of the talents: rich in metaphor, it is the story of a man traveling in the far country who calls his three servants together and entrusts to each, according to their character, a number of talents (a Hebrew measure of monetary value.) They are told to watch over the master's money until he returns. The servant receiving two talents and the one guarding over the five talents each made investments and doubled their amounts. The servant entrusted with one talent buried it until it was redeemed.

When the master returned, he was presented with the two talents that had grown to four and the five talents that had grown to ten. He was sorely angered when the servant entrusted with the single talent returned the same, without even having deposited it with a lending institution that would have paid interest. His talent was taken from him, he was sent away in disgrace, and the talent was then given to the most profitable servant.

Recently, while rereading Matthew chapter 25, I was able to see how closely that parable related to the goals of our guild. Our members were given writing talents to use and increase—and we have. How? By using our God-given talents to improve ourselves, our families, and the world community in which we live. The book you are holding is an example. By daring to step out and take the challenge of writing, even outside of our natural genre' and preference, we are multiplying our gift and sharing the increase with people far beyond the walls of our meeting rooms.

How did this miracle happen? Most club meetings include a lesson related to an element of writing, presented by professionals, who show us how to: become successful authors, get an agent, write a query, use word processing tools, market our work, and how to do countless other valuable things that improve our writing. Awards are given, not only for getting published, but for receiving rejections (which shows that the writer is at least trying.)

The bi-monthly meetings are well-planned and include time for refreshments and socializing with each other and with the speaker of the evening. It is a time of uplifting and of strengthening, a time of sharing and inspiring, and a time of breaking through the bugaboo of writer's block that we all occasionally experience.

Although I have been a published columnist for years, I felt this club would be a place where I could strengthen my existing writing and grammar skills. I found myself looking forward to these meetings and have been able to publicize the guild through my articles. The word is spreading that the Christian Authors Guild has something going for it, spirit and service, and both new and experienced writers want to be a part of it.

Several sponsored chapters are being planned and will be raised up in the proper time. These new groups will benefit from receiving the monthly newsletter, *The Wave*, from visits from our own professional speakers, and from guidance given by our officers as they grow into their own.

Today, we are a group of individuals ranging in age from writers in their twenties to me—age 77. We encourage one another, we critique one another in a loving manner, and we pray for one another and for one another's families. That's because we *are* family, a family of Christian writers who live in a secular world, but have a Christian message that needs to be spread around the world with the power of a tsunami wave—a Christian tsunami.

Donald Conkey

No Small Miracle
by R.T. Byrum

The year of the miracle, the assigned site for my family to attend our church's worldwide conference was in Pensacola, Florida. The sermons had inspired my wife and me, and the worship services had even impressed our four school-age sons. The final message was the call to be a witness—to spread the good news, not by preaching on a street corner, but by serving others as an example. Along with the congregation, I prayed that God would open doors for me to witness for Him.

Not that I needed help. After all, a well-worn bible was prominently displayed on my desk at work. If a client or vendor asked if I studied the scriptures, I would nod and smile. They might even ask me a bible question that I could answer, and we would talk about God over lunch. Maybe that wasn't exactly the proactive witnessing the church had been admonished to do, but I *was* spreading the word, and that had to count for something. God would understand.

The conference had ended, and, following the closing prayer, my family and I had returned to our rooms for the last time before checkout. That afternoon we would finish packing and leave the beautiful Gulf Coast for our home in Atlanta. For now, my sons were enjoying a swim with friends they wouldn't see again for a whole year, and my wife was browsing through the hotel gift shop. As for me, I was relaxing on our ground floor patio, enjoying the latest Clive Cussler novel.

I don't know why I glanced up from my book to notice the lone figure several hundred yards down the beach, but I did. The barefoot girl, possibly in her twenties, was dressed in faded blue jeans and a long-sleeved flannel shirt, which protected her against the stiff morning breeze that rolled the waves shoreward as a child with a stick rolls a hoop. Eddies of wind-tossed sand danced around her, making her turn this way and that to avoid the stinging grains, but she never retreated.

Her dark shoulder-length hair, soaked with spray, hung limply around her face. Something else that I noticed was the way her shoulders seem to sag as if carrying a heavy burden. I tried to return to my book, but my eyes kept straying to the girl. I wondered what was driving her to endure such discomfort.

She would walk a few steps, pause, and then stoop to sift sand through her fingers before moving on. As she neared, the unexpected sound of sobbing separated itself from the rush and fall of waves and constant moaning of the wind. My book, now resting on my lap, was urgently summoning me to discover how Dirk Pitt would get out of the sacrificial well where he had been thrown by terrorists, yet a stronger urge was lifting me out of my chair—and my comfort zone—and onto the sand.

I crossed the fifty yards or so of beach, mirroring the girl's dodging and turning movements to shield my face from the driven sand. The sky was filling with dirty cotton clouds, tempting me to run back to the hotel, gather up my family, and leave before the storm hit. An even more powerful force kept pushing me forward.

She didn't notice me until I touched her arm. Startled, she quickly dabbed at her eyes with her shirtsleeve. I introduced myself and asked if she needed assistance. "No, thank you. I—I lost my keys, that's all."

I nodded my understanding and asked, "Room keys?"

She sighed and wiped her eyes again. "No, I could deal with losing those. I'm supposed to be on the road back to Georgia to meet my grandmother. She's flying in this evening from Indiana—her first time on an airplane, and if I'm not there to meet her, she'll be very frightened."

"And that has something to do with your keys?"

"They're for my Volkswagen and for my apartment back home. I didn't bring any spares with me…I feel so helpless."

"I'm sorry. I wish I…" My tongue froze. YE SHALL BE WITNESSES…the words of the sermon rose above the wind and waves. Glancing over my shoulder at miles of beach, I opened my mouth and blurted, "Let me help."

Why did I say that? We had eight hours of travel ahead and nasty weather closing in.

"What did the key ring look like?" I asked. *What was I thinking? She might have left them back at the pool or in the gift shop, and I just committed to searching this endless sand pile for them.*

Suddenly it dawned on me. I had prayed this morning for opportunities to witness. Maybe God was testing my sincerity. *What did your key ring look like?* Yes, I was committed.

"Oh, a—a round chrome thingy that the keys fit on, and…umm…a blue and white plastic disk with a VW emblem. You're very kind, but this is my third trip up and down the beach to as far as I've gone since coming here. I guess I'll have to fly back to meet Grandma, get a locksmith for my apartment, and then fly back with a spare key to pick up my car."

I didn't want to fill her with false hope, or cause her to miss a flight, but a powerful presence was driving me. "Tell you what, Miss…"

"Janet."

"Janet…you finish your search as far as you've been in that direction, and I'll trace back the other way to your hotel. It's worth one more shot with two pair of eyes."

"Are you sure? I don't want to take up your time."

I nodded. "I'm sure." By now, I really was. What's more, I saw a touch of the sun appearing between the clouds. We humans love signs, and this looked like one.

"My hotel's the tall light green one next to the board walk." She pointed it out, smiled weakly, then continued her start, stop, stoop, and sift motions away from me. The sky continued to clear.

Raising my face into the slackening breeze, I silently prayed; "Lord, I know You're not in the business of recovering lost keys, but if You're giving me this chance to witness, then use me to help this girl."

Even before opening my eyes, I heard a metallic tinkling; the sound a ring full of keys might make when being coaxed ashore by the fingertips of a dying wave. When I dared to look, jewel-like reflections from brass and silver sprinkled up my shirt and across my glasses.

I stooped and grasped a plastic disk embellished with a VW symbol. Suspended on the round chrome *thingy* were car and apartment keys. Now *I* was sobbing. I held the ring high and waved it back and forth through the narrow beams of sunlight. I could see her suddenly stand and turn as if I had shouted her name, although I hadn't.

She ran. I ran. We met—we cried, and then we laughed.

"Are you some kind of angel?" Janet asked, her eyes searching my face.

"Not hardly, but I *do* know their boss, and He occasionally sends an angel to help me out. You see, my family and I are here for our annual church convention, and with so many believers in Pensacola, I know that God walks among us."

"That's so amazing. Grandma belongs to that same church and she is flying out after her conference ends, too. She's tried to get me to attend at least once with her, but I've always been too busy. Maybe this small miracle with my keys is a wakeup call for me. Thanks, again. I'll never forget what you've done for me."

"Don't thank me, I'm only His instrument." I pointed skyward. "However, you might take your grandmother up on her invitation when you see her. Then you can thank my angel's boss in person."

She smiled as she shook my hand, then with a wave she sprinted back to her hotel.

I glanced up at the last of the gold-tinged clouds still masking the sun. "God, You have all the power to create a universe, to calm the seas, to raise the dead, and yet You took the time to return a small ring of keys. As I've witnessed your power and mercy to Janet, You have witnessed to me."

That happened more than twenty years ago, and I still think about what Janet called "this small miracle with my keys." Her life may have been forever changed by the experience. And me? I *know* my faith and trust in the infinite mercy of the Father grew that morning. Think about it. A God-sent angel may have stooped to fish a set of keys out of the limitless reaches of the ocean to drop them at my feet in answer to a ten-second prayer. To me, that's no 'small miracle.'

Lessons in Listening
From a Two-Carrot Writer
by Scarlett Smith

It is hard to pinpoint just when I started using carrots for earplugs. Maybe a teacher caught me daydreaming and asked if I was paying attention, or if I had carrots in my ears. The origin of the analogy is a mystery, but carrots are a good choice because they are obvious and uncomfortable. The present term, which sounds as though it originated in academia, is selective hearing.

Bad reception, low battery, carrots, or whatever; I was guilty of avoiding or denying God's voice many times in my life. When I listened for an answer and did not get a response, it was because I stayed tuned in only for words I wanted to hear or ones which made sense to me. My lessons in listening not only improved my hearing but also my vision to see God's creative work in my life.

The bittersweet tragedies of giving birth twice to premature babies who died, inspired me to write the story, *The Gift of a Child,* which was printed in the Atlanta newspapers. Not only did God bless my husband and me but, perhaps half a million readers who we will never know. God marketed my story. I just put a pen to paper and wrote what I experienced.

Writing has always been my passion but I decided not to pursue it as a career because the college professor of my Journalism 101 class required students to interview people living in the area. Being an introvert, I retreated from the challenge. I did not think creative writing required verbal communication skills but the Journalism Department did, so I dropped the class and switched my major.

My next choice of curriculum was art. Drawing was fun, but I had no idea what I would do with an art degree. It did not matter because all my instructors gave my projects the same comment, "messy." Late in my third year, I found the most suitable alternative was Family Services with a Counseling option. Making academic decisions had been a struggle and although I prayed about them, I was not perceptive to God's answers.

Whatever job I had after graduation, I incorporated my writing skills in business letters, newsletters, reports, inter-office communications and all of my activities. As I matured, I felt the increasing pain from the carrots in my ears. They restricted my relationship with God.

The regular trials of being single and independent woman were normal, but continued for a much longer period than I had hoped. When I was 33 years old, I needed an operation to explore my reproductive system and remove a large tumor, which looked cancerous. I was devastated. If there was a chance I might marry, I did not want to lose my ability to conceive but I also did not want to be bitter at God regardless of the outcome,.

My conversations with Him were one-sided because each time, I automatically put the carrots in and did not listen. While in recovery, my mother softly put her head to mine and whispered, "They didn't take anything." Surely, having children would be in my future or God would not have let me keep all the necessary parts.

I was lonely and miserable by age 36. I did not want to be an elderly spinster with no family to look after me. Even at this age, I could still get married and have children, but God needed to hurry up because time was fleeting. I implored Him to fulfill my longing for marriage or take away the desire. Once weeping, I vowed never to date again unless God brought the right man to me. I followed with a query, "God, when will you do this?"

Feeling sorry for myself, I did not expect a reply. But, I finally heard one. It was as if God spoke so quickly my mind understood what He said but my ears could not hear it fast enough to consider it audible. God said, "Three."

The word was clear but I did not understand if I would meet the guy in three years or be married in three years. If it was three years for each event, it would be another six years of waiting. Before I could formulate another question, God countered, "If I told you, would it make a difference in how you live your life now?" I bit my lip and shrugged.

I could not speculate God's will. Three months later, I met Chris and three months afterward, we were married in the third month of the New Year. We wanted to have children but I had infertility problems for a few years. After two early miscarriages and passing my 40th birthday, I was consumed with empty womb anxiety. I convinced my husband to let us try in vitro fertilization. Maybe I was right to step out and see if God blessed this choice. I presumed He did not object or He would clearly let me know. I was not listening for His direction, I just wanted Him to okay my decision.

Spending mega bucks, controlling my reproductive system by forcing it with drugs, and making daily visits to the clinic was draining on our marriage. My old female anatomy could only produce three eggs, which was pitifully low. Three embryos were implanted but none attached. The doctor concluded it was highly unlikely I would ever get pregnant and advised me to quit the program. Disappointed, I wondered why God had allowed me to waste all that time. Possibly, my impatience denied I heard Him as though I had cultivated carrots in my ears.

Three months later, complaining of flu-like symptoms, I was shocked by the announcement I had morning sickness. After giving up my attempt to manipulate God's timing, I was pregnant by natural means.

My water broke before six months into the pregnancy. A week later, a son arrived surpassing everyone's estimations. The baby was three months early but he had developed adequately and was given a good prognosis for survival. He thrived for 18 days then suddenly died. My heart was broken, but I was thankful God allowed me to have the pregnancy and time to bond with my baby.

Three months later, I was pregnant again! God did it before and He was doing it again. Chris and I were cautious about our expectations, but we were hopeful. I was in the fourth month when my water broke but I carried the baby for four more weeks. My second son was perfectly formed but his lungs were not developed sufficiently. He held on for 18 hours before his tiny body could not continue. It was a short, but significant life.

Chris and I were stronger in our conviction to remain ardent and we accepted the peace that only a loving creator could give. Wanting to share my perspective with others who experienced similar losses, I helped start the first Parent-to-Parent Volunteer Group at a hospital. As a volunteer, I edited the Perinatal Loss Department's newsletter for five years and wrote many articles about grief. Writing was healing.

I also worked a few hours a week in a nursery to dote on babies. Chris cut his office hours short to coach middle school basketball at a Christian school. Working with children attributed to mending our sorrow.

Both of us appreciated being asked to explain how we remained tenacious in our faith. It was not our measure of faith but it was God being faithful to us. That trust sustained our expectations for some new demonstration of His love.

The mother of a player on Chris's team approached me after a championship game asking if we would be interested in adopting. Appropriately named Faith, she knew of a college student who was pregnant and needed to find adoptive parents for the baby. Although she did not know us personally, Faith had heard about our losses and was sensitive to our situation because she was our age and had two adopted sons. She was encouraged to meet us by a friend who coincidentally happened to be our attorney's wife. Chris and I were honored for the consideration. Hopefully, we thought, Faith would call us soon with the next step.

A month later, we read a notice of Faith's death. Apparently, she had been very ill but Faith persevered that day to watch her son's final game of the season and to meet us. A few weeks later she was gone. Not knowing the names of the people involved in the adoption situation, I thought my hope had died with Faith.

Nevertheless, God carried out His plan. Knowing she was close to death, Faith had told her husband to contact us with the information we needed to pursue the adoption. Her last mission was completed. Everything, every detail, progressed in meticulous order. My daughter practically dropped out of heaven, into my heart and rested in my cradling arms. My life's story needed updating to include what it was missing—Joy.

Even though I had the beautiful baby I long awaited, I wanted to continue aiding and encouraging other mothers who experienced pregnancies ending with demise.

Part of the healing process is sequencing the events around a loss and trying to see how each one affected another. Journaling helped me. From my notes, I wrote an essay about God's grace through my adversities. Every few months, I would retrieve the pages from a stack of unfinished projects and edit the story. I wondered if it had a purpose. Carrots were interfering again or God was too quiet. If only one person benefited from my writing, it would be worthwhile.

One evening, my husband and I planned to meet at a restaurant for dinner after I completed some errands. Using idle time between stops, I sat in the car and organized my purse, which as usual, was full of lists, notes, receipts, coupons and miscellaneous papers. Signs of an unfocused writer. In a side pocket was a check my mother-in-law had sent for Christmas. My routine was to put deposits on my visor. After the last errand, I rendezvoused with Chris to eat. Returned to my car after dinner, I glanced up at the visor and did not see the check. It was not there.

Frantically searching the car and my purse, I concluded I dropped it some place on my route. The amount of the check was not a concern, but I would feel awful telling Chris's mother I lost it. Guilty of carelessness, I repeatedly asked God to help me locate the check. I wanted Him to show me where it was, I did not think to listen to Him. The word "sweatshirt" popped into my mind, but I dismissed it because I had already checked my waistband and my pockets. I thought about what I did at the places I had been to in the last few hours, and returned to each one retracing my steps to no avail.

It was very late when I drove back to the restaurant and inspected every inch of the empty parking lot. Defeated, I sat in the car not wanting to give up. For some reason I patted down my sweatshirt where it bunches up in front when I sit. There was the check, tucked between two rolls of fleece. All this time, it was right on me. "God, why didn't you tell me when I asked you instead of letting me waste hours hunting?"

As soon as I realized how the question sounded, I sat up straight, knowing a lesson was congealing. My subconscious was speaking for God. "I told you it was in the sweatshirt. Does my voice have to be blaring for you to pay attention? You are the one who needs to adjust the volume by keeping your ears open."

The comment must have implicated the carrots I always stuck in my ears. Curiously, I looked up the Bible verse referring to "God's still small voice." I yanked a carrot out as I was assured God speaks loudly and He speaks softly, whichever decibel He uses, He does speak in different ways. I needed to listen.

A Christian writing group advertised in my community's newspaper. I promptly joined and found the encouragement I needed to keep writing. A couple months later, in December, the president of the club announced an opportunity for submissions to the Atlanta Journal-Constitution ("AJC"). The search was for a Christmas story concerning sadness and joy. Mine definitely conveyed "weep and leap" feelings but I did not think it had much of a chance with a liberal paper.

The editor called me the next day and said everyone in her office cried over my story and she wanted to publish it. She explained how unusual it was to receive a piece not needing editing and chopping, even coming from the newspaper staff. Mine did not need any changes, which she emphasized was a high compliment. It was hard for me to believe because my writing was not polished. Twice AJC photographers came to take pictures. The publication date was set the Saturday before Christmas.

My husband got up before daylight to purchase copies. The sign on the newspaper stand read, *Local Mom Gets Miracle Baby!* We had to laugh envisioning a 1930's newspaper boy waving and yelling, "Read all about it! Baby drops from sky!" My blatantly Christian story was the lead on the front page of the Faith and Values section and ran over to the second page. It was amazing.

A narrative with sensitive content, referencing God, not especially written well and likely had limited appeal, was published in mainstream journalism. I would have been satisfied if one person read it, but more than 600,000 issues were printed and distributed over many states. God was using his amplified voice and I clearly heard. With the carrots out, it was almost too much. The essay was not impressive semantics but by honoring Him, it was like the light over the manger shining on his son.

A woman in my writing group encouraged me to send my article to a contest sponsored by the Amy Foundation, which supports the formation of church writing groups and the commitment to discipleship. The Amy Writing Awards program annually recognizes authors presenting Biblical truths applied to current issues in secular publications. Mine fit the basic criteria so I sent a copy of the article, not anticipating success, but then I received a notice that my story was in the top 15 winners out of 1000 entries. It won a national award.

When I read the anthology book including my entry, I was humbled by the biographies of the other winners. All of them were seasoned; published authors, clergy, columnists, scholars or combinations of those professions. My biography invaded a very respectable group of esteemed professionals. I had no previously published work. I was a homemaker and volunteer, a latent writer with no credentials.

My lessons in listening came from the curriculum of life in an imperfect world. God granted me the gift of writing, therefore faith will influence what I write. I continue to find carrots growing but now I eat them.

The Diamond
by Diana J. Baker

My mother and I have always had a great relationship, and as I grew up, she often blessed me with unexpected surprises. My most treasured surprise came in the form of a graduation gift.

Just before I finished high school, the band on mother's wedding ring wore through, prompting my dad to buy her a new set of rings for their anniversary.

Mother then had a jeweler mount the main diamond from her original engagement ring in a ring for me. When she presented me with the ring, she shared the following story:

"When I was pregnant with you, the diamond fell out of my engagement ring. Fearing that it had gone down the bathroom drain, I knelt beside the sink to see if there was a way to take the drainpipe loose. Much to my relief, I felt the diamond on the floor under my hand.

I took the ring and the diamond to a jeweler, who reset the diamond. I wore the ring for eighteen more years, until the day the band wore through.

When your dad bought my new rings, I had the diamond from my original engagement ring set in this ring for you."

I treasured my ring, a daily reminder of my parents' love for each other and for me, and was very protective of it.

One weekend, I went home from college with a friend. That night, while I was crawling around the floor playing with her little sister, I happened to glance at my hand. My heart sank. The diamond in the ring was gone!

I had no idea if I had just lost the stone or if it had been missing for awhile.

My friend, her little sister, and I crawled around their living room floor frantically digging in the dark shag carpet looking for the diamond. Silently I prayed, "Please, God, you know how much this ring means to my mother and to me. Please let me find the diamond,"

Within minutes, God answered my prayer, and I found the diamond buried in the carpet. You can believe I was praising the Lord.

I took the diamond and the ring home with me the next weekend. My mother took it back to the jeweler to be reset and then returned it to me the following weekend.

A number of years passed during which time I married a great guy and birthed four beautiful children. God called my husband into the ministry, so we moved to New Orleans, where he attended the New Orleans Baptist Theological Seminary. During that time, the diamond fell out of my ring again. This time I heard the stone hit the floor and quickly retrieved it.

Since we had a large family and a limited income, I knew I would have to wait for awhile before I could get the ring repaired. I placed the diamond and the band in a small, brown envelope, sealed it, and stuck it in my jewelry box for safekeeping. There it remained for several years.

The Lord opened new doors for our family after Larry finished seminary, and we moved from New Orleans to Canton, Georgia. We rented an old, run-down farmhouse until we were able to buy a home of our own.

One afternoon, I walked into my bedroom and found my jewelry box setting on the bed. Without my permission, one of my children had gotten it down to look at my jewelry. There lay the opened envelope on the bed beside the jewelry box.

My heart began to pound as I hurried across the room. One peep into the envelope confirmed my worst fear. The ring was inside—but the diamond was missing! My daughter tearfully confessed that it had fallen out on the floor.

My husband, my children, and I spent hours digging in that three-inch red, shag carpet looking for the diamond—to no avail.

I dreaded the thought of calling to tell my mother about the loss, so I put off the call for several weeks. I also put off vacuuming our bedroom. However, when I began to have unbearable allergy problems, I knew I had no choice but to vacuum.

Reluctantly, I pulled the vacuum cleaner, a wonderful old hand-me-down with a long hose and a thin nozzle, out of the closet and drug it into the bedroom. I set the vacuum near the bed where the diamond had been lost and plugged it in. I uttered one last prayer, "Lord, please let me find my diamond."

I turned on the vacuum, got down on my knees, leaned my weight on the back of my left hand, and began swishing the nozzle back and forth across the carpet. To my utter amazement, the diamond popped out of the carpet and landed squarely in the palm of my left hand.

As you can imagine, there was rejoicing in our house that night. My guilty child was restored, and I had a great opportunity to share with my children about how faithful God is to hear and answer our prayers.

It was a joy to call my mother and give her a praise report instead of a negative report about the lost diamond.

God is faithful, and He loves to answer the prayers of His children—especially when the answers strengthen our faith and create deeper bonds of family unity and love.

The Drug Lord
by Jennifer Evans

Mom was in her mid-forties when she and my father parted ways. Since my sister and I were already settled in our own homes, she did not ask for alimony. Instead, choosing to work, she first taught high school art classes and later served in a girls' shelter as a counselor, and also acquired experience as a recreational therapist in a nursing home.

As an Air Force wife for over half her married life, Mom learned to use her creativity to fix whatever problem came along. She told me she learned to repair things by following her father around and watching him work. She fixed toilets, teddy bears, cords on appliances, and any furniture that needed to be reupholstered. After keeping a tight budget for groceries all those years, she could write a book entitled: *One Hundred Ways To Cook Ground Beef.*

Mom always loved to paint, and when I was in high school, she went back to college to earn her bachelor's degree in studio art. Some people may have a nostalgic moment when they smell brownies baking, chicken frying, or a certain perfume that reminds them of their mother. For me, that happens whenever I smell turpentine or see brushes standing in a jar. During lean times, she bought canvas from a sale table at a fabric store and stretched it across her own hand-made frames. Then she treated them with a white, pasty stuff called gesso to make it possible to paint them with oils. While we were stationed in Alaska, she even did paintings on pieces of tree bark. "Where there is a will, there is a way," she would remind us with a smile.

Music is another of her passions. Throughout my childhood, a reel-to-reel tape recorder stayed available to fill our house with the mellow tones of Jim Reeves or Perry Como. When I was eleven, Mom and Dad bought a secondhand piano. I wanted to learn to play, but Mom decided to find out how serious I was about it first. She taught me for several months until I mastered the basics. Growing up, I assumed there was very little my 'mommy' couldn't do.

I was working overseas when Mom took a job selling insurance. I never understood the advantages of commissioned work over a salaried job but knowing Mom, I reasoned there was method in her madness. Although she often admitted that money was tight, her simple faith carried her through. She always trusted God to make ends meet, or to give her a creative idea to fill the gap.

It was on a Monday night in one of those two-week periods between commission checks that her tithe and the telephone bill had finished off the last of Mom's money. She was grateful for a freezer full of food and enough gas in her car for the interim. She knew how to be frugal. At 10:30 she had begun her nighttime routine: feed the cats, be sure the doors are locked, turn off the TV, then go to the kitchen to take her medicine.

She opened the Atenolol her doctor had prescribed and gently tilted the bottle without thinking. Out rolled one pill. Her heart skipped a beat as she poked her index finger into the empty bottle to be sure none of the precious blood pressure medicine had stuck to the bottom. Not one pill was left! Her creative mind kicked in—*Maybe I left some in a suitcase when I went to visit the grandkids.* She checked. Nothing.

The medicine cabinet in the bathroom yielded the same result. She searched through dresser drawers, a nightstand beside the bed; through coat pockets and retired purses stored on the closet shelf. Finally, she had to admit that there was no more Atenolol in the house, and she couldn't buy any for two weeks. Anxiety gripped her heart, but she refused to let fear take over. This time, she couldn't fix it. No amount of ingenuity, creativity or artistic license could provide a solution to meet this crisis.

"Lord," she prayed aloud, as she often did, "You know I need this medicine. I don't know what You're going to do about it, but I am not going to worry. It's in Your hands." With that said, she felt a calming peace settle over her. Since there was nothing further she could do that night, she laid the empty container on top of her purse, intending to fill it when her check came in. Then she brushed her teeth and went to bed.

Tuesday dawned bright and clear. She dressed carefully, knowing she had clients to visit that day. *I wonder what time I need to leave,* she thought, and went to find her purse to check her day-timer. There lay the prescription bottle, just as she'd left it the night before. She lifted it to unzip the bag, but halted in her tracks. Something inside rattled as it shifted. She shook it more intentionally. There was no mistake: something was inside that bottle. With trembling hands, she gently pried off the lid. There inside were sixteen Atenolol capsules! Chills washed over her body as tears welled up in her eyes.

See how much I love you, she heard the Lord whisper to her heart. *Ask, and you will receive.* It was the miracle of the widow's oil, except it was the widow's prescription. The medicine lasted two days beyond when her check arrived.

People inherit all kinds of things from their parents, but the one thing I would like to inherit from my mother is her faith. Perhaps I should just follow her around and watch her Father work.

A Journey of Discovery
by Lloyd Blackwell

It happened in 1945, at an old historic country Methodist Church near Oneonta, Alabama where my paternal grandfather and great-grandfather had preached many years earlier. My twin brother Floyd and I had walked the mile to Lebanon Methodist Church for Sunday school and preaching the previous three years, until dad gave up his career as a sharecropper, sold his mules and moved closer to town. The four-mile walk back to church was a little too much so Floyd and I gave up church attendance for about two years.

When dad eventually got an old beat-up automobile—a 1936 Plymouth coupe – he still never drove us to church nor offered to do so. He was not a bad dad, he just did not go to church, nor talk about religious matters. In fact, I never remember it being discussed until he developed cancer the second time at age 77. Even then I was the one who brought it up to him, concerning his salvation. He insisted he had accepted Christ as a child, but did not care for "organized religion." I finally accepted this as fact.

Mother was a Christian but was generally unable to walk to church because of bad health. She did attend church in her older years when they moved to Birmingham. The local Methodist Church was only three blocks from their home after their move. However, I never remember dad going to a church, except for a funeral. He did not object to the rest of us going, it was just not one of his great interests.

Our grandfather Blackwell was a bi-vocational preacher and a farmer most of his adult life. Granddad and grandmother would usually drive from Pueblo, Colorado to visit us for two or three weeks each year. Ever since I could remember—about age five—they came, usually in a Model-A Ford. However, this particular year they came in a black 1941 Chevrolet four-door sedan, a certain sign of prosperity so soon after World War II. Our first ride in it was something very special, and a memorable event for two impressionable boys with little experience with automobiles.

This was our grandparents first visit to the new house we had just built out of used weathered lumber from a greasy automobile repair shop dad had salvaged. It looked like Joseph's coat of many faded colors. We did have a sink with running cold water in the kitchen, our first. However, there was no indoor toilet. Our familiar basic outhouse was located behind our house, near the small barn where we kept our cow. The house had a good roof, a front porch and three bedrooms. For the first time in our lives Floyd and I did not have to sleep on the floor in the living room when our grandparents came to visit.

I am convinced God has a sense of humor; and has his own timing. Granddad and grandmother were visiting us during the late summer of 1945. When visiting us, they would go to Lebanon Methodist Church for Sunday services. They not only knew most of the people there, they had several relatives who were members. My grandfather and great-grandfather had even preached there in previous years. They would occasionally attend another old Methodist church that my grandfather and great-grandfather helped establish in the early 20th century. We had relatives there, too.

On this particular Sunday afternoon granddad asked Floyd and I to attend Lebanon with him, as there was to be a revival meeting that evening. Floyd and I both chimed in with hurried adamant excuses. "We don't have any Sunday clothes to wear and we don't have any shoes or socks to wear to church. We can't go barefooted," we responded with some truth. We could afford only one pair of cheap shoes each year, and they were always worn out by the time school was out for the summer. The rest of the year we went barefoot including spring and fall, except when we attended school.

Granddad was not easily sidetracked. He disappeared into his bedroom and returned promptly with two extra pairs of large black shoes and black socks. Mother appeared shortly with two clean pairs of blue jeans. Our excuses vaporized and we reluctantly returned to our bedroom to change clothes. We were unaware that our fate was about to be sealed in a blessing we could never anticipate.

On that fateful evening in August 1945, at age 13, and in the church of our ancestors, Floyd and I accepted Christ into our hearts and lives. In faded blue jeans and in shoes and socks at least three sizes too large, we received a new life and a new beginning. It was a joyous occasion. Our grandparents and former Sunday school teacher were especially pleased. None of us realized the even greater significance of the timing of the event until a much later date. Floyd, my beloved identical twin brother and best friend, was accidentally shot and killed three years later by another youth. My only consolation was that I *knew* we would be together again in heaven some day. However, it would be many years later, at a seminary in a foreign land, before I would know what God had in store for me; another new beginning and an even greater commitment as a lay missionary.

My family suffered through fires, tornadoes, accidents, the early death of my infant sister and the tragic death of my twin brother. Three years later my six-year old brother died of tetanus, even though he previously had his shots and booster. My mother, always sickly, became paranoid and would spend several months in a mental institution. She eventually developed Alzheimer's disease and finally died of a stroke. My father was disabled at age 54 and had cancer twice before he died of the disease—and the list goes on and on.

In spite of a childhood and youth filled with hardship and tragedy, I consider myself one of the most blessed persons on earth. I grew up with no hope but yet achieved probably 95% of every goal I ever made for myself. This came about through an event I consider a miracle in my life.

A sharecropper family obviously would not have much in the way of earthly goods. Floyd and I became hard workers early in life through necessity. We were never able to participate in school sports because of our afternoon and Saturday employment. I graduated from high school in 1950 with no money or hope of going to college. It seemed only natural for me to continue my part-time job at the grocery store on a full-time basis. It was at this grocery store in 1951 that the incident occurred that changed my life forever. I will never be convinced that this was not a "God thing."

It was a Saturday in late summer and I was at work in the grocery store in Birmingham, along with a coworker. Bobby was a high school dropout and had worked at the store several years. As Bobby and I were talking a man that knew him approached us. After Bobby introduced him, the man asked me, "Lloyd, what do you plan to do with your life?" Before I could respond Bobby replied, "Lloyd is just like me, he will never amount to anything." Bobby was joking but I made an immediate commitment to myself and to God that I would do whatever it took to become *somebody*. I do not remember the gentleman's name and I am sure he has no idea what an impact he made on my life. However, I am convinced God sent him to be the right person, at the right time, and at the right place, to turn my life around completely. I can say with absolute certainty that this was the defining moment that led me to a purpose-driven life and I will always be grateful.

In those days in Alabama, to become *somebody* you had to graduate from the University of Alabama. Within 10 days I had resigned my job at the grocery store, and took 300 silver dollars I had saved to enroll in the University of Alabama in Tuscaloosa. I did not have a job or a place to stay but I continued on in blind faith and determination. I had to earn my own way and overcome many obstacles, but I eventually graduated from the University of Alabama. Finally, I was *somebody*.

During those early years I was active in church but I could not be called a great witness for our Lord. Soon after I married, my wife and I became youth Sunday school teachers. In 1967 our church pastor resigned to go into the foreign mission field, and for the first time I became interested in foreign missions. I became a member of our missions committee and grew even more interested in mission work. I sensed a tug at my heart towards the mission field, but had no thought about becoming a career missionary.

By 1970, I had developed two passions; one for adventure travel, and another for mission involvement. During June and July of that year, I was in Brazil to set up an expedition into the interior of the Amazon Jungle. The expedition fell through because Indians had killed four white people in the jungle a couple of months before my arrival. Part of my backup plan was to visit the Baptist Seminary while I was in Brazil.

I asked for directions to the seminary and took the proper bus to the end of the line. A walk of a few blocks took me to my destination. I was then escorted by one of the missionaries who explained the operations, and introduced me to other missionaries, students and their families. I was fascinated and convicted. I made a commitment to God at the Baptist Seminary by the banks of the Amazon River in Belem,

Brazil, to devote a good portion of my life's efforts to mission involvement around the world. It has been 35 wonderful years of blessings, one after another. As long as God gives me health and strength I will keep on serving.

I've had many invitations to speak on missions, often being asked about where I've been and how many mission involvements I've participated in over these many years. Although I have never really kept count, I believe a conservative number would be 200 mission involvements. I have been involved in possibly every mission activity known including constructing churches (for 19 years), witnessing, distributing Bibles, participating in prayer walks and children's programs, renovating churches and church buildings, delivering airplane parts and many other missionary supplies around the world.

I have participated personally in mission work in 51 countries and 42 states over those 35 years. I became a Gideon in 1987 to combine my love of missions and travel. I've distributed Gideon New Testaments in 42 countries and 38 states under almost every circumstance imaginable. I have given out New Testaments aboard a transcontinental train, crossing America coast-to-coast and border-to-border, on a refurbished 50's train across Australia, coast-to-coast, across Canada on another vintage train, across six South African countries, and on an ultra-modern train speeding at 186 mph across France.

I have never planned an adventure trip just to give out Bibles under unusual circumstances. However, I do give them out on all of my travel journeys. I have given out New Testaments on the Concorde while flying at mach II (1,346 mph—twice the speed of sound), and at a height of eleven miles. You could even see the curvature of the earth up there.

I have distributed Gideon New Testaments on all continents of the earth, even giving a New Testament to a member of my expedition team at the North Pole in 1995, and others to the crew of the ultra-modern Russian scientific-discovery ship we were on in Antarctica.

I presented a Gideon New Testament to the captain of our scientific submersible vehicle while the two of us were 1,000 feet below the ocean surface, and others on ship voyages across the Atlantic, West to East on the Queen Elizabeth 2, and a second voyage aboard the Queen Mary 2, East to West. I distributed New Testaments the entire 278-mile length of the Grand Canyon while whitewater rafting the Colorado River, and gave another to my jumpmaster after skydiving from a plane three miles above the Mojave Desert in Nevada. There are others but these were the most interesting.

Some of the most interesting countries where I gave out Bibles would include places like China, Russia, and Cuba, where I distributed Gideon New Testaments openly without challenge. Some would say God watched over me, others might say I was incredibly stupid and lucky. What really matters was the fact that many seeds of God's salvation plan of hope and faith were scattered in a dark world. Only God can reap or judge the harvest.

Our hearts and beliefs are reflected in the lives we live and the words we speak. I have been persistent and God has been faithful in blessing me with these wonderful experiences in travel and missions around the world. Most certainly it has been, *a Journey of Discovery.*

Bones of Contention
by Judy Becker

Look here, Mrs. Becker," she said as she grabbed me by the arm and drug me over to the table to look at the x-rays of my neck. "You have a very bad problem. You can't quit coming yet."

"But you are not helping me," I replied. "It's just a waste of money." I left determined to find another chiropractor.

I had one more errand to run. I needed some art supplies at Dick Blick's Art Store. It was late in the afternoon and traffic had thickened. I waited to make a left turn into the shop and took my first opportunity. A man coming up the ramp out of the parking lot (the store was below road level) looked directly into the sun and did not see me. He slammed into my left front fender as I was turning. The impact jolted me. I thought *here am I just coming from the chiropractor all soft and flexible, what will this do to me?*

After filing an accident report and getting the car towed to the shop, I called my family to come pick me up. At the time I seemed to have suffered no effects from the accident. But as time wore on I began to notice a severe strain on my muscles in my back. I went to several chiropractors. One finally x-rayed me. To explain the problem he picked up a model of a back bone. He said, "This is what your backbone looks like," as he rotated it into a twist.

I said, "How do we fix it?"

He replied, "I don't know."

I left his office discouraged. I thought back on the accident and realized that when the car hit me from the left, the jolt rotated my right hip to the left as well. I went to a new chiropractor telling him my problem. He tried to right it, but he failed me also.

My back hurt when I bent over, it also disrupted my sleep, because I couldn't sleep on my back without strain. I arose each morning with a backache. But after trying many doctors I decided it was something I would have to live with.

I don't remember if I asked God to help me, but I probably did since I was not bashful about making my needs known.

We took our annual trip to the November Charismatic Conference at Ridgecrest North Carolina. One of the speakers, Derek Prince, who was known for his power in healing and deliverance, would be ministering. I didn't think of it as an opportunity to have my back healed until the night of the healing service.

Then he began to call for those who had back problems to stand up. I stood. Then he questioned us. He pointed to me and asked, "What is your problem?" I told him I had been in an accident and twisted my back, but none of the doctors seemed to be able to straighten me out. He told me to come up to the platform.

Many others were called up with me. We were all seated on straight-backed chairs in a large semi-circle on the speaker's platform. He and his wife made the rounds laying hands on the outstretched legs and praying. Many legs lengthened, equalizing the position of the hips.

When he got to me he asked me to extend my legs. He prayed. My legs began to move side to side and turning toward each other and then away with out any help from me. It was a strange sensation, awesome to watch, because no one was touching me. His wife's remark was, "Oh my, She is getting a major adjustment." And I suppose I was, but not for my twisted back, because it didn't improve.

Several months later I saw Derek Prince's wife again at a woman's conference. I told her I still didn't have my healing.

Her words to me were, "Keep believing. Have faith. He will heal you if you believe." She herself had been healed of a back ailment.

I turned the whole thing over to God and went on with my daily routine.

My husband, Harvey, came home from work one day with the news that his boss wanted him to go to Puerto Rico on business and I was invited to go along. We would fly first class, no less. Did I want to go? Boy, did I ever. It would be in a week or so.

Shortly after, with the trip on the horizon, I was out in the pasture checking on the cows. I had put up a dust bag in the open shed part of our barn. The idea was for them to pass under the bag letting it drag across their backs depositing the insecticidal dust, to keep the flies off. However, I failed to get it quite low enough.

Queenie, our gray and white cow was standing directly under it with several inches to spare. It was an opportunity to get some dust on her at least. I looked around for a stick. I found one and gave the bag a whack. I got dust on her back all right, but what I didn't expect was her reaction. Frightened by the noise she let fly her two back legs kicking out in a scissors action. She caught me squarely on the right hip and knocked me to the ground.

My first thought was *oh no, I'm hurt, now I won't be able to go to Puerto Rico.* But as I began to assess my injuries, I realized I didn't feel that bad. In fact, I felt good. *Did that cow straighten out my backbone?* Sure enough she did.

Later as I thought about it I knew it was a divine appointment. How else could that cow have hit just the right place with just the right impact to rotate my hip back to its normal position? What if she had kicked me in the soft tissue of the abdomen? I probably would have been ruined for life or killed. Only God could have been so precise.

Needless to say, I went on the trip to Puerto Rico praising God and giving him the credit. God is faithful and ever mindful of our needs. He is even able to straighten out bones of contention. To this day I tell people that God is my chiropractor.

Something Better
by Brenda Thompson Ward

As a mother, I remember watching my children grow and wishing I could keep them from every hurt, but I could not. I remember praying for God to send the right mates into the lives of my children. It was easy when they were small to guard their lives, run interference, and stay the hurts. It was so easy to say, "Here, let Mommy kiss it and make it well."

As my children matured and grew into young adults, it was much harder to be their guard and keeper. They had to learn from their own mistakes and heartaches. I cried when they cried, but I could not always heal the hurts as I did when they were small. I found that out when our youngest daughter was planning her wedding.

In the summer of 1995, romance filled the air of the Ward household. It was the middle of July and the entire family was involved in preparing for Leigh's wedding in September. Leigh and Guy had been engaged for almost a year. As we grew closer to the day of the wedding, everything was going smoothly and we all relaxed a bit.

The invitations were almost ready to mail, the bridesmaids' dresses were being made, and the cake was ordered. Everything was proceeding as scheduled. Leigh had decided to wear my wedding dress, which was thirty years old. We had the dress restored and I started the task of sewing on thousands of sequins and pearls.

Our daughter had met her fiancé, Guy, over a year earlier in Montgomery, Alabama. Since then they had seen one another every weekend, except when he had military drills. He seemed as devoted to her as she was to him.

31

In the middle of July Guy had to go to Florida for Air Force Reserve drills. Through the days following his departure, Leigh would hear from him on an irregular basis. She reasoned that she did not hear from him everyday because of his schedule.

Midway through this time, Leigh told me she felt something was wrong. I told her it was probably her imagination, but she replied, "No, Mom, something's not right. He doesn't sound like his usual self."

The day he was to come home Leigh waited patiently by the phone to hear from him. By late afternoon, she still had not heard from her young man.

Later that evening my son dropped by for a visit. As Doug left his sister's room, he turned and said, "If I had not seen my wife for two weeks, I'd rush to see her as soon as possible. Now find out what's wrong."

Leigh, wanting to give Guy the benefit of the doubt, did not call immediately. When eight o'clock had rolled around and there was still no word for her finance, Leigh became deeply concerned and decided to call his home. When Leigh did call Guy's home, his younger brother told her he had gone out for a ride to think things out.

You would have to know my daughter to understand her reaction. I cannot remember her ever being critical of other people. She wants to believe the best about others. Leigh is one of the most tenderhearted people I've ever known.

Leigh stayed in her room while the rest of the family, my husband, my son and his wife, and I went into the den to wait. Without warning, I heard Leigh crying as if she were in great pain. She was. Her heart had been broken. I ran to her bedroom. Leigh was sitting on the floor, leaning back on the wall. She clutched the phone close to her chest, and sobbed. I wanted to reach out and hold her, but she pushed me away.

Giving her a few more seconds to calm down, I stood by and waited before I asked, "Does he want to postpone the wedding?"

"No, Mom, he wants to call the wedding off."

"Did he give a reason?"

"Yes. He says he doesn't think he's ready," she answered through a deluge of tears. Finally, she looked up and asked, "What did I do wrong? Why is this happening?"

I am not always capable of giving the right answer in an instant, but the Lord was gracious that day and I replied, "Leigh, all I can think of is that God has something better."

Looking through tear soaked lashes, she said, "There's no one better than Guy."

At that point we were in disagreement. In my opinion, it had only taken a split second Guy's popularity rating to fall considerably. This young man was not even in the top ten. Yes, he possessed such extraordinary good looks that when he entered a room, all the females noticed. He was pleasant and charming. But, now, he had broken my daughter's heart and I was not feeling benevolent.

Two stressed filled days later, Guy and his father came to our house. His father stayed in our den while my husband, John, Leigh, Guy, I went into the living room. When I saw the pained expression on Guy's face I found myself feeling compassion for him. Leigh kept wiping tears away.

I wanted the meeting to be calm and without anger. My husband had other plans. The young man and Leigh were seated on the couch. I was in a chair in the corner across from the couch and my husband was on the piano stool across from the young man.

My husband was the first to speak in an intimidating voice, "Now, you want to explain why you did this?"

The young man mumbled a few syllables and finally said, "Mr. Ward, I still like Leigh."

"Like her! When you asked to marry her you told me you couldn't live without her. What happened?"

Neither Leigh nor I had ever seen my husband this angry. I believe he would have enjoyed crossing the room and doing physical harm to the young man.

"I just don't think I'm ready for marriage," Guy finally said.

Realizing that there was nothing else to be said, my husband and I left the room. Leigh was saying goodbye to the young man she felt she wanted to spend her life with and he was rejecting her. Her heartbreak was visible to all who saw her.

Leigh attempted to return the engagement ring, but Guy would not take it back. During the goodbye, Leigh had asked Guy if he was sure this was the right decision and he assured her that his mind was made up.

After that meeting, life fell into a semblance of normality. Leigh continued to go to work everyday, but when she was at home she would stay in her room. Leigh did not want to go anywhere or see anyone. Most of all she did not want to talk.

There are times in every life when you need solitude to thrash all your feelings. Leigh became withdrawn. She was deeply depressed, lost her appetite, and would not open up to any of us. I wanted to do anything I could to help, so I cancelled the florist, the bakery, the stores where her china was on display, and all the little details in an effort to relieve some of her feelings of depression. I made phone calls to all our friends who had received invitations to the upcoming bridal shower. Despite the fact that she had done nothing wrong, she was humiliated about the situation. Rejection is never easy to face.

I tried to encourage her by telling her God had someone special for her and all she had to do was wait. When I did try to encourage her, she would say, "I'm not getting involved with anyone. I don't want to go through this again."

Several days after the break-up we decided to take Leigh to West Columbia, South Carolina to visit with her older sister DeeDee. It would get her out of the house and maybe she would cheer up being away from all the fuss.

It amazes me how God can send certain circumstances and people into our lives to change our outlook. After the visit with her sister, though still depressed, Leigh would at least talk about things. One particular night stands out in my mind.

Leigh and I were in the den watching television. The doorbell rang and there stood the son of one of our friends. The girl he wanted to marry had broken off their engagement.

As he entered the den, he looked at Leigh and said, "Hey, we've both been dumped. Let's go out and talk about them like the low lives they are."

We were surprised that she actually went out that night and when she returned she was smiling. It had felt great to talk about the situation with someone who is not a family member and had experienced the same pain you are feeling. It seems that it upset her to talk to us because her sister and I would cry. That is usually what a mother does with her baby is hurt.

Several day later Leigh walked into the kitchen and announced, "If Guy doesn't want me, then I don't' want him."

I reminded her what I had said about God having something better. I was told, once again, in no uncertain terms that she was not getting involved with anyone anytime soon.

However, that something better was lurking right around the corner. Leigh had started to work at Wal-Mart. She would come home each day and tell me about the people she worked with. I asked her if there were any cute guys working with her.

"There's a guy named Mason who says he wants to date me."

"What does he look like?

"He's cute, Mom, but forget it. I mean it when I say I'm not getting involved with anyone."

A few weeks later Leigh, my husband and I were in Wal-Mart and a good-looking young man walked by and greeted Leigh. As we continued to walk I asked, "Who was that?"

"Oh, that was Mason."

My only reply was, "Do you have rocks for brains?"

"Mom, drop it. Okay?"

I did not mention it again until a few Sundays later when Leigh and I walked to her car after church services and there, on the windshield of her car, was a card and a rose. She panicked and actually became physically ill.

"Mom, open the note. Please tell me they belong on another car."

There was no mistake. Mason had left the note and flower and told her he would call her that afternoon. Leigh was so terrified of the prospect of dating someone that she almost did not talk to him that day. Her father was not thrilled about this young man at first. He did not want his daughter hurt again. I was excited simply because I had seen my child sad for so long I wanted her laughter back.

Mason and Leigh stated dating and after a year became engaged. At first I think Mason must have thought we were all watching and waiting for him to do something wrong. My husband was not overly friendly in the beginning. Mason thought he hated him personally. At that time he did not like anyone who might hurt his daughter.

Mason won me over when he wanted to buy a devotional book and read the Bible and pray with Leigh on a daily basis. I did not tell Leigh at that time, but I told her Dad "Mason's a keeper."

It is ironic that four months after the broken engagement, Guy paid a surprise visit to Leigh at work. She walked out of the store to go home, and there he stood with a dozen red roses. She had already just starting dating Mason. His visit was to no avail. The trust she once had in the young man was gone.

Looking back on the harsh reality that had smacked Leigh in the face before she met her husband, I remember that it not only hurt her, but our family as a whole. However, I have always believed that God does not make mistakes. During the hard times God is teaching us to lean and trust in Him. Through this experience God taught us all that with love, support, and prayer, God would answer in His on way and in His own time.

It frightens me to think of what might have happened if Leigh and Guy had gotten married. We were all angry when he hurt Leigh, but I must thank Guy for doing the right thing. It was better to realize you were not ready before you go through a marriage ceremony. Although painful, a broken engagement is easier than a divorce.

On July 21, 1997, Leigh and Mason were married. A short time before the ceremony we had talked about her past experience and she smiled and said, "You were right, Mom, God did have something better."

God's Gift For Guy
by Burl McCosh

The word spread through the family. "Dad really looks bad. It looks like he's not going to make it." My wife knew that it was necessary that she go to be with her father at this time. The children, all eight of them, left their work and homes to be there. They consoled their mother and each other and took turns keeping a constant watch on their father.

Getting them all together was not easy to achieve. Some of the children routinely made the trek to the middle of Florida to visit their parents; for others it was a relatively rare occurrence. Due to the gravity of this situation, however, they came because the doctors' diagnoses and reports form those children who had seen their father first-hand, they expected that this was the last time they would see him alive. This gathering was not for an all inclusive prayer vigil either. Some of the children may have said prayers in their own way, but it was not a way of life for them nor did they realize the power of prayer. Their mother, along with others, prayed fervently. They realized that the only recourse at this point was hope and the only hope was through prayer.

This situation started so innocuously. Guy, who had already had several surgeries and who had been close to death's door on a couple of those occasions, had some abdominal pain. As this pain became more intense, it became evident that he needed medical attention. Upon being admitted to the hospital, the doctor's diagnosis indicated that the cause of the pain was gallstones. Even though Guy's gallbladder had previously been removed, a few gallstones had escaped removal and were now lodged in his body, causing him great pain. The doctors were

38

able to find and remove some of these gallstones, but left those that could not easily be retrieved.

Following that later surgery, pancreatitis and infection in the liver occurred. Nothing more could be done until his condition stabilized, which hadn't happened. The pain persisted and Guy's health weakened to the point that his life was in jeopardy. The attending physicians gave up any hope of his recovery and so did Guy. The primary doctor's position at this time was to put him in a nursing care facility to await his demise.

Guy was always the kind of person willing to lend a helping hand. Being a superb mechanic and carpenter, he used his skill over the years to supplement his income. If someone had a need, they knew that he was willing to help. If they couldn't pay, he didn't charge. If they couldn't pay a lot, he charged a little. On many occasions, he pitched in to help me with projects, some of which I couldn't have done without his assistance. In short, Guy had a giving spirit. One of the things that probably sustained him over the years was his willingness and ability to contribute. When his small community church acquired a defunct nightclub to convert into their worship center, he was instrumental in the renovation.

Because of Guy's giving nature and my love for my father-in-law, it was very hard for me to see him in this condition. My wife had the love for her father that comes from a close relationship over both the growing and mature years of her life. It was particularly painful for her hear of and then see her father in this condition. She and I prayed earnestly for his recovery, if it was God's will. We both knew that if there was any hope for improvement in Guy's health it would have to come from God. The doctors had demonstrated that they were powerless to help. While God will and does answer prayer from one who earnestly asks and lives in accordance with His will, it certainly helps to have the support of other Christians in petitioning Him. Thus, my wife and I placed Guy on the prayer list in our church and in our Sunday school class. I respect and admire the people in our congregation in their daily walk with God, and was immediately comforted that these people would also be praying for Guy's recovery. I still did not know if he would recover or not, but knew that God would hear and consider our request and, that if it was His will, it was in His power to heal Guy.

God began to work in Guy's life. The family made a decision to take him from the hospital in Florida to one in Greensboro, North Carolina where one of his daughters lived. No one was confident at this point that he would be able to survive the trip. However, placed in the hospital in Greensboro, God's therapy began to work immediately.

The treatment by the physicians not only addressed his physical recovery, but also revived him spiritually. They told him about God's healing power and prayed for him. Finally, Guy recovered to a point where the operation to remove the remaining gallstones could be performed successfully. Recovery from surgery went well. What a joy it was to offer praise to God in Sunday school class and to thank the members for their prayers that helped Guy recover from his health from a near death experience. His family was happy and relieved that he made it through his ordeal, but not all realized the direct blessing of God in causing it to happen. Still, Guy fully attributes his recovery to the power of the prayers offered on his behalf. This experience has not only served to strengthen Guy's faith but that of my wife and myself as well.

Close Encounters
by Judy Parrott

Dad scrounged around for a hunk of wire to tie up the Buick's dilapidated muffler, found some illegal license plate for the trailer, and plugged its brakes into the car. In his haste, however, he didn't reveal to me that the only trailer on hand to carry this twenty-seven foot houseboat was 'way below capacity to haul such an enormous burden. Consequently, Dad forgot to advise me to tighten the wheels' lug bolts every hundred miles or so during the trip from Michigan to Georgia. *What tiny wheels*, I observed, but never considered why they appeared unusually small.

My dad was a forgetful but lovable businessman who often flew by the seat of his britches, and took chances that conservative people would never consider, especially this one, gambling with our very lives for the sake of a boat sale. His traits passed down through the family. We are fearless- and often pay dearly for this 'infirmity'.

Dad's escapades have become legend. We still tell entertaining stories of his antics at parties. (I hope he is laughing up there in heaven.) Every spring, for example, he took our boat out of storage and forgot to put the plug in the bottom. I recall many times as a child being in the middle of the lake watching water flow in through that hole, and Dad rushing toward shore before it filled up and sunk.

Dad had a good heart, and would never hurt anyone on purpose. He just tried too hard sometimes to give everyone a good time. Usually Dad's risky decisions turned out all right, but this time I may not have been here to tell it if God had been hard of hearing.

I took off that hot July day with my twelve-year-old co-pilot, our son Rob. A Seacamper houseboat had been sold and Dad had asked if I would like to pull the boat to Georgia, where we lived. I didn't mind driving instead of flying back, since he offered to pay me a healthy bonus to deliver it. I had never pulled such a giant before, but was impressed that Dad trusted me with his treasure.

We woke the next morning after a pleasant night in the elegant new houseboat, parked in a Kentucky RV park. After buying breakfast, we headed to the Tennessee Mountains. The trailer was struggling to stay straight behind the car. *Maybe I am just over steering. I have to relax a bit,* I thought.

Climbing the first high mountain was difficult for the Buick, but we finally got to the top, but trying to keep control as the boat shoved the car down the steep slope was quite another story. Our speed kept increasing in spite of pumping the brakes, and the smell of rubber warned me to scan frantically for a ramp where trucks can coast upward off the road when they can't slow down.

I realized with sudden horror that I'd lost control when the car suddenly began bucking and swaying across the four-lane highway. Rob said later he knew we were going to go over the cliff and die a horrible death, but was too scared to speak. Too panicked to pray, I could only scream, "Jesus!"

Without my assistance the car, heading for the ravine, as if shoved by some gigantic hand, spun completely around toward the median, and some large object flew over the hood. Fifty feet of car and trailer abruptly stopped, spanning the entire highway. Rob and I braced for the inevitable crash as vehicles came flying around the curve.

The car stalled, but incredibly it started just in time for me to drag the trailer to the median inches from traffic whizzing around the curve. We didn't yet realize the trailer axle had cracked almost in half, and the flying object had been a tire! The boat, untouched but listing, loomed in the air like a protected queen on her throne. The only immediately visible damage was a badly twisted trailer hitch.

A trucker, expecting a wreck, was ready to help and stopped nearby. " I saw the wheels wobbling," he told me, "and I knew you were heading for trouble." The kind man separated my car from the trailer and handed me the twisted hitch parts. Rob and I headed for the nearest town a few miles off 75.

After I called my husband at a gas station in Lake City, Tennessee, an eavesdropping stranger warmed my heart by offering to weld my broken hitch and repair it at no charge. A policeman in the gas station gave me a stern order, "You are required to place warning triangles around that trailer immediately or you will be responsible for any accidents it may cause."

Rob and I went shopping for triangles, but the two hardware stores we found would not take a credit card, and I hadn't carried much cash with me. A still small voice spoke to my spirit: *Walk around the block.* A sign in a store window announced those very triangles on sale for *exactly* the amount of cash Rob and I had pooled together- nineteen whole dollars and fifty-three cents. The Shepherd had been there ahead of us, leveling our path.

After setting the warning signs around the boat, I went to town and called my dad. He felt so guilty when I told him what happened.

"It's all right, Dad," I said. "All's well that ends well." But it wasn't over yet.

"Mom, there's a motel pool with a slide. Can we stay there and wait for Dad?"

Rob asked. I was happy to settle somewhere, have a nice dinner, and swim a while after all the trauma. To top it all off,

God painted us a picture: a magnificent peachy gold sunset framed by craggy mountains reflecting in the glistening pool. What a way to end a supernatural day of deliverance from certain destruction.

In the meantime, after many phone calls, Rog finally located an axle two hundred miles south of our home in Alpharetta, Georgia. The unusual size axle we had to have was being tooled right then, and would be finished by the time someone arrived. What was the chance of that?

Our son Dave, who lived near us, offered to pick it up with a borrowed van. It took until two in the morning for him to get back to his dad. Dave relayed the van to my husband, who left Alpharetta for the motel in Tennessee.

Not until he arrived in Lake City at six in the morning did Rog realize Dave hadn't given him the gas cap key. With great difficulty, he had to take apart the pipe leading to the gas tank to fill it.

I was jarred awake early by a knock on the motel door, but so thankful to lay groggy eyes on my weary husband. After a yummy breakfast we drove the few miles to the highway to check out the boat and trailer. Gone! Not a sign of it anywhere. I was in shock. I knew right where I'd left it, but Rog thought I was confused.

"How could anyone move it with a cracked axle and no tire?" he asked.

We drove back to Lake City and asked a gas station attendant if he had seen a huge boat on the side of the road while driving to work. Just then a woman walking by happened to overhear us, and said she had seen one being towed by a wrecker up the highway against traffic at 8PM the evening before. She even happened to know it was Brown's Wrecking Company in nearby Clinton, Tennessee. She gave us directions, and we found it just where she had said.

We learned from Mr. Brown the police had ordered him to haul the hazard off the highway, so he had taken it to his shop. It was a great relief to have a safe level parking area in which to repair the trailer. As owner of the lot, Mr. Brown charged us a fair towing fee, and even loaned us his tools. Any mechanic will attest that never happens.

While Rog tore the trailer apart to replace the axle, Mr. Brown directed me on my search for two tires, since a second one of the four had also been destroyed, and a bearing was needed. The tires were a unique size, and not one was available within a fifty- mile radius. I stopped at a junkyard in desperation, but to no avail.

Sitting on a pile of tires to call places further away, I asked the Lord what to do, and just then the clerk yelled out, "Wow! Can you believe this? Lady, you are sitting on the very tires you need!" He sold me two brand new tires for only ten dollars. I often pondered how new tires came to be in a junkyard.

Following advice from every helpful clerk, I finally located a bearing and several other items. I was disturbed on my return to find the bearing not in the bag. Rog examined the wheel and realized he hadn't needed one after all; I was relieved to find the parts store had also not charged me for it. That again affirmed God's invisible presence, and thrilled me to know He was so involved in every detail of our lives.

Before sundown the new axle was in place, so Rog and Rob took off with the car and trailer. He had been unable to repair the trailer brakes, however, so I was very fearful about him driving through the mountains.

"How do you expect to get down those mountains without trailer brakes? Please sleep in the boat overnight and fix them tomorrow," I pleaded.

He insisted they would be fine, and was determined to be home by midnight. "The brake parts are not available, so we have no choice. The lug bolts are tight. God is with us, isn't He?"

The trailer was no sturdier than before and I was not in the mood to put God to a test. Off they went, with me following in the van, praying fervently.

They climbed the first steep mountain, but on the descent the car started fishtailing as I watched in horror. They were soon out of control just as I had feared, heading for a steel rail and beyond, a huge chunk of nothing! I screamed for Jesus again, and in an instant, they stopped wobbling and straightened out as if nothing had happened. Rog said later he had told Rob, "Duck! We're going to crash!"

I turned into the next rest area, which Rog had passed up, turned off the engine and wept with relief. After a few moments, I turned on the key to catch up with them, but there was no response. I was flabbergasted. The battery was stone dead. Eventually the entire rest area population took notice when I opened the hood, and surrounded me, trying to help. Nothing worked.

Then I remembered God, and all the miracles I had just experienced, stood in the midst of my new companions and humbly asked Him to start the van. I slammed the hood shut, got back in, turned the key on, and away I flew, like Elijah in the chariot! My advisors just stood there staring at my rear window. What a perfect sermon that was.

At that point, I noticed my gas was nearly gone. "Lord," I prayed, as if He had no clue, "I have a problem here. I have no gas cap key and no cash. What do I do now?"

A voice somewhere inside said: *Follow that semi-truck ahead of you.* It turned off an exit, so I did too. There in front of me was a gas station, though I had seen no sign of one. The attendant listened to my tale, reached in his pocket, and amazing me, opened my gas cap with his own key! He also accepted my MasterCard.

Entering our hometown, I stopped at a light, and there went the boat through the intersection, heading safely home.

I have recorded only some of the many miracles God did on this trip. Whenever I am tempted to get discouraged, I remember what He has done for me in the past. The list is long and still growing. He promised to turn all things out for good for those that love Him. He surely showed me the truth of that promise.

Whether He guides us with thoughts, people, words, or inspirations, God can speak any way He wants. That's His business.

Please, Lord, Don't Let Daddy Die
by Charlene C. Elder

"Your daddy has cancer." Those four terrifying words took my breath away. I knew that cancer was terrible.

"This isn't supposed to happen," I cried. I was only in ninth grade, and junior high school graduation was just a few months away. I was scared. My stomach hurt, my head heart, and my heart felt like it was breaking.

Even mom's hug didn't take away the fear that I felt deep inside. I loved my daddy. I didn't want anything to happen to him. After all, daddy was supposed to be there as I grew up.

"Will he be all right?" I asked, needing reassurance.

Mom hugged me and said, "We'll just have to trust the Lord and have faith."

My daddy had smoked for years. Growing up in the south, he had picked up the family example of his relatives. I remember watching him smoke his pipe or cigar in the backyard because mom wouldn't allow smoking inside the house due to her allergies. The consequences of years of smoking loomed larger than life when the doctor affirmed the tests showed that the tumor inside my daddy's cheek was malignant.

"What does that mean?" I asked mom.

"That means your daddy has to go through radiation treatment to kill the cancer cells in his body. The doctor suspects that your daddy bit his cheek at some point when he was smoking his pipe or cigar. The irritated area formed a lump that became cancerous. That's why daddy looked like he was holding a golf ball inside his cheek. Now the lump has to be removed because it is growing inside and getting bigger."

"Will he be okay?" I asked once again.

"We'll have to put our faith and trust in the Lord," she repeated.

That answer wasn't enough to squelch the rising fear in my heart and devastating thoughts in my mind. Every day after hearing the doctor's decree, the horrible cancer reminded me that it was going to kill my daddy.

Even with a solid foundation of faith from my upbringing, the continual thought of the cancer killing my daddy nagged me. I knew God loved me and that he was a good God, but I questioned *why* he would allow this to happen. Negative thoughts crossed my mind like a store's blue light special advertising a sale, but they advertised death – the death of my daddy.

We'll just have to have faith in the Lord. My mom's words echoed in my mind. As I heard the words, my mind replayed memories of my childhood with my daddy like a favorite movie. I heard him give his unique, shrill whistle when I was outside playing in the neighborhood to let me know to come home immediately. I thought of the special hikes we I took in the hills near our house. I remembered the neighborhood kids knocking on the front door to see if 'Charles' could come out and play. The funny, sweet memories came to mind night after night, and I wanted to add more of them.

This crisis was the hardest thing I had to face as a child. I knew I would have to lean on my faith and let that faith in God be the controlling factor if I were to get through this difficult time. This was a turning point in my walk of faith. I realized I wouldn't be able to get through this trial on my own. I would have to trust the Lord and release my daddy into His care.

The doctor scheduled chemotherapy with hospitalization for my daddy. Mom did her best to encourage me and so did my grandparents. Meanwhile, graduation drew closer.

"Charlene, you know that daddy won't be able to come to your graduation, don't you?" mom asked.

I nodded as the tears formed in my eyes.

"But I want him there!" I insisted.

"I know, sweetheart," mom hugged me. "Daddy would rather be with you, too, but he won't be able to this time."

I was terribly disappointed, and I cried. I didn't want to be the only one at Graduation without her daddy there. I even had a new dress for graduation, but he wouldn't be there for my special event. Thinking back now I'm sure he was more disappointed that he couldn't be there than I was. I was his little girl, his only daughter, and he loved me.

The weeks prior to his hospitalization were a blur. Final exams took place; graduation pictures were scheduled; and graduation practice filled the hours during the day. But no one knew the mental turmoil I was going through every night.

I continued hearing the negative thoughts in my mind and experiencing a heaviness in my heart. Would I let this situation steal my faith, joy and peace, or was I going to fight for everything I believed in?

Prayer and faith were my weapons. I loved my daddy, and needed him. I didn't want my daddy to die!

One particular night, I tried to pray, but words wouldn't even form on my lips. Instead I cried and cried. Finally in a feeble attempt I managed to verbalize seven little words that scared me so much. *Please Lord, don't let my daddy die.* Hearing those words come out of my mouth opened the floodgates on my emotions, and I cried some more. But just as instantly as I had spoken those words out loud, I felt God's presence surround me in my bedroom. It felt like God Himself enveloped me in His arms, holding me close. Waves and waves of peace flooded over me, like the ocean waves drenching me in its foam. It was so peaceful, so reassuring.

My tears stopped. I *knew* my prayer had been answered. I never had such peace and assurance as I felt at that very moment. Instead of hearing the cancer tell me it was going to kill my daddy, I found myself speaking back to it with certainty and resolve of faith. *My daddy won't die.* The waves of peace again flooded over me, through me, and throughout my room. I had no doubt that my daddy would be okay.

I knew people in our church who had suffered with cancer, and whose prayers were not answered for reasons not understood. They went on into the presence of the Lord. Those thoughts came into mind, but waves of peace continued to flood over me. My daddy would be okay. God, in His infinite love and grace had answered a little girl's prayer of faith.

Ninth grade graduation day came. The chemotherapy was going well, but my daddy was still in the hospital. I talked to him on the phone before we left for the ceremonies.

"I love you, daddy," I said.

"I love you, too," he told me. "I'm very proud of you."

"I miss you, daddy, and I wish you could be at my graduation" I said, trying to hold back the tears.

"I know, and I miss you, too, but I'll be there with you even though you can't see me."

I hung up, and went to my graduation knowing that my daddy was thinking about me. On the way mom said the doctors were confident that they had eliminated all the cancer. My daddy would live and not die. And I would continue to trust the Lord no matter what I would face.

A Good Answer
by Cheryl Davis

While promoting my historical, inspirational novel *Hope Is Constant*, I have often been asked why I enjoy writing books. I do not think I ever gave anyone a good answer to that question. Maybe evasion occurs because answering that question *honestly* would mean I would have to share my testimony. Speaking about the spiritual direction of my life has always been a trying, and perhaps an embarrassing, ordeal for me.

I started writing long before I became a Christian. The content of my books use to be spicier, what the publishing industry jokingly calls "bodice rippers". But today the characters in my books have a *spiritual* life, not just a *romantic* one, and moral convictions are not just plot inventions. I think the change in my writing style occurred because I was forced to come to terms with the idea that what I was doing and saying in my books was not in accord with my Christian faith.

I did not grow up in a family that attended a church. I do not even remember God being mentioned too often in our house. Unlike most people, I can pinpoint the exact moment my family stopped going to church. There was no casual drifting away. My parents regularly attended services until I was six years old. There was an abrupt end to formal, religious observance of the Sabbath in our household.

My brother and sisters had all been baptized on schedule. Once the child hit a certain age, it was time to make a commitment. When I turned six years old, my father became convinced that I needed to be baptized.

My father did not listen to my mother's argument that I was terrified of water and baptism for a very young child by submersion was not a good idea. I had almost drowned when I was four years old. I really do not have any memory of the incident. But I do remember my family talking about it...*again*...*and again*...*and again.* I was positively terrified of water. My mother wanted to wait until I was a little older and requested baptism.

But my father firmly insisted that it was time for me to be baptized. When I went in front of the church, I panicked. I started to struggle, wanted to run away. I had no idea what baptism meant. All I could think of was those Sunday school stories about Abraham and how he almost sacrificed his son Isaac on an altar.

The pastor intervened. My father insisted I be baptized. The deacons had to get involved. Apparently there was quite a scene. I was not baptized. And my family stopped attending that church—or any other church.

Only after I married did I resume church attendance. Though I might have my difficulties with formal religion, I wanted my children to grow up in a church and know why they were there.

When my sons were still preschoolers, I discovered I was going to have another child. I was unhappy. I did not know how I was going to go through another tortured pregnancy—the hormone treatments, the sickness, the anxiety.

My attitude began to change from dread to anticipation. This new baby became the confidant that was always there with me. I talked to him quite often. I told that unborn child all my misgivings, all my fears, all my secrets. I was overjoyed when the baby moved inside me in the fourth month of the pregnancy. I started to look forward to the birth of this baby and to seeing the face of my new friend.

Then the worst happened. Something just did not feel quite right. In the hospital, the doctor grimly informed me that the protective bag of water had broken. There was no way a baby only halfway into a pregnancy was going to survive.

So what do you do, lying in a dark room with beeping monitors, waiting for the labor pains to start and for your child to die? What do you say to someone who is never going to have a birthday party, attend a first day to school, and hear a bedtime story much less ever take a breath of life?

I will tell you what you do and what you say; you talk about your faith in your God. You tell your friend how much God loves you both. And you tell him about *His* son. You tell your child that he must go on ahead without you. He will be in the Lord's care, not yours, and you will meet him a little later than you hoped.

If I live to be 100 years old and write 100 books, I doubt I will ever be able to touch another life the way Adam touched mine. He helped me discover a strength I did not know I had— and how much I loved the Lord.

Long after Adam's death, something felt 'undone'. Having to tell Adam about my love for the Lord made me realize I needed to be baptized—me, with that little girl cringing inside me that was still so terrified of water. I needed to make that profession of faith. I could no longer avoid it. And I had to do it the right way, make a complete commitment. I could have settled by just being sprinkled, but I think I *needed* to face a baptism by submersion.

I practiced putting my head under water in the bathtub the week before I was supposed to be baptized. That did not help. In fact, I just grew more apprehensive because I never did manage to get my head below water level. I grew extremely afraid I was going to panic and embarrass myself in front of another church congregation.

The morning I was finally baptized is very vivid in my memory. Though I was anxious and nervous, the amazing thing is I was not scared at all. In fact, I do not even remember my head going under the water. There was no gagging, no thrashing about and no panic. A protective bubble seemed to engulf me.

I think there was a reason I waited so long to be baptized. I had to learn how little there is to fear when I put myself in God's hands.

I insisted that there be a dedication at the beginning of my novel *Hope Is Constant*. It reads, "To Adam, who taught me life does not have to be long to be of great value." That is a lesson I do not want to forget or waste. And it needs to be shared with others.

So the next time the three children that God *did* entrust into my care tease me about my passion for my writing, I just smile. I now have a good answer for them. "Every story I should ever tell should reflect my faith in the lord. And even if I should write 100 books, the *best* story I should tell *should be my own.*" In fact, the *best* story *any of us* should tell should be our own—and that should include a testimony of our faith and trust in the Lord.

From Skeptic to Teacher
by Cynthia L. Simmons

As the pastor spoke, Ray glanced around the congregation. His former Sunday school teacher sat nearby nodding his head and smiling in response to the sermon.

I wonder what he would say if I asked him to reconcile Genesis with evolution? he thought curling his lip. *Would he get upset? I doubt he could answer me.* Ray had walked down the church aisle at nine to ask Jesus to forgive his sins, but now he was fifteen and skeptical. *My school teachers present a good case for evolution. If evolution is true, we don't need the Bible.*

"Amen! Preach it brother," shouted several men in the front pew. Members of the congregation named this spot the 'Amen Corner.' *They're shouting again,* Ray thought frowning. *They sound spiritual but their choices stink. What's the problem? Doesn't this stuff work?* He had heard several men from the 'Amen Corner' cursing after the service. Another man in the group stopped going to church after leaving his wife to live with his secretary.

Christianity doesn't make sense, Ray thought cocking one eyebrow. *It's just a long list of things you can't do. But people don't live the way they talk.* Crossing his arms, he watched the preacher pounding his Bible. *Say something. I want information! I don't know if this stuff is true,* Ray said to himself as he tried to focus on the sermon. *But I'm giving it one last chance. I'll go to all the services for a while to see if there's any truth here.*

Ray's family lived in a low-income part of Rossville, Georgia. His father was almost blind, but worked at a textile mill where the boss gave him jobs that he could still do. Most of Ray's school friends lived in his neighborhood. They hung around the 'smoking area' outside the school, cursing and bragging about their conquests. Ray did not participate in any of these activities. However, he did not feel comfortable elsewhere, so he stayed with his old friends.

In 1971 Ray enrolled in Biology and discovered that his teacher was the notorious Mr. Westcott. Ray had heard he was the hardest and weirdest teacher in the school. The first day of class the pungent odor of formaldehyde drew Ray's attention to his teacher's collection of dissected and labeled specimens stored along the walls of the classroom. Rising from his desk, Mr. Westcott strode toward the students and plunged into his lesson.

"Biology is the study of life." He pointed to the jars lining the classroom. "We are living beings who think and learn," Mr. Westcott said. "Learning is a process," he explained as he walked over to a huge reel-to-reel tape recorder. "Learning to think begins with simple thoughts like this one finger melody." He pushed a button and the class heard a tune. Turning off the machine, Mr. Westcott said, "Then a person adds to a simple thought just like the composer dressed up this melody." Cueing the tape, his teacher played the melody again with chords added. He turned off the recorder. "Finally, we layer in more complexity." Once more he pushed the play button and the class heard the same melody enhanced by the symphony. He turned off the music and faced the class. "While we study biology," Mr. Westcott said tapping his forehead, "we are going to use our minds – and think."

I can't believe he used music in biology class. I like this, Ray mused. He cradled his chin in his hand and squinted his blue eyes, devouring every word.

"In college I used to drive my professors crazy." Mr. Westcott gave the class a triumphant smile. "I pointed out their errors and it made them mad," he said with a mischievous

57

twinkle in his eye. He stepped over to his desk and picked up his book. "Turn to page 403 in your textbooks. Look at the pictures of the vertebrate embryos. The text says these embryos look alike in the early stages, which points to a common ancestor. We've known for fifty years that vertebrate embryos don't look the same at this stage of development. These drawings are faked, but the author included them in the textbook anyway."

Mr. Westcott also brought several books on evolution to class. Opening each book, he read statements and then showed the students how the author contradicted himself later in the text. In addition, Mr. Westcott taught methods of reasoning so they could spot the same sort of error.

I'll read carefully from now on, Ray thought pressing his lips together. *I'll catch the sloppy reasoning.*

"God could have used evolution to create the earth," Mr. Westcott said, "but He didn't. The discovery of DNA destroyed the theory of evolution." He pointed to the text. "Scientists are ignoring the fact that the DNA code would prevent these progressive changes." He motioned toward the stack of evolution textbooks. "Scientists must now rely on mutations to explain these changes, but mutations can't do the job." Ray raised his hand and Mr. Westcott nodded for him to speak up.

"Why couldn't a number of mutations over long periods of time produce evolution?" Ray asked raising his eyebrows.

"Mutations are almost always bad and most cause death." Mr. Westcott looked him directly in the eye. "If we give evolution a billion years, it's still not enough time to produce even a simple species."

One day when Ray entered class he noticed another student had drawn a cartoon on the chalk board. It pictured a lake with a fish that had sprouted legs, but still used gills to breathe.

"Well, here goes nothing," the fish said frowning at the shore. The artist showed the fish flapping its tiny fins preparing to jump. Ray, laughing along with his classmates, had begun to understand evolution's flaws.

In biology Ray had the freedom to ask any question and probe until he was content with the answer. Over time he understood that some of his queries were not hard to resolve. Biology became his favorite class and he worked hard to earn the best grades. However, other classes did not get the benefit of his new study habits. Ignoring difficult assignments, Ray studied just enough to make average grades.

Classmates told him Mr. Westcott had a Bible study at his house after school. Ray decided to try it. His teacher, a seminary graduate, interpreted each verse from the Bible showing the students how to live what they learned. Ray realized he knew very little about the Bible although he had attended church all his life. Listening to Mr. Westcott teach, Ray began to grasp the incredible depth and scope of scripture. He recognized that Christianity is a relationship with God, and set aside time for his own Bible study and prayer.

Ray felt a growing restlessness about his old friends. Even though they had grown up together, he could not get them to understand his new excitement. He wanted to talk about God and they didn't. He managed to stay in touch, but he ended up spending more time with his new friends from the Bible study discussing and debating ideas from the Bible.

Bored with his pastor's sermons, Ray started going to Mr. Westcott's church. The minister explained scripture and Ray enjoyed hearing him speak. One evening he sat by Mr. Westcott. Lowering his eyebrows in concentration Ray scribbled fast trying to record each word. His hand ached.

"How much of that are you evaluating?" Mr. Westcott whispered. "Pastor is a good teacher, but he could make a mistake. You should check out what he says."

Oh! Yeah, I remember that passage in the book of Acts. It was about the Bereans. His hand shook as he adjusted the hair that fell over his forehead. *They didn't accept what they heard unless they could prove it in the scriptures.*

One Sunday evening a member of Campus Crusade for Christ came to speak to his new youth group about ancient Biblical manuscripts. *This is amazing,* Ray thought leaning forward. *He's saying we are more certain about the accuracy of the text of Scripture than we are of other historical writings. I want to know more because this validates the Biblical content we use today.* The lecture lasted an hour, but it gave Ray a thirst for more information. Right away he bought two books by Josh McDowell which gave evidence for the truth of Christianity.

When Ray returned to school after Christmas break he discovered that Mr. Westcott had started a new program for gifted students and had included him with the smart kids. His teacher had fought a battle with the school principal to get Ray in the program.

"You can't have Ray Simmons," the principal snapped frowning. "He doesn't make those kinds of grades. He's just average."

"I want him," Mr. Westcott insisted. "He's a scholar."
At last the principal relented and let him add Ray to his group.

Mr. Westcott supervised all of Ray's school work except math. Since gifted students were self-motivated, Mr. Westcott allowed them to direct their own studies. He answered questions and gave tests. Knowing his teacher had high expectations, Ray worked hard and loved the challenge.

Most of the pupils completed their school work early and pursued subjects they found interesting in their spare time.

One boy studied astronomy; another studied Egyptian hieroglyphics; and yet another studied electronics. Ray looked around at the other students, who had their own pet subjects to research, and felt left out.

"Mr. Westcott, I want to study something extra." Ray asked one day. "But I don't know what to do." He shrugged. "Do you have any ideas?"

"I think you should study Biblical Greek," Mr. Westcott said. "My Greek books are here." He pointed to a huge bookcase overflowing with textbooks. "If you have any questions, just ask." Under Mr. Westcott's direction, Ray learned Bible study methods and learned how to use the original Greek text.

Longing to study at home in his free time, he made a list of Mr. Westcott's books. Ray started to purchase Greek lexicons, grammar books and concordances using money earned at part-time jobs.

Ray lived in a tiny house with his three brothers. He tossed their clothes out of his room onto the kitchen floor. "Get your clothes out of my way," he shouted to his brothers. "I can't study when you throw clothes all over my room." His father had enclosed the back porch to make an extra bedroom. While two of his brothers slept there on bunk beds, all of the brothers shared a closet in Ray's bedroom.

Ray's father had dropped out of school after eighth grade to work on the farm. "Ray's working on his books again," his father said to his wife. "I'm not sure how much you can learn from books." Mr. Simmons sighed. Nevertheless, both his parents were pleased that Ray wanted to study the Bible.

After completing his school work, Ray covered his desk with Greek books and studied scripture for hours. As a teenager he filled many spiral bound notebooks with his study notes. In college he added history, philosophy and politics to his personal studies as well. Reading and thinking about ideas became a lifestyle as he examined the history of man's thought in the light of the scripture.

Ray completed college in December of 1977 and a few months later married his sweetheart from Chattanooga. He and his new wife moved to the Atlanta area and found a church in Marietta. Before long, the pastor got to know him and recognized his ability.

"You have the gift of teaching," the pastor said, "I'll help you get started."

Soon the Sunday school staff, which the pastor supervised, asked Ray and his wife to substitute for the preschool teacher. Later, he agreed to teach the school age children.

"You've had some experience. I think you need to teach adults now." The pastor assigned Ray an adult Bible study which met during the week.

The pastor helped Ray navigate technical points of preparing a lesson, but Ray developed his own presentation style while teaching the Sunday school children. After he asked a difficult question, Ray walked the children through the answer a step at a time. His wife attended his classes and gave Ray comments afterward.

"How did my lesson go today?" Ray asked.

"Your material was great," his wife responded, "But, you have one awkward gesture. When you adjust the hair over your forehead, you cover up your face."

"Okay, I'll have to watch that," Ray said with a grimace. "What do you think of the way I handled the story about Jesus discussing Scripture with teachers instead of going home with Mary and Joseph?"

"I liked your question," she said. "You got them interested when you asked if Jesus sinned when He stayed at the

Temple. You made their dilemma worse when you pointed out Jesus couldn't sin, yet His actions made His parents worry."

"All of them looked puzzled," he said smiling, "but they stayed with me. I wanted them to understand that Jesus obeyed God."

"If you had just explained that Jesus had come of age, the kids might have fallen asleep," she said. "I like the way you guided the discussion. You're teaching the Bible and showing them how to think."

"That is exactly what I want to do," he said. "Thanks for your input."

Twenty years later, Ray had developed a relaxed and candid approach to his classes. He encouraged discussion, and he loved questions.

"Yes," Ray pointed to a man in his class who raised his hand. "Do you have a question?"

"I know this is off the subject, but this has always bugged me," the man said rubbing his chin, "Why did God say the sins of the fathers would be passed down to their children? That doesn't seem fair." He shook his head.

"Let's see, that is in Exodus," Ray flipped the pages of his Bible until he came to the passage. "First, let's get the context and then we'll read the whole thing. This is where God gives the Ten Commandments. It says 'I, the Lord your God, am a jealous God, visiting the iniquity of the fathers on the children on the third and fourth generation of those who hate Me,' Keep reading and you find the contrast–look. It says 'showing loving-kindness to thousands who love me and keep my commandments.' "

"Oh, I never knew about that part," the man's face broke into a smile.

"God is comparing the consequences of sin with the benefits of righteousness. The point is–choose to do right. It brings blessings," Ray said smiling, "Thanks for asking. Good question. Does anyone else have a question?"

"I've got a friend who is studying philosophy." A lady raised her hand and spoke at the same time. "Doesn't that scare you? That stuff is dangerous. She says she is seeking for truth but I don't know what to tell her. How did you learn all this?"

"I asked questions and found answers," Ray said. "No, I am not afraid of philosophy. Christianity is strong. It can stand up to examination because God is real. If someone searches honestly the answers are there."

Looking back, Ray knows God guided him during his quest for truth and believes God prepared him to teach. "Ideas matter," Ray says, "Things you don't know will hurt you. People who don't know the Word of God are walking in darkness." Ray spends hours preparing to teach because he believes the verse "You will know the truth and the truth will set you free."

Breaking the Chains of Addiction
by Donald S. Conkey

October 1960 was a major turning point in my life, a time when a wrong decision would have led me down the wrong road for the rest of my life. I was married, had three children, and lived in a new three bedroom, cement block home in a new subdivision in Sanford, Florida. Many outside observers could have been envious of my status. But inwardly I was torn apart, caught between the addictions of the flesh and a strong yearning to become a disciple of Jesus Christ.

Two years earlier I had graduated from Michigan State University, accepted a job in Florida, 2,000 miles to the south, that paid $75 a month more than a job offered in Fort Wayne, Indiana with a large international corporation. My job was to represent the dairy farmers of Central Florida before the Florida state regulatory boards. Effectively I was a lobbyist.

To my dismay I found out soon after arriving in Florida the organization did not have enough money in the bank to pay my first month's salary. My first assignment was to go out and collect enough member dues to make the payroll. I did, and for the next four years I never missed a payroll. But in spite of never missing a pay roll, I hated my job. The profession of lobbying lawmakers was hard for me. Outwardly the job seemed glamorous: lots of travel, the best hotels, the best restaurants, and gourmet meals always with wine and champagne, but underneath that shimmering camouflage of glamour lay most of the sins of humanity the influencing of legislation with wine, women, and party money.

I was good at my job and soon developed a reputation of being one of the best lobbyists in the state, especially after winning a significant number of high-pressure confrontational battles in the industry. But for a young man who had lived a sheltered life this lifestyle was negatively affecting me. My use of cigarettes grew to four packs a day and my consumption of alcohol increased. Social drinking was an occupational hazard, and excessive drinking of caffeine beverages soon became a serious health hazard.

In September of 1960, I began a serious investigation of the doctrines and beliefs of the Church of Jesus Christ of Latter-day Saints. This was a different church from the church I had been born into, or was then attending. It was a religion I had never heard of before their representatives knocked on my door and offered to share a message. I accepted their offer and spent several months discussing the Bible, Jesus Christ, church doctrines, and the mysteries of life with them.

My spirituality quickened. The more I pondered the biblical doctrines the more I studied the Bible. The more I studied the Bible, the more I compared the foundational doctrines of this new-to-me religion to the orthodox dogmas of the church of my parents, which I considered both my family and cultural church. This church was just beginning its expansion program in Sanford, but did not have a chapel yet. Its local leaders were in the process of building a new chapel, one chicken dinner at a time, and were, like many new churches, meeting in a borrowed building, the City Hall of Sanford, Florida. After a few weeks of study and discussion I was invited to attend their church and see it in action. I accepted. It was an invitation that changed my life, my life style, and the lives of five generations of my family my generation, my parents, my children, my grandchildren, and my great grandchildren.

And, surprisingly the focal point of my change was not doctrine or life style, but an eight-year-old girl who stood ramrod straight at the makeshift pulpit that day. In the assembly room of City Hall, not even in a formal church, she delivered a message that touched my heart, a message that has lived with me for nearly 45 years. It wasn't the length of her message, only two and a half minutes, it was her demeanor, her bearing, her confidence, her assurance as a child, to deliver a talk before this audience: and it was her testimony of her belief that God lives that really touched me. An eight-year girl had touched my heart. When she finished, I had tears in my eyes.

Although I don't remember her words, I do remember saying to myself, *If this is what this church teaches its children this is what I want for my children.* From that moment on my focus changed from studying beliefs and doctrines to preparation in becoming a member.

But, there were hurdles for me to overcome, real stumbling blocks, stumbling blocks that almost derailed my enthusiasm for this anticipated lifestyle change. These stumbling blocks were in my lifestyle: the use of habit-forming stimulants, cigarettes, alcohol, and drinks containing caffeine. I soon learned that to become a member of this church would require me to give up my addictive habits. Common sense told me that my use of these stimulants was causing serious damage to my health, but being highly addictive, they were proving very difficult to give up. Today, 45 years later, the ghosts of those habits still haunt me. As I write this story, I am nearing completion of a 30-week chelation treatment program to undo the damage I did to my body in those early years of abuse. And it seems to be working. At least I have hope again.

What was I to do? As much as I wanted to give up these stimulants, the addictive hold they held on my body proved more then I could overcome alone. Giving up alcohol was not a problem, but quitting smoking was. I tried to stop, but whenever I quit smoking for a day the shakes would take control of my body. It reached the point where it affected my job. I couldn't think, I couldn't concentrate, I couldn't meet my obligations. I had to do something, and quick.

On one particular day in early November of 1960, when my shakes were so obvious that my secretary commented on them, I decided to do something. It was then I remembered one special night in July of 1956, a night when I had gone to the Lord with my first prayer. I had asked Him to help me make a career decision. He did, in a very spectacular way. He helped me then, and my faith was still strong enough to believe He would once again help me this time to overcome my debilitating and extremely offensive habits.

I left my office, got in my car and drove north toward Sanford. Between the office and home was a small park where people would stop to observe the scenery and to meditate. I drove into the park and began to ponder my dilemma of how to quit smoking. I then prayed for divine help to overcome this deadly habit. I prayed as hard as I had during my first prayer. I could feel my prayers reaching upward.

The feeling of that moment is as clear today as it was in 1960, more than 44 years ago. After I had offered my prayer, I lay over on the front seat and fell asleep. It was still hot in Florida in November and the sun was shining through the car windows. This was in the days before air-conditioning and the car soon became very hot. After an hour of sound sleep, I awoke completely wet with sweat, so wet I could have wrung a quart of water out of my totally drenched clothing.

But during that hour a miracle happened. God heard my prayer. My nicotine addiction was removed from my body. Never again would I be plagued with this addiction, not even for one moment. The urge for cigarettes was gone—totally gone. Never again have I craved a cigarette, even in a room full of smoke. The Lord cured me. Now it was up to me to stay cured.

This was a second strong testimony for me on how, after I did everything I could for myself, God listened to my individual prayer, stepped in, and helped me solve a serious problem. It was a lesson I kept close to my heart. On many occasions in the next 44 years I have remembered that hot afternoon sitting in a car asking God for help with a serious personal and physical problem. It is a lesson I have shared with my children and grandchildren knowing full well that they, no matter how well taught by good parents, will one day have to go to the Lord in sincere and humble prayer and ask for help on resolving a personal problem. After all, He tells us, in Revelations 3:20, that He stands at the door waiting for us to knock. I knocked and He let me in—again.

God's power to help individuals with addiction problems: tobacco, alcohol, drugs of all kinds, pornography, or sexual deviations is real. He helped me, and as no respecter of persons, He will help anyone who approaches Him in sincere prayer, and asks for His help. For me His help was immediate, and I have been extremely grateful. As sure as I sit here at my computer in the year 2005, writing this Testimony, I know my mortal life would have ended many years ago without His intervention. I have lived through eight heart attacks, two near-death experiences, two open-heart operations, and was told in October 2004 that seven of my eight bypasses were again closed off, and there was little the medical community could do for me.

Again, the Lord stepped in and led me to a doctor who practices alternative medicine and now, once again, I have hope, the very essence of life. I, along with millions of Christians, testify He lives and loves each of His children. He lives and He loves me, in spite of my many imperfections. This I know.

From Cooties To Christ
by Shelley Hussey

"Half the world is nutty—the rest are squirrels." Anonymous

Let's be honest—I had some pretty strange childhood quirks. The collective cultural name for these quirks is "cooties," or in more formal circles, "*the* cooties." I'm not referring to lice or creepy-crawly bugs here. Having the cooties is like being afflicted with "emotional leprosy," or "bugs in the brain," a term my husband once coined to describe my nervous habits. In Cleveland, Ohio during the 50s and 60s, kids could avoid catching other kids' bugs or cooties by simultaneously yelling "Detours!" while holding up their thumbs.

It's possible I was born with the cooties, but they remained dormant until second grade, when I got glasses. My mom made the mistake of letting me pick out the frames for my spectacles, and I was a spectacle, all right. The Coke-bottle-thick lenses sported fins that looked like they came from a pimp's '58 Cadillac. My self-esteem plummeted from the moment I put on my glasses. Low self-esteem tended to set off an internal alarm, provoking nervous tics and twitches.

When I was eight or nine, I developed some slightly painful and disturbing habits, such as compulsively scratching and itching mosquito bites. I scratched with one hand, and typed on my face with the other. I also twitched my nose like a rabbit. The typing and twitching annoyed people. I know this, because many twitched right back at me. I was be-twitched, bothered, and bewildered I was doing this stuff, but I couldn't begin to stop.

One of my most embarrassing childhood moments happened when I was eleven. I tinkled on the piano bench while tickling the ivories during a piano lesson. You see, I was too bashful to ask to use the bathroom, even though my bladder was ready to burst. Towards the end of the lesson, I soaked the piano bench. My teacher didn't notice the puddle on the bench, but she did notice that I suddenly began playing off-key. I went from C-minor to P-major. On that note, the lesson ended. I backed out of the room, and then out of the house, so the teacher wouldn't notice my whole backside was wet.

So maybe you never squirted a piano bench, or exhibited other quirks when you were a kid, but I know we'll find some common ground here: *Puberty*. I was not into puberty. Puberty was the launching pad to adulthood, and I *never* wanted to be an adult. From what I observed, adulthood was too much responsibility and not enough fun. (I got that right.)

With my own weird thought processes operating, I thought I could stop myself from growing up if I quit wearing deodorant. I took things one step further and also quit taking a bath for several months. I really did. I ran the bath water and made splish-splash sounds, but I frequently forgot to get the clean bath towel wet. My clever parents eventually caught on to "Smelly Shelley."

But maybe I wasn't as weird as I was rebellious—to all things clean and Godly. Around the same time as my Bath Party of One Rebellion, I decided I didn't want to go to Sunday School. Every Sunday morning I hid in the church ladies' room, worshipping in my own way at the porcelain throne, and praying that (A) my mother wouldn't need to use the restroom, or (B) if she did, she would not recognize my Mary Janes under the stall.

My shyness and nervous habits followed me to junior high school—that time of life when everyone gets weird. I continued to wear the glasses with the Cadillac fins—now the upgraded '61 models with all the options.

Our local junior high school administrators didn't concern themselves with children's self-esteem issues. Instead, they organized kids in sections; ranging them from section one for smart kids to section nine for special ed. I was in section eight. (My dad says that "Section Eight" was a qualification for a mental discharge from the military.) On the first day of school, everyone asked everyone else, "What section are you in?" Whenever I was asked, I lied. I told them "section seven."

As puberty continued to engulf me, I realized life was becoming more painful, so I decided that twelve years old would be my age limit. By age fourteen, I observed that my plan wasn't working. I needed to take drastic measures to stop the age progression, so I decided to try anorexia nervosa, an eating disorder which is actually a form of addiction.

Eating disorders were not popular in the 60s. The popular diseases—mono, strep throat, or tonsillitis—happened to normal people. People like me had bizarre things happen to them. As a typical anorectic, I was satisfied with my emaciated appearance. For the first time, I felt I was in control of *one* area of my life—my food intake.

I was also lacking in mental clarity, partly due to my state of malnutrition. I thought seventy-eight pounds looked good on my 5'4" frame. Our family doctor wasn't impressed, however; and recommended a psychologist. One day after I arrived home from school I noticed a couple of gifts on my bed. I remember one of them being a manicure set. "Uh-oh," I said to myself, having that instinctively uneasy feeling that dogs get when they know they're going to the vet. The gifts were my mom's way of smoothing over my initial visit to the psychologist.

As I sat stiffly in his office, wearing my red winter coat with the real fur collar, I waited apprehensively for him to speak. Once he finally did start psycho babbling, he lost me and I never went back, but I did go see the Beatles.

I was so obsessed with the Beatles, that I begged my parents to drive 300 miles to Chicago to see them perform. They succumbed, thinking the trip might be a form of shock therapy. Unfortunately, the Beatles did nothing to change my ingrained, diseased thought patterns. I didn't snap out of my anorectic stupor until my parents threatened to put me in the hospital.

During my twenties, I continued to have weird eating habits. My diet was sugar in the morning, sugar in the evening, sugar at suppertime. I felt jumpy, edgy, irritable, unfocused, and restless during this high glycemic time of my life. The addiction to sugar was so strong that for five years I woke frequently in the middle of the night and went into the kitchen to devour brownies, cookies, and M & Ms.

In desperation to stop myself from collapsing into a chocolate coma, I visited a hypnotist. When that failed, I insisted that my apartment roommate lock me into my bedroom at night. The locked door strategy kept me out of the kitchen for only a week because my roommate was evicted for attacking her mother, who happened to live in our same apartment complex.

Apparently I had "bug charisma"—an innate ability to connect with highly unstable people. Or perhaps being around such people raised my self-esteem. Or maybe my bugs attracted theirs, kind of like a porch light in the summer.

So how did my parents deal with all my nervous habits and anorexia? They were supportive, but mostly puzzled. Connecting with me was very difficult. My mother was the perfect "June Cleaver" type, minus the formality of the pearls and shirtwaist dresses. Her life was wrapped up in doing typical 50s and 60s stuff for our family. Sometimes she worked herself into such a frazzle with cooking, cleaning, washing, ironing, and yelling at us kids that she came to the dinner table exhausted, laying her head down on the table while the rest of us ate.

Mom stressed herself out trying to keep up with June. My dad used to warn us: "You kids need to behave or Mom is going to have a nervous breakdown." I later learned that Mom's monthly migraines contributed to her frazzled state for years. An imbalance of hormones combined with severe pain is enough to make any woman go tilt. In any event, Mom finally got happy after her major stressors left—us kids!

My dad was the typical dad of that era, except he was a lot more fun than Ward Cleaver. When he came home from work, he always found time and energy to play "I'm Gonna Get Ya!" Dad chased us through the house while we screamed and ran to the closet. His great imagination fabricated games like: "Make a slaff" (Make us laugh). He'd line us up and make faces or weird noises until everyone laughed. Both Dad and Mom made valiant efforts to connect with me during my childhood, but they were, unfortunately, "Clueless in Cleveland."

If you lived in a home environment similar to mine, neither you nor I can blame our parents for our problems (except possibly in a genetic sense). I know my family would not have been classified as dysfunctional in the cultural framework of that time period. We did normal 50s and 60s things: ate meals together, played board games, watched Ed Sullivan, lived in a middle class neighborhood, and owned a neurotic beagle who had dog cooties. What could be a more normal home life? Well, I don't know, because I didn't live in anybody else's home.

In retrospect, it's obvious to me that my mom was suffering from bouts of anxiety and depression, and of course I swam in that gene pool. Additionally, my paternal grandmother was hit with a blast of anxiety genes, which skipped my dad, worked their way into my brain, and implanted bugs.

If we believe in the God who loves us and is in control of our lives, then we know we also have the power to swat and smash many of the cootie bugs that land on us. I know I would have benefited from knowing that God loved and accepted me unconditionally, cooties and all, and was helping me from His lofty position as the Sovereign Fly Swatter in the Sky.

Unfortunately, I had little awareness of God throughout my youth. He and I finally connected when I was twenty-five years old. For several months I attended a youth ministry with my boyfriend, a new Christian. I never planned to make the altar call to "get saved." I was divinely tricked. I misunderstood—possibly due to having fallen asleep. I thought I heard the pastor say: "Please come forward if anyone in your family needs prayer for healing." So I went to the altar to pray for Grandpa's pre-cancerous bladder polyps. I wasn't saved at the altar—I was too stunned. The purpose of going forward was to save Grandpa from his bladder polyps. But darned if I didn't end up getting saved five minutes later.

Those of us at the altar were led to a back room, where a sensitive counselor explained the gospel in a few minutes. One verse clinched it: "That if you confess with your mouth, 'Jesus is Lord,' and believe in your heart that God raised him from the dead, you will be saved." Something clicked when the counselor said, "confess with your mouth Jesus is Lord . . . " and of those seven words, the three key ones were: "confess, mouth, Jesus."

My life changed overnight, literally. I began to have a calmer outlook and experienced temporary moments of peace. I still had bugs in my brain, but God had done a work in my heart. My brain is still a work in progress, but I'm thankful the work in my heart was completed twenty-eight years ago.

The Unwelcome Visitor
by Brenda Thompson Ward

In December 1999, the world was abuzz about Y2K. Some people were preparing for a catastrophe. My own father had bought everything the disaster seekers had advised world population to purchase while waiting for the worst. He made certain he had plenty of bottled water and a variety of canned food. Dad was certain a catastrophe was on the way.

I was not concerned at all. I was not going to get upset because of all the frenzy over the subject. Just to prove everyone wrong, I was determined to stay awake until the year 2000 started. On New Year's Eve, I go to bed and welcome the New Year the next morning. However, wanting to have the certain joy of saying, "I told you so", I stretched out on the couch to wait for whatever would happen.

As Dick Clark counted down the last few seconds of 1999, and watching the ball fall in Time Square, I rubbed my right eye. I was shocked into a wide-awake state. Something was not right. I had vision only in the upper left eye. I covered my left eye and the vision in the right eye was all right. Once again, covering my right eye, it became obvious that something drastic had happened to my left eye.

Suddenly, anything else slipped into the category of the unimportant. Even Y2K. An uninvited and most unwelcome visitor had dropped into my life. I'm a people person and I have always enjoyed having guests drop by for a visit, even unexpected visitors. They are always welcome at out home. This new visitor spelled trouble from the beginning.

My ophthalmologist appointment was two days later but I would have sixteen days to wait and wonder. That gave me plenty of time to get my heart and nerves settled to face whatever was ahead, and I thought I was ready for anything.

The day of my visit to the eye doctor I taught my scheduled Bible Study at our church. We were studying the different gates in Chapter Three of Nehemiah. As I look back, I can see that God was preparing me for what was ahead later that afternoon. In the middle of the class I said, "We don't always understand why we have to go through valleys, but we must trust God and believe that He has a reason for what happens in our lives."

A couple of hours later I had to practice what I had taught that morning when I heard the doctor say, "Mrs. Ward, you have a mass on you left retina. I don't do masses, so I'm sending you to the Georgia Retina Center next door."

I remember thinking that I was a "walk-in" without an appointment, and would have to wait for hours. That was not the case. The receptionist met me at the door and whisked me into the first examining room. No waiting. Just whish, and you are under lights being checked out for two hours.

The idea this was serious kept dancing through my mind. When a doctor immediately sends you to a specialist and you have no appointment, but you are given priority status, you know you have a major problem. Suddenly, my bravado began to crumble. Now I was scared.

"I'm sorry, Mrs. Ward, I must tell you that you have a malignant melanoma on your left retina and it doesn't look like any benign tumor I've ever seen."

I found myself thinking, *Well, Brenda, looks like you're facing a valley. What are you going to do about it?* At that moment I became a statistic. Each year six people per million population will develop a melanoma of the eye. We all are known for something, but this was not what I would have chosen. My next thought was, *Oh Lord, I'm going to die.*

Although my husband and the doctor were in the room, I was in another zone. I could vaguely heard Dr. Lampert and my husband talking. I remember hearing something about Philadelphia.

Whenever you find out you have any form of a cancer in your body I firmly believe your next thought is of death, your own death. Then cancer becomes very personal. This unwelcome visitor brought the gift of fear.

My next thought was, as a Christian, do I not believe that if I died I would go to heaven? Yes, I do believe that, but I didn't particularly want to rush the situation. Finally, the last thing I remember thinking before I mentally returned to Dr. Lampert and my husband, was *but I'm not yet a grandmother.*

Before a definite decision could be made about treatment I had to have a complete physical, which included a mammogram, chest x-ray, and a liver function test. Just to make certain there were not other cancers. I also had to be checked by a doctor in one of the other offices of Georgia Retina Center.

By the time John and I got to the car, I was crying. That made me angry because I always wanted to be strong in the face of danger. I was not as upset about the cancer as I was angry because I was crying as if this were the end of the world.

It was only after taking time to catch my breath that I finally realized that God was, indeed, in control and that for some reason He had decided for me to go through this particular valley. It was up to me to react in a way that would either honor or dishonor Him.

The next two weeks were spent going to the physician for tests. All the results had to be sent to Dr. Lampert's office. The good news was that there were no other cancers in my body. Other than needing to lose some weight, my only problem was the melanoma on the retina. After all the tests were finished I once again visited Dr. Lampert. I was given a choice between different places to go for treatment. We chose Wills Eye Hospital in Philadelphia. My appointment was for February 7th at 8:30 A.M. I was informed that the testing would take the entire day.

John and I arrived in Philadelphia on Sunday night during a freezing rainstorm and strong winds. By the time we made it to our hotel a few blocks from the hospital, John was running a high fever. For some reason, I had brought a thermometer with me. I gave my husband Tylenol for the fever, and prayed he would be better the next morning. Monday morning, though bright with sunshine, was terribly cold and windy. John was still running a fever as I arrived a few minutes early for my appointment. This gave me a chance to observe several things about the other patients that came into the office.

The door opened and a large athletic man carrying a tiny infant walked into the office, and immediately walked back to the examining room. From what I could hear, the baby was about three weeks old and had tumors in both eyes. In the back of my mind I stopped and thanked God for fifty-four years of good vision, even if it took corrective lens to have that vision. It amazes me that in the midst of any trying situation, God can send someone across your path to point out that we should never complain about problems. There is always someone worse off than you.

After hours of testing and examinations from Dr. Jerry Shields and Dr. Carol Shields, the gravity of my situation was put into prospective. It was confirmed that I did indeed have a malignant melanoma on my left retina. I was told, "We're not here to save your eyesight. We're here to save your life."

Even though I thought that I was at peace with what was going on, hearing those words reinforced the importance of the situation. This was a life and death matter and I wanted to choose saving my life.

The treatment was Radiation (Plaque Radiotherapy). While in surgery, a small radiation plaque, the size of a dime was placed directly on the tumor. It is secured on the eye over the tumor to directly treat the tumor. It would be there for four days and I would be in isolation while undergoing the treatment.

Arriving at my room the night before the surgery, I was placed in a room with a large sign that read Hazardous Material on the door. I also wore a wrist ban with those same words. I remember asking my husband if he thought the sign was biographical.

Even though I love to be around people, I also value my "alone time". I remember thinking I'd have four days to lie around, read, listen to music, and think about my life. Being a writer, I took a journal to record my thoughts.

My husband could visit me for only three hours a day and he had to stand across the room. My alone time suddenly seemed a bit restrictive. Especially when you have live radiation in your body and even the cafeteria workers all but throw you food tray on your bed. One of the men that brought my food one day, smiled as he put the tray on the bedside table, and said, "Nothing personal, but, see you later."

Four days after entering the hospital for the implant, I had a very short surgery and by nine o'clock that night I was back home in Woodstock, Georgia.

It has been five years since I was a patient at Wills Eye Hospital in Philadelphia. I've been faithful to keep all my check-ups. It is a great thrill to leave the doctor each time knowing the tumor did shrink and that the treatment stopped its growth.

I was blessed to have doctors who were experts in their fields. I thank Dr. Lampert, Dr. Jerry Shield, Dr. Carol Shield, and my new doctor at Georgia Retina, Dr. Mark Rivelese, for their care. I feel God had them in the right place at the right time.

I look back on that experience and can still recall the fear I initially felt when hearing I had a cancer on my eye. I do not believe that things happen for no reason. Radioactive material was placed on my eye and has caused permanent damage to the left eye. The tumor has shrunk to a small speck. Hazardous material was placed in my body, but it would have been must more hazardous had I not allowed myself to see God walking me through this valley.

I believe in The Great Physician and I know He can heal, but I also know I was guided by Him and great doctors through what could have been a terrible tragedy. Out of this valley, I was forced to draw on the treasure chest of God's grace and peace that He alone provides. I found His grace is more than sufficient.

Also, my great fear of not being a grandmother has been satisfied. I now have four beautiful grandchildren and another on the way.

We've Got the Power
by Bonnie Greenwood Grant

It was about 70 degrees out side. The blue sky was filled with small-scattered clouds. It appeared spring had come. I was driving home from my four-year-old son Jeremy's swimming lesson. He was securely buckled in his car seat. His white blond hair was still wet and slicked back from his face. I turned up our street and slowed.

My friend Mary was outside in the yard with her son, Sean. They looked up from the flowers they were planting, waved a greeting and started walking across the street toward us. Sean, a blond haired enthusiastic four-year-old boy, was Jeremy's best friend. He had a joyful smile and a frequent giggle. Jeremy was frantically winding down the window as Sean and Mary came over to greet us. I pulled over to the side of the street and stopped. Sean was standing on his tiptoes and had both hands on the top of the open window as he chattered excitedly to Jeremy. His mother, Mary, a pretty, young blond woman, stood beside my window and we talked.

Cars came and went around us. Suddenly Sean let go of the window, turned and raced back toward his yard to show Jeremy his new toy. Mary and I both turned toward Sean and yelled in horror "No Sean!" at the same time. A black sedan with a woman driver appeared. The street had been recently blacktopped and still had gravel on the road. We could see the lady's look of terror as she tried to stop, but the car kept sliding toward Sean. There was a sickening thud as she hit him. His little body was tossed like a rag doll up on the hood of her car. We heard his head slam against the windshield. He slid off the hood on the far side of the street.

Just as I was getting out of my car, a guy ran his car into the back of my car. He jumped out and started yelling, "You backed into me." I looked at my hand brake, which was pulled up and just shook my head. Sean could be lying there dying and this bozo is trying to get out of paying for damages he caused by not paying attention.

"Get out of here," I said.

I ran over to Mary, Sean and the poor distraught motorist, who was sobbing. She kept saying, "He just darted in front of me and I tried to stop, but I couldn't."

I heard the guy start his car, pull around my car, and drive off. Sean was lying still on the gravel. His little body looked crumpled and his eyes were closed. Mary was starting to lift him.

"No, he shouldn't be moved." I remembered some things from my first aid classes. I ran back to my car and grabbed a blanket from the trunk.

"Here, cover him with this. I'll go call 911." I raced up her front steps and into her kitchen. I called 911, hoping my mind wouldn't go blank when they asked for the address. I ran out and told Mary they were on their way. She asked me to call Cliff, her police officer husband who was working out at the gym. My hands were starting to shake and my voice was getting weepy as the situation began to sink into my brain. My voice was quivery as I asked for Cliff Walters. The receptionist said she couldn't reach him and asked if she could take a message.

"Tell him that his son was hit by a car and that he'll be taken to Sacred Heart Hospital."

"Oh, I'll find him some how, even if I have to go into the men's locker room."

I could hear the ambulance arriving. A man's voice reverberated in the kitchen. "I'll stay and wait for him. I think Mary might need you outside."

.

I looked up to see Ken, my stepbrother. My widowed mother had married his father the year previously. Ken lived three houses away.

Ken looked like an angel standing in the doorway, granted, not the conventional angel. He was tall and slim with dark hair and small mustache. His angelic traits were appearing out of nowhere and taking care of everything. *Thank God, Ken would take care of notifying Cliff.* He gave me a quick hug, and then took the phone to wait for Cliff to come on the line. By this time, I wasn't capable of speech. Sean could be dying.

I ran outside. The ambulance was there and the stocky, dark haired female paramedic was forcing Sean to walk. My jaw dropped. Surely that was not the way to treat a person hit by a car. The paramedic put Sean in the ambulance and told Mary that she couldn't ride with them but would have to follow in her own vehicle. Mary rushed to her own truck and climbed inside.

"Mary, you shouldn't drive. You're shaking worse than I am. Let me have my stepbrother, Ken, take you." Ken had just come out of the house.

"Cliff said he'd meet you at the hospital." He said.

"No, I'm going to drive down. I'll be OK. Honest." She pulled out behind the ambulance. I looked over at my car. Jeremy was still buckled in his car seat. I leaned in and hugged him. He was worried about his friend. The week before he had seen a little white dog hit by a car and killed. The incident had really upset him. It was only natural that he would be worried about the same thing happening to his friend. He wanted to know if Sean would be all right. I told him he would be. He must not have been hurt too bad if the "experts" had him walking around.

I drove the block to our house, parked the car in the garage and fed Jeremy his lunch. After I laid him down for his nap, I went to call the hospital to make sure Mary had arrived safely. I had prayed for her safety so I was pretty sure she was all right. I told the operator that my friend's little boy was hit by a car and brought in by ambulance. She put me through to the emergency waiting room. Cliff, Mary's husband, answered the phone.

"Did Mary get there ok?"

"Yes."

I breathed a sigh of relief. As an afterthought, I asked about Sean, thinking that he must be fine because he'd been up and walking about.

"How's Sean doing?"

"He's not responding."

"What?"

"He's not responding. He was unconscious by the time he got here and when they stick him with a pin he doesn't respond. He's not going to make it"

I stopped breathing. I could feel my body growing cold, but my mind was racing. I thought immediately of the county wide prayer chain. Every church in the county was part of it.

"Cliff, I'm going to hang up right now and call the prayer chain. Will you be alright?"

"Yes", he said after a short pause.

I immediately called the prayer chain.

"Please call us back and let us know how he is," the prayer chain captain said. Her voice was full of concern. It was a mother's voice.

"I will."

I went to my bedroom, closed the door and knelt, praying fervently. I could feel the power as I prayed for Sean. I knew I was not alone. At least a hundred others were kneeling with me. I was still shaky and crying, begging God for Sean's life. Gradually, a peace and a surety crept through me, then gladness, then joy. I got up and almost skipped to the bedroom door. As I opened the door, I heard the phone ringing. I had a premonition as to who it was.

"Cliff?"

"He's responding! He's conscious. He'll make it."

"Thank you, Jesus, thank you." I said quietly.

"No, it wasn't that," he said. "They must have made a mistake. That's what happened. They made a mistake."

I wanted to say, *don't be absurd.* I had felt that power. I had felt the prayers rising like incense before the altar of God. I had felt God's presence. Why would you not want to believe that there was a creator who loved you and would answer your prayers or your neighbor's prayers, on your behalf?

I called the prayer chain back. The lady said to me, "You know it was the strangest thing. I knew he would be healed the moment I started praying for him. Maybe it was because I knew there were a lot of mothers in the group who have four-year olds and you know, "Fervent prayers of righteous mothers availeth much."

I smiled.

God's Amazing Grace
by Diana J. Baker

God's hand has been on my life for as long as I can remember. I grew up in a Christian family, was introduced to Jesus at a young age, and accepted Him as my Savior at the age of ten. I loved going to church and can remember crying on the way home from a Sunday family outing when I realized we wouldn't be home in time for the evening service.

By the time I was seventeen, I knew I had a call of God on my life. I dedicated my life to full time Christian service that year at a youth camp in Pensacola, Florida (my birthplace).

I majored in music in college, because I knew it was an avenue through which I could minister. I remained active in church during my college years and regularly participated in Christian groups on campus.

My senior year at the University of Southern Mississippi, I met Larry Baker, and in less than a year we married. I knew God had put us together, but I wondered how God's call on my life for full time service would be fulfilled. Women were not allowed to serve in pastoral positions in our denomination, and Larry had no plans of entering the ministry. Larry was a Christian, but he was also an accounting major with aspirations of becoming a CPA and eventually a lawyer. I decided to rest in God and trust Him to bring about His purposes for my life.

The week before Larry's graduation from USM, he secured a civil service accounting job at Ft Benning in Columbus, Georgia. The day before his finals began, our first child, Shannon, was born. Larry took his finals, and on the following Saturday, when Shannon was six days old, we moved out of our college apartment. Larry drove Shannon and me to my parent's house in Jackson, Mississippi to stay for a few weeks, spent the night, and then left on Sunday morning with a full rental heading for Columbus.

He arrived safely in Columbus, parked the rental at his new boss' house, and spent the night in a motel. On Monday he started his new job. His boss took him to lunch and to see a vacant house near where he lived. That afternoon, Larry bought the house and moved in. Shannon and I flew to Columbus and our new home two weeks later.

Later we found out that the house had been vacant for six months and the strong Christian couple across the street had been praying that God would put a Christian family into the house. God answered our prayers and theirs, and we enjoyed weekly Bible studies and great fellowship together.

Eighteen months later, Larry was transferred to Ft. McClellan in Anniston, Alabama. We had our second daughter, Jennifer, three weeks after that move, and only a week after we had moved out of a motel and into our new four-bedroom home.

We joined and became active in a great church, growing stronger and stronger in the Lord. We also taught couple's Bible studies in our home. During that time, I became pregnant with our third child.

Imagine my surprise when Larry came home from work one day and announced that God wanted him to quit his job and go to seminary to prepare for full time ministry. My response was a resounding "YES!" The mystery was solved. God had been at work all along, and full time ministry was on the horizon.

Larry gave a two-week notice the next day, and we put our house on the market. Within two weeks the house had sold, and we were packing to move to my parent's new home in Gulfport, Mississippi, until time for us to move to the seminary.

When we got to Gulfport, God had a surprise for us. Larry's cousin owned a fully furnished house there that she rented out, and it *just so happened* that her renters had moved out the week before we arrived. We rented the house for three months, while we purchased a mobile home and secured a place for it on the seminary campus. Our son, Stephen, was born in Gulfport on October 1st, and we moved to the seminary campus the last week in December.

During Larry's second year in seminary, I became pregnant with our fourth child. We were excited about the prospect of a new baby, but the big question was 'where are we going to put the baby bed?' Not only were Larry and I and our three children living in our single-wide mobile home, but another seminary student, Fred Vann, had moved in with us after his wife had left him.

Since all of our bedrooms were full, Fred had been sleeping for five months on a cot in the living room with his feet under his grand piano. Yes, you read that right. Fred's grand piano took up half of our living room, so we couldn't get the hide-a-bed opened out for him to sleep on.

A new home was a must, so Larry and I began searching for a house to rent or buy. Of course, our search was faith-based, as our finances were limited.

Newspaper ads led us to an older home in a neighborhood not far from the seminary. When we found the house, no one was at home, and there was no "For Sale" sign in the yard. Larry talked to the next door neighbor, who informed him that the house was not supposed to be on the market until the following week. However, she called the owners and let Larry talk to them.

The surprised owners, who had just built and moved into a new home, came over and toured us through the house. We asked if we could rent the house with the option to buy it.

However, they explained that the house was under contract, and we would have to go through the realtor. We knew we couldn't afford the realtor's asking price.

We went home disappointed and unable to get the four-bedroom house, with its fifteen-by-thirty-foot den and fenced back yard, off our minds. For the next six months we prayed that if God wanted us to have the house, He would hold it for us.

Amazingly, the house didn't sell. When the contract expired, the owners called us to see if we still wanted to rent the house. We rented it for two years for $150 per month and were then able to purchase it for only $29,000. Our daughter, Mary, was born a few weeks after we moved in. God's perfect timing once again.

We lived in the house for three years, during which time Fred married Debbie, a wonderful Christian girl, and Larry and I opened a macramé and craft store in partnership with friends in Canton, Georgia. Those hectic days were some of the happiest days of our lives.

At the end of 1978, our business partner asked us to move to Canton to help with his mushrooming business. After several prayerful months, we hired people to manage our shop in New Orleans and moved to Canton. Our house in New Orleans sold six months later for an unbelievable $45,000. We rejoiced in God's abundant blessings.

Soon our business partner opened stores in Acworth and Alpharetta, but God had other plans for us. Larry was asked to be the interim pastor of a fledgling church that we were attending. He accepted the job. Eventually, he liquidated our shop in New Orleans, turned our other business interests over to our partner, and began to serve God in full-time ministry.

In 1986 I was ordained as Larry's Co-Pastor. We have served as the pastors of Prayer and Praise Christian Fellowship, originally called Word of Faith Church, for the past twenty-five years. Through those years—filled with joy and sadness, blessing and sorrow, success and failure—God has been faithful to us.

God miraculously provided the finances for our small church to buy fifteen acres of property in Woodstock, Georgia and to build a large church building on it, without incurring any debt. With the exception of three months during the bricking process, the church has remained debt free through the past twenty-five years. Currently the property is valued at around eight to nine million dollars.

Larry and I bought an acre of the property from the church in 1986 and built a five-bedroom home for our family. That house has been a great blessing, as we have raised our family and hosted many bridal and wedding showers, parties, and ministry guests.

In 1989, God comforted and sustained Larry and me when our sixteen-year-old son, Stephen, was hit by a car and killed. We found out then that God is faithful in every circumstance of life. Though weeping endured for a night season, God restored our joy. He has since blessed us with eight wonderful grandchildren—five of them boys.

Larry and I can identify with John Newton, the author of *Amazing Grace*, as we sing, "Through many dangers, toils and snares, we have already come. 'Tis grace hath brought us safe thus far, and grace will lead us home." As Andrea Crouch, sang, "Through it all, we've learned to trust in Jesus, we've learned to trust in God."

God is forever faithful to His children, and I thank Him daily for His great love. I am blessed to be called His servant and to know that His hand is upon my life for good. No matter what I have given up or given out, I could never out give my awesome God. My life is a testimony to His amazing grace.

Recognizing His Hand
by Robert W. Ellis

It is exciting to see God's hand working in your own life, but it is especially exhilarating when you can see His guiding in the lives of your children.

My wife and I have three children and five grandchildren. We discuss weekly how God has blessed each of them in special ways. Our oldest son has a wife and sweet family as a direct result of God's blessings in his life. Our youngest son's career has, on many occasions, been directed by God's hand.

A few years ago, he had decided to move from New York to Los Angeles to seek more opportunities for his acting career. A series of annoyances had occurred prior to his leaving for the West Coast. He confided sometime later that he had decided that if one more thing went wrong regarding the trip, he would take it as a sign from God not to go. On the day of his departure, his Jeep and rental trailer was only twenty miles from home before the engine fan belt broke. He canceled his plans and currently lives in the Atlanta area taking advantage of "gigs" here.

Our daughter, her husband and their three girls are another living testimony to God's grace and mercy. We have watched His hand move in her family for fourteen years. The following, in the words of my daughter, Kimberly Ellis Golden, is only part of the story.

* * * *

"Seminary was never a word that I ever thought would be associated with my name. It was where the really holy 'other'

92

people went to learn more about getting holier. The path that I took in life was drastically changed because seminary became a place that God had chosen for my new husband and me.

"I met a wonderful man at church, Todd Golden, and knew that he was the one after the first month of knowing him. We had a two and a half-year courtship, before becoming engaged. I vaguely remember him mentioning a call to the ministry during those two plus years, but conveniently dismissed the conversation. My mind would never willingly accept moving more than 100 miles away from my mama. To emphasize this fact I drew a 100-mile circle around Marietta, Georgia. on a map for my beloved.

"We married in March 1991 and by August of that same year were living in a foreign place called Memphis. (It had a pyramid). How did it happen? One day I was a five minute drive from my parents, and the next, a rental moving truck was leaving Georgia dragging my little Toyota Corolla.

"I am like most people and would never outright say no to God. Another generalization that I would like to make is that most of us will not say no but we go kicking and screaming into His will. That is what I did through the first three years of our move to seminary. I was one of His brattiest kids.

"Todd was having the time of his life in seminary. He loved the whole experience. That made me even madder. He was soaking up all the knowledge of a loving Father that he could get. I was looking for anything that I could fit into what I like to call my "bag of bitterness". It was full and heavy to carry. I would try to get Todd to help me carry it but he never would. Seeing the joy that he was finding made me realize that I had to lose the bag. How? God gave me two words—repent and recognize.

"I could not live with the misery any longer so I had to fall on my face and repent and ask forgiveness. After a flood of forgiveness was loosed in me, I began to recognize how God was sustaining us even through my rebellion.

"There were so many ways that He had blessed us even in my bitterness. I had failed to see it and thank Him. We had very little money in seminary but there were only two semesters that we had to pay tuition because of anonymous donors.

"Our little Corolla broke down and we had to take out a loan to pay for the repair. The same day we took out the loan, a check for the exact amount came in the mail.

We had no medical insurance, but I got a job that offered full coverage the month before we found out we were to be parents.

"A lady in our church volunteered to keep our daughter for free while I worked. The record of His goodness to us during seminary is endless. God wanted me to trust Him as my Father and recognize Him as my Sustainer. His plans have never failed to amaze me. Now my eyes are always searching to recognize His hand in my journey."

* * * *

In the beginning, my wife and I would marvel at how God was working in Kimberly's family, but no more. Each time we hear such stories, we simply smile and nod and say, "thank you, God" for this daily miracle.

Prodigal
by Farrow Beacham

"I have wasted the wealth, which the Father gave to me, and in my wretchedness, I have fed with the dumb beasts. Yearning after their food, I remained hungry and could not eat my fill. But now I return to the compassionate Father and cry with tears: I fall down before Thy loving-kindness; receive me as a hired servant and save me!"

This hymn, well known among Orthodox Christians, is sung A cappella every year on the Sunday of the Prodigal Son. Saint John of Damascus most likely wrote it before 700 AD. It reminds the Orthodox faithful of repentance and forgiveness, which are central to the parable of the Prodigal son, and central to our salvation. Every time I hear the hymn, it reminds me that my life has been a lot like the Prodigal Son. My story is a long one, but I have wanted to tell it for several years. I joined the Christian Author's Guild a couple of years ago with only one goal — that I would write an article that might help others like myself, who had left their church or worse, quit Christianity altogether. Maybe one person would hear my story, and perhaps change their thinking.

When the announcement was given at a guild meeting, that we were writing the book of testimonies I was overjoyed at a chance to write what I had to say. After I thought about it for a while, I feared putting my testimony in this book with other people's wonderful, sudden, and clearly defined events, because my salvation was not an intense, instant transformation. It is just the exact opposite — a slow moving, ongoing process.

I started out brought into the Presbyterian Church with the sprinkling of water on my head as an infant. I stayed close to that church until I graduated from high school. I loved going to Sunday School, and I got several perfect attendance pins, Bibles, and similar awards. When I became eligible to join the church at nine years old, I jumped at the chance. I attended a couple of Saturday classes, which enabled me to start taking communion four times a year. On those Sundays I usually helped my father pour grape juice into all the tiny glasses, and I helped him break the matzo crackers into small pieces onto the silver trays, I thought this was all the preparation needed to take communion. Nobody ever mentioned repentance or confession of my sins prior to communion.

Although I went through the motions of receiving the Lord's Supper, I always felt guilty and worried someone was going to find out that I was faking it. I watched my father and all the other elders who distributed the silver trays, and I could see that most of the grownups would partake of communion, and then hold their temples or bow their head. At first I thought they had a headache, and I always felt guilty because I never felt a thing, headache, joy, or some kind of religious feeling. Nobody mentioned that this was supposed to me symbolic, so I kept expecting more. However, I went to church every time the doors opened, because my parents went, and I tried to be a good kid and do what they wanted.

About the same time I joined the church, I remember my parents went to see, A Man Called Peter, a movie about Peter Marshall, the famous Presbyterian preacher, who was chaplain of Congress. When I learned my parents were truly inspired by the movie, I planned to become a minister in the Presbyterian Church. As a start I worked for my church for a year, earning the Boy Scouts' God and County Award, and then I went away to college to a Presbyterian school with intentions of joining the ministry.

When I went to college, my roommate was a Yankee, and since he was from "up North", he had instant credibility over my teachers and preachers. He claimed to be a beatnik. He sure wasn't much of a Christian, and several other kids I met also challenged all the spiritual things I had taken for granted — the miracles of Jesus, the virgin birth, Christ's crucifixion, and resurrection. Several other students told me, that they didn't get much out of communion either. At some point, I convinced myself that the act of taking communion, and getting nothing out of it was breaking one of the Ten Commandments — taking God's name in vain. Then I started questioning everything related to Christianity and the church, and I started skipping my freshman Bible class. Next, I stopped going to daily chapel services, and then I made up my mind that I was no longer a Presbyterian nor any kind of a Christian. I left Jesus and His Church just like the rich son left his father, thinking I could have a better relationship with God by myself.

Some months later after I was academically suspended, my draft status went to 1-A, and since the Viet Nam War was in progress, I soon found myself at the reception center for new soldiers at Fort. Jackson, South Carolina. My first Sunday there we were given a choice of peeling potatoes on KP or attending church. Instantly all 400 of us in my battalion decided we wanted to go to church. They marched us there and ordered us to sing Onward Christian Soldiers, as we went, which I objected to, but not as loudly as Private Moskowitz, a conservative Jew from Chicago who marched beside me.

The chaplain's message was abrupt, shocking, and unpleasant. "Men, half of you are going to be killed in Viet Nam in the next six months. If you haven't given your heart to Jesus, you had better do it right now, or you will burn in hell forever. After all, the Christian thing to do is to kill the Viet Cong, who are nothing but godless communists," he shouted.

His next message was that he was going to take up a free will offering for the wives and children of servicemen killed in Viet Nam. I looked at Moskowitz, who gestured to me that this person was a crook, because there was no organization to channel the funds to the needy people. As they marched us back to the barracks singing Onward Christian Soldiers, I promised myself never to go in a Christian church ever again.

After basic training, I spent the next three years overseas. Even though I studied most of the other religions, I couldn't find anything I could believe in for various reasons. While I was in foreign countries of course, I did everything I think the prodigal son must have done, and much more than a usual share of excesses and sinning. I survived several bar brawls, often woke up in wrong places, and almost drank myself to death a couple of times. Of course I squandered every dime I made. I came home financially broke and spiritually broken, but when I came back to my hometown, the girl I left behind agreed to marry me. Even though she was a Christian, I made her marry me in the Unitarian church. She asked me, "What do the Unitarians believe in?"

I proudly replied, "They say they pray 'to whom it may concern'; and their creed is that they have no creed." She must have loved me an awful lot to have put her own faith on hold, and we did not go into a Christian Church for several more years, due to my problems with Christianity, but she never pushed her beliefs on me. Since my study of religion had produced no results, I realized that even though I didn't believe in Jesus Christ, I knew she did. Therefore, I told her I had always believed in God, and that I would go to church with her, but that I would never take communion, nor would I ever join another Christian church.

We started attending an Episcopal church, one that was high church, also called Anglo Catholic. There was plenty of incense and bells, kneeling to pray, genuflecting, and the order of worship was complicated to my church experience. My wife took communion every Sunday, but I just watched, because it was a closed sacrament just for Episcopalians. I started having good feelings about the warmth and holiness of the services. I started wanting to be a part of it, but I knew I didn't deserve to, with my past rejection of Christianity and all the sinning I had done. I started wondering, if communion could help me believe in Jesus Christ, or if communion would seem as empty as it had been for me previously. Eventually, I went to see the priest, and told him I wanted to take instructions, but I told him that unless I felt at some point that I would have a genuine religious experience, I was sure that I did not want to take communion.

When Father Morley told me that I had to come to class every Saturday for a year, I was flabbergasted, because it only took a couple of one-hour classes to become a Presbyterian, and I could easily take communion at any Presbyterian church I wanted to attend. He asked me, "Well, do you really want to find out about this or not?" I told him that I did, so he spent the whole year teaching me a lot about theology, the Trinity, the Creeds, preparation for communion, repentance, forgiveness, and the order of worship. I may have missed one or two Saturdays, but when the year was over, he told me that the bishop was coming to confirm me, if I wanted him to. By this time I seriously wanted more than ever to receive the Holy Gifts. Unfortunately, I came down with the flu and missed the bishop's visit. A couple of weeks later, when I was well, I came again on Saturday morning and asked Father Morley what my next step would be.

He calmly said, "You need to continue to take instruction until next year when the bishop comes back." Again, I was astonished, but at this point, I had realized that turning my back on Jesus and his church was sinful. Because I had separated myself from the church, I was sorry, and I had asked for His forgiveness, but even for a while I felt the waiting was my punishment for what I had done.

I continued to take instruction, and I had repented, but I felt like I had not yet been forgiven nor welcomed home yet. I prayed for a conclusion of my training. All of a sudden, Father Morley decided to retire, and the bishop sent a new priest, Father Johnson. I told him my life story and about my life of sin and having turned my back on Jesus. I had repented of my sin, but I felt hungry for communion, like the prodigal son -- hungry and still far away from home. Like the prodigal son's father, he was forgiving, and he said," Your formal training is finished, and you will take communion this Sunday. We will get the bishop to confirm you the next time he comes."

That Sunday he got up to preach the sermon, his first ever in a church he would later preach at for many years, but he was struck speechless from emotion. No wonder people said God works in mysterious ways. Father Johnson's subsequent sermons were wonderful, wonderful enough that he is now a bishop in the Episcopal Church. That day was very special for him and for me. Twenty minutes after his silent message, I had an incredible holy experience with tears, joy, and an absolute feeling the presence of the Holy Spirit when I received the Divine Gifts. I had finally come home, just like the prodigal. My wife and I were now a Christian family, but this story isn't over yet.

A year or so later, I was unexpectedly promoted and transferred to Wisconsin. At the same time, the Episcopal Church drastically modernized their prayer book, which was central to their order of worship. Everything was modernized, the hymns, the worship and the holy traditions. In Milwaukee we looked for a high Episcopal Church, but after more than a year, but we never found one. We were lost in a very liberal, minimalist Episcopalian diocese. I had a hard time feeling the sense of sanctity that I had grown accustomed to, and communion started to seem empty again. Our former priest, Father Johnson, came to Wisconsin at our request and met with the local bishop and us. Our conclusion was that there were no Anglo Catholic parishes in Wisconsin, and we could leave the Episcopal Church or leave Wisconsin. We started going to every different kind of church festival we could find. And one Sunday after another less than wonderful service, at another new church, I asked God to give us a sign of what we should do. The car was pointed South, and in the dead of winter, with a light snowfall, all of a sudden there was a beautiful rainbow that arched all the way across the horizon. I told my wife that a rainbow in the middle of winter was something I had never seen. We felt if we headed south our spiritual problems would be solved. Instantly, I realized that the new job wasn't as wonderful as I it should have been, so, I quit my job and we decided to come home to our old church.

I was able to find a job about 60 miles south of our old parish. We even tried to fit into the local parish, but the local Episcopal Church had about that time ordained a woman priest, thus it was not the service or traditions we were accustomed to, so we commuted 60 miles each way on Sunday to go back to the high church services. However, even our old parish had adopted the new Episcopal prayer book and had made major changes in the order of worship. We were disappointed that we just couldn't seem to find what we had lost.

I had made the change from being a non-Christian to a traditionalist Christian. Communion had gone from a pretend experience into a genuinely mystical one for me, but at that point, with the new, less formal service, the mystery was not there very often. I started to be afraid, because I felt that if I returned to just going through the motions, that I was back where I started. I prayed as hard as I could for God to help me find a way to keep my newfound faith alive. I began to have serious worry about my faith once again.

One morning at work, IBM called on me for our usual monthly meeting. I was a Data Processing Manager in a large carpet mill. During the prior decade, IBM had told me about more than a few situations to make extra money by doing work for other computer users, since this was long before personal computers. This time IBM asked me to volunteer to assist a local monastery, where the monks had started a company doing computer service work. This was the monastery's way to earn their daily bread. IBM explained that the local branch office had given the monks all the training they could afford to donate, but the monastery still needed considerable hand-holding. I sympathized with their computer problems. IBM told me they were Orthodox Christians, but I had absolutely no idea what that really meant.

I was afraid of cults, and suspicious of the monks and their religion, but I really owed IBM many favors, so I started teaching them. I showed them how to program their computer better, and they asked me to be their technical advisor. I agreed to continue to work with them. One day they asked my wife and me to attend one of their services. My wife almost always went with me to the monastery due to my concerns about them, and she would read or sew while I taught. We told the monks that we were high church Episcopalians, and that we thought that their services must be more complicated than ours, and that we might not know when to sit or stand or kneel.

Father Michael, one of the founders of the monastery told us, "That won't be a problem." He took us into their chapel. "Notice anything different?" he asked. I told him that it looked like someone had stolen his pews. When he told us they didn't use pews, I asked him why. He then asked me, if the President of the United States walked into the room we were in, would I stand up? I nodded affirmatively, and he asked me when would I sit down? He told us that at all of their services they expect Jesus, God the Father, and the Holy Spirit to be there with us, along with a cloud of witnesses, all Christians that have gone before us.

He asked, "Wouldn't you show them as much respect as you would the President?" This, was the first I learned of many Christian traditions, preserved to this day and still used, that came from as far back as the disciples and the early church. We went to church with them that Sunday, and it was very different, with an unusual feeling of holiness. Almost every word of the service was sung or chanted, and every word sounded like it had come out of the King James Version of the Bible. Later, I found out that was truly the case.

My only problem was that it was also a closed communion, and only Orthodox Christians could partake of the Holy Gifts. On the other hand, without even receiving communion, I had the most significant religious experience that I had in years. Years later, I would read that a Russian Orthodox Saint said that the presence of God is as obvious as a tooth ache. When I read that, I instantly recalled that first service, and every one ever since. .My wife and I felt immediately that we had finally found the Church for us. We had been looking for the sense of tradition and holiness we had missed for a long time. We would later find that little had changed in the Orthodox Church in at least fifteen hundred years. Most interestingly, we found that Orthodox Christians were not surprised by a religious experience in every service. Instead, they always expected one, and if it didn't happen, they felt in a state of separation (sin) from Jesus and his church.

We had to tell Father Johnson that we had left the Episcopal Church. This was a difficult task, but we are still good friends and godparents to his son. We rarely went back to an Episcopal church, and after almost 25 years, we have continued to attend church at the Monastery of the Glorious Ascension in Resaca, Georgia. After at least another 6 months of instruction every week and after significant preparation, we were Baptized and received communion during a typical Christian Sunday service.

At 17, I was sure I knew all I needed to know about Christianity, but forty years later I continue to learn about it one day at a time. Some of the lessons are from the Bible, and some are from the ancient worship, the hymnography, the oral traditions of the Church, not merely what is in the Bible alone -- sola scriptura. The theology is ubiquitous in the Bible, the written word of God, and in the oral traditions, the worship, and ancient hymns, like the one that started this testimony. All of these were created by the same people who were divinely inspired to write and compose the Bible, many centuries before the reformation even prior to all of the Ecumenical Councils.

In the last two decades, I have been able to grow spiritually from every communion, and in every service to prepare for communion. . Others who believe that communion is just a symbol of what Jesus taught us, and that his presence is not included may feel this way because the reformers rejected the medieval Roman view of transubstantiation. However, Eastern Christians never analyzed or tried to define the mystery in the Eucharist. They just remembered Him. They remembered Him in two ways: They thought about his presence in the past, but they also put him back together for the present. In doing this the Body of Christ meant more, but the mystery was not analyzed or defined, and it still has no need to be.

My feeble mind and soul need to have communion be mysteriously revealed to me through deep and sincere repentance and preparation, and by holistic worship that involves the whole person with all of our senses. There is incense to smell, holy relics, bibles, and other things and each other to touch, icons to look at that are windows into heaven, hymns to hear making a joyful noise and teaching us, and the wonderful taste and spiritual food of the holy gifts, the body and blood of Jesus Christ (John 6:53-56). This bringing forth of our entire person, humbly and obediently before Jesus Christ is not just attending a service, but complete participation in the worship at the throne of God. Through the Divine mysteries of the church we are able to worship beyond time and space far beyond our mere reality as fallen humans. We are called to come before Christ and the cloud of witnesses with humility and love, with awe and with thankfulness to worship. He who made Himself like us for us, now calls us to make ourselves like Him for our sake too.

When I finally returned to my Father's house, He received me warmly, and treated me even better than before I left. He put the gold ring on my finger, and he had them kill the fatted calf for me. Surely I do not deserve his grace and mercy, but I found out one thing, that if you come home to Him, you will have far more than you even imagined you could get on your own.

911 Angel
by R.T. Byrum

In hindsight, canceling the canoe outing on the Miami River that day would have been a wise decision, but our church youth had planned this six-mile whitewater trip for months. They had raised canoe rental money, and had attended water safety classes with growing anticipation of this day. Besides, there was no hint of disaster on the morning's pine-scented breeze. The sky was a Thomas Kinkade painting, awash in red and gold, with only the occasional cloud drifting across the waking sun.

Earlier in the week a drought-breaking rainfall of three inches had deluged southern Ohio. Streams once diminished to trickles were now surging to within a hand's span of flood stage. Downstream from us the Miami drank hungrily from its tributaries, and the swollen current carried rafts of branch and leaf debris to the Ohio River and beyond.

The pastor raised his hand for silence. "Father, your children delight in the fresh air, the cool water, the green trees and the blue skies. Today, we are here to enjoy all of your bounty and ask that you place your angels about us to deliver us safely to our destination downstream. Amen."

A chorus of "Amens" followed. After life jackets were double checked, a caution against horseplay delivered, and water safety rules reviewed, we were *go for launch*. Novices entered the canoes first followed by teammates, and then each craft was pushed out into the quietly flowing current near the ramp.

Shouts and good-natured ribbing greeted awkward attempts to guide the canoes while trying to establish a paddle rhythm. Two of the craft collided less than twenty feet from shore and the first of several unplanned baptisms took place.

Fortunately, the shallow water made it simple to upright the craft, and the soaked crews regained their seats and some of their pride.

"I'm no novice," I informed my canoe partner a short time later, "having paddled a kayak around a large lake, but I admit that the way the current is increasing each time we pass a stream emptying into the river is making me uneasy." He nodded his accord. The two of us were at the rear of the flotilla to assure everyone's safety, and to aid anyone in difficulty.

The first heart-stopping incident occurred several miles downstream. A young man and woman, not of our group, had collided with a pile of driftwood and their canoe was entangled in the jagged branches. Rope ends had been tossed to them from the towering bank by rescuers, and the two frightened boaters were being lifted to safety. Before our startled eyes the surging river violently twisted the canoe into a crumpled mass of aluminum and oak.

I breathed, "Oh, God. Thank for your mercy on your children." My partner and I increased our paddling tempo. We needed to stay close to our young people for fear that they would become the next victims of the river. Heavier debris, including entire trees, was either flowing along with us or was caught up on the bank or on a bottom obstruction. I breathed easier when I saw that our group was staying well away from those deadly traps with only a mile remaining to the recovery landing.

Rounding the final bend, we were stunned to see one of our chaperone couples in extreme danger. A huge walnut tree had washed from the bank, and was now wedged against the bottom. Its serpentine roots protruded above the surface downstream. The massive trunk and branches were aimed like spears toward the onrushing water and people-laden boats.

The chaperones' canoe had been bent and twisted around a thick branch, and the man and his wife had been flung into the river and then washed up against the tangle of roots. They were both balancing on the trunk, pinned up to their waists by the swiftly flowing current—unable to escape.

The sight was so frightening and overwhelming that I failed to act in time to prevent our own craft from colliding with the same tree. "Watch out," my partner screamed as he was jolted from his seat, swept along the tree, and instantly wedged between the other two captives.

My canoe was pivoting around a branch, and was being drug beneath the surface by the merciless pressure of the swollen flood. Struggling against the fear of drowning, I managed to pull myself from the doomed boat by a handhold on one of the branches. My face was barely above the surface, but the drag on my shoes and life jacket was pulling me under.

My mind screamed—*If I lose my grip, I'll be swept under this tree and be jammed into the roots.* A terrifying mental picture flashed before me; recovery divers prying my body out of the tangle while curious onlookers gathered along the twenty-foot high bank to watch.

"Help!" I choked as muddy water filled my mouth. On the tree the others watched my struggle in horror.

My arms and hands were tiring from the relentless strain until my thoughts began to surrender to the peace of letting go. Between choking gasps, I finally cried aloud, "Oh, Merciful God, I can't hold on. Save me. I know You won't let me die this way."

The strong pair of hands that suddenly gripped my upper arms was also strangely gentle. My eyes were still closed in prayer when a calm masculine voice said, "Let go and relax—you're in my hands, now. You're safe."

Unbelievably, I obeyed. The sun and water made it difficult to open my eyes, but when I did, I saw a young man with short blond hair. He looked to be in his mid-twenties, well-built, yet not muscle bound. He held me effortlessly and told me that on the count of three, he would lift me onto the trunk.

Those next moments are still very fuzzy in my memory. I do recall making my way down the length of the tree toward my three companions. My rescuer moved behind me with his hands firmly on my waist. Then, we four shipwreck victims stood pressed side-by-side against the roots and stared in wonder at the stranger who had appeared from nowhere. Clad in red swimming trunks, he stood before us, unmoving against the deadly current with nothing to brace him.

His quiet voice instantly filled us with a peace and confidence that defied the logic of our hopeless predicament. "Listen to me. One at a time, I'll boost you out past the roots. Don't fight the river. Let yourself drift past this tree, then swim with the current and you'll be carried to the beach where your friends are waiting to help. Do not fear—you will be safe."

There is no other way to describe what happened next. The mysterious champion literally picked each of us up and tossed us the ten feet or so needed to clear the spoke-like roots. We drifted and swam, and were soon pulled to safety as promised.

Amid cries of joy and tears of relief, we all turned to watch for the one who had saved us to make his way to the beach. There was no one there. The tree and the river were empty of any sign of the handsome young athlete in red trunks. A staff member from the canoe livery called 911 to report an apparent drowning, but there were growing whispers of understanding beginning to flow among the group gathered at the landing.

A young woman spoke. "I saw the man standing on the bank above the tree right before he dove into the water, but I don't remember him climbing onto the tree." Another described witnessing our rescue to the accompanying nods of the rest.

As I told of my desperate prayer, and described how I had been pulled from the water, the other survivors spoke of their own desperate prayers for deliverance.

Perhaps when this life is over, I'll encounter an angel with short blonde hair who once appeared before me in a pair of red swimming trunks. I hope so, for I'd like to thank him personally for the extra years that I've been given, and for the deeper awareness of the gift of life. In the meantime, I have given thanks many times to the One who sent him, and asked that He pass on my gratitude.

Do I believe that God through one of His ministering angels answered our 911 prayers? Of course. The Bible relates a number of miraculous rescues. I'll never forget that when I was unable to help myself and was ready to surrender to death, the quiet voice that said to me, "Let go and relax—you're in my hands now. You're safe."

In the Eye of the Storm
by Susan M. Schulz

A fast approaching storm weighted the air in Atlanta. The phone startled me. I glanced at the caller ID and quickly lifted the receiver. "Hi Dad, what's happening?"

"Suzi, the hospital here in the Keys is unable to do anything more for your mother." I could sense the helplessness in his voice. "They are ordering an ambulance to transport her to Mount Sinai Medical Center on Miami Beach tomorrow."

"I'll pack today and leave for Miami first thing," I said. "I'm bringing the kids with me, OK?"

"I've arranged for you to stay with your cousins. They have plenty of room for all of us, so I'm sure it's fine for you to bring the kids. But I'll let them know."

I didn't have the heart to tell my dad why I would bring the children. My husband and I were prepared for the worst. We had decided that I would drive with the three children from Atlanta to Miami, and he would fly down later, if Mom didn't make it through.

Outside raindrops began to fall; the storm was upon us.

The kids and I finally reached Miami. Soon after settling the children in, my father and I headed for the hospital. At Mount Sinai Medical Center, we located my mother's wing. As the automatic door whooshed open, a blast of antiseptic air met us head on. Immediately I began looking for the chapel. True to hospital pattern, a plaque on the doorframe to my left identified the Surgical Waiting Room, and another door on the right, Chapel.

"Hold on a second Dad," I said, "I want to take a look in here."

My gaze was drawn straight ahead to the far wall, where coral rocks covered it like a fireplace surround, but without the hearth. Against the mottled beige rocks, words made of brass stood out, first in Hebrew, then in English—*Out of the depths I cry to you, O LORD.*

Many worried hearts had been there before me. Prayers, written on pieces of paper and folded neatly, were stuffed into the crannies of the rocks, making it a miniature Wailing Wall.

At my mother's bedside, I saw she was so ill she could barely communicate with us. I watched my dad wring his hands. My own frustration rose.

It had been only a year since my mother had become critically ill following esophageal surgery. The surgery resulted in a multi-organ failure; her heart, kidneys and lungs had shut down. She lay in a coma for over a month while the Lord repeatedly assured me through His words in John 11 to Mary and Martha, the sickness would not end in death.

Now, a howling wind and torrential downpour pounded against my heart.

All I wanted was for the surgery to correct the intestinal blockage to happen immediately. Doctors studied my mother's complicated medical history, and had ordered many pre-surgery tests and procedures.

As we waited, I took in the view outside her window.

The imposing complex of Mount Sinai Medical Center with each wing named for its Jewish patron, did not obstruct a breathtaking view of the causeway over Biscayne Bay, distinctive beach homes, and pristine Miami Beach. The beautiful scenery accented by bright sun and blue sky contrasted the storm raging in my life.

When mom was put to sleep during one of her tests and was so groggy she didn't recognize that my dad and I were there, we decided it best to go to our temporary home and rest.

The accommodations God generously provided through my cousin were a tropical paradise. The property encompasses three acres of land covered with lush vegetation and tropical fruit trees, there was a golf cart for transportation, an incredible swimming pool rivaling any plush island resort, and even a hot tub. My children had plenty to do on the days they remained away from the hospital.

The next morning I woke up early to spend some time alone with God before facing another grueling day at the hospital. I kept the verse I saw on the chapel wall in my heart and mind from the moment I read it—*Out of the depths I cry to you, O LORD.* Inspired, I got dressed quietly, grabbed my Bible, journal, and a pen and headed outside to pray beside the pool. Whether at home or away, a journal remains close to my Bible. Writing in it as I read God's word generates keen hearing of his voice. That day I desperately needed him to speak a message of assurance in my ear.

As I walked past huge rock waterfalls cascading into the pool, the sound of falling water and swaying palm branches soothed my worried soul.

The eye of the storm directly overhead brought with it a temporary reprieve from my inner torrent.

I sat down at an iron patio table, opened my Bible to the book of Psalms, and started to skim. As I turned the pages, my mind focused on God's faithfulness. I thought of the countless souls through the ages that, like me, had received comfort through the storms of life from these ancient songs of prayer.

Getting close to the end of Psalms, I finally found the verse in Psalm130 and discovered the word "wait" used five times. The Lord spoke his message clearly; He commanded me to wait upon Him without knowing the outcome.

My experience with this illness was quite different. I never felt abandoned by God, but He had been silent until He spoke the message of "wait." Until then, all I knew was that I had to be prepared for anything.

Later that afternoon, I found out mom's surgery would occur the following day. The nurse said to call early in the morning for the time of the surgery. Since my mom was being worked in to the operating room schedule, the time wouldn't be available until then.

My dad remained a nervous wreck and left the calling up to me. Up early, I phoned first thing. I was shocked when the nurse casually informed me that mom had already been taken to surgery. A rush of hot anger ran through my body. The eye of the storm had moved, and the tempest beat harder and harder against my heart.

I couldn't remember the last time I had been that angry. I had driven over 900 miles, with three children, to see my mother the morning *before* she was operated on, only to have my mother sent into surgery without anyone calling me or my dad, her husband of 50 years!

I desperately wanted to hold her hand and pray with her right before she was rolled into the operating room. As soon as I heard the news, my father and I ran out the door. We had a chance in a million to see her face before she went under. Flustered, I took off without grabbing my Bible.

After my father and I explained what had happened, the woman at the waiting room desk tried her best to get us in to see her, but to no avail.

The high winds continued to blow; sheets of rain drenched my soul.

I borrowed a Gideon Bible from the front desk and sought refuge in the chapel. My father stayed in the waiting room with other family members who, like us, had loved ones in surgery.

Bible in hand, I walked into the empty chapel next door, and stopped before a chair closest to the wall of prayers. There, I dropped to my knees and laid the open Bible on the bench. Resting my head on folded hands, my heart screamed the words before me—*Out of the depths I cry to you, O LORD!*

As I prayed, the Spirit of the Lord calmed the storm raging in my heart. I remembered the message to wait. I settled down. God then began filling my heart and mind with understanding. In a place where I felt the strong influence of the Hebrew people, yet I and all people were welcome, my thoughts carried me back in time.

My spiritual journey began figuratively on Mount Sinai, in a Bible study of Moses, one of the Hebrew heroes of faith. From Moses I learned how to pray. He taught me how to hear the voice of God clearly and showed me, by example, that I must obey what I hear to have a life of great adventure. Moses' grand adventure spanned 120 years; most of his life and ministry built on obedience and a lot of waiting.

Through this hospital visit, in a way only God can communicate, I recognized a new dawn breaking on my horizon. A new stage in my service to God, a beginning of the ministry He called and trained me for—freelance writing. Through my years of journaling and recording the magnificent voice of God, I believe I should now turn to endeavoring, as it is written in Psalm 96, to declare His glory among the nations, His marvelous works among the peoples.

Time flew by and soon the surgeon came into the chapel with my father to tell me that my mother had pulled through. The surgeon explained how he had removed a huge gallstone the size of a hen's egg that had made its way out of her gall bladder and into her intestinal tract, completely blocking it. Although she was extremely sick, with close, intensive care, Mom would survive and heal yet again.

He told us that this type of surgery is rare and that he had filmed it. The video will be used to teach new physicians training to become better surgeons. The very thing that harmed my mother, God had used for good to accomplish the saving of many lives. As God has done since the time of the Patriarchs of old, He used the hard things His children endure for the good of I now understand the meaning of personal hurricanes. Whether the squall is blowing wildly on the horizon, or just passing, God uses such storms to display His glory. He is able to carry His children safely through each one.

The marvelous works He performs are without end.

Here Am I, Lord, Send...Someone Else
by Anita C. Lee

"If I rise on the wings of the dawn, if I settle on the far side of the sea, even there your hand will guide me, your right hand will hold me fast." Psalm 139:9-10 (NIV)

"Is there someone here to meet you?"

We looked at the Chinese airport official and then at one another, determined to remain calm. There already had been many mix-ups and much confusion in trying to get here. Now we faced a new challenge.

"I certainly hope so," my husband, Daryl, answered.

We had been sitting in the dimly lit holding room for almost an hour, as one by one, or in small groups, those who had shared our flight from Los Angeles to Shanghai were met by their Chinese hosts. Finally, our family of four sat alone. The children dozed, caught in a time warp created by our 21-hour flight that had originated in New York.

The stern official looked at our young children and at my husband and me then said to Daryl, "You. Follow me."

As I watched my husband disappear behind a door with frosted glass, prohibiting me from seeing farther, I practiced deep-breathing exercises and fervent prayer. It was the first of many times during our year in the People's Republic of China that I would rely on a deep-seated belief that we were in the center of God's will, and therefore anything that happened would be within that will.

We had arrived in China in August 1982 and it was the culmination of years of praying and waiting, waiting and praying. Almost three years earlier, as Daryl was finishing his Ph.D. degree in electrical engineering, I had increasingly felt a tug towards some kind of mission work abroad. I argued with God, saying, "But Lord, I've already done my bit overseas. It was great, but I was single then. Now there are two kids and a husband to consider. And what about all those other people out there who've never been out of this country? How about calling some of them!"

God must have chuckled at my ranting, telling Him what I wouldn't do, knowing how pivotal my two years in Japan with a mission board had been for me. I could almost hear Him say, "But you loved living abroad. You love trying to learn other languages. You love the adventure of experiencing new cultures. I *made* you that way for a purpose."

For several months I tried to push the thought of our going to another country out of my mind. Surely I was imagining this feeling that God was calling us to service in another land. But if this was from my own mind, wouldn't I *want* to go? Instead, I was resisting it mightily. Day and night I wrestled with God. I kept the struggle to myself, not wanting to bother Daryl with my mental tug-of-war while he was finishing his degree requirements.

Finally, in tears, I said to God, "If you want us to live and work abroad, I'll go gladly, but you'll have to call Daryl. I won't call him for you."

Imagine my surprise when shortly after my latest discussion with the Almighty, Daryl came home from work and announced that his company was going to do some extended business in China, and his boss had tapped him for heading up the project.

"It would mean a one- to two-year stay there," he explained. "What do you think?"

I thought God had a very keen sense of humor.

We started reading everything we could about China— from ancient history to contemporary news events. We saturated our lives with all things Chinese—food, customs, language. We began meeting weekly with a young Chinese man who was in America to study business practices. We exchanged English lessons for Mandarin lessons and shared American customs for information on Chinese culture. In the process of learning, we developed a deep appreciation for one another.

Then, after two years of the company's negotiations with the Chinese government, the whole plan fell through. Company executives reluctantly gave up on the idea of sending people to China.

We were devastated.

After preparing for over two years to go to China, it seemed we would have to give up our dream. God, however, had other plans.

When we shared the disheartening news with our Chinese friend and language tutor, he paused only a moment before asking, "Would you come to China to teach at my alma mater? My government pays transportation and living expenses, and a small salary for foreign experts to teach in our universities. Will you come if I get you an invitation?"

We were amazed at this turn of events. We praised God for His faithfulness as we continued to ask for strength and wisdom. There were still setbacks and delays, but finally we received the airline tickets and the official invitation from the Chinese government to teach at the university. Daryl would teach computer science and I would teach English. Instead of going to China with an American computer software company, as we had expected, we would step out on shaky legs of faith, quit the job, sell the house, and rely on God to lead us.

So, now here I sat in the Shanghai airport in the middle of the night. I had never felt so small and helpless as I did then, sitting with my arms wrapped around my two children. I trusted that my husband would not be gone forever and that there would indeed be someone from the university there to meet us, as our official letter of invitation had stated.

None too soon my husband returned with a young Chinese man by his side.

"This is Xiao Jin," Daryl said with obvious relief. "He has come from the university to meet us."

Here was someone who could speak English and Chinese and could usher us through the red tape necessary to exit the airport. He would be our guide around Shanghai for a few days, then we would all fly to the city of Hefei, in Anhui Province, where we would begin our year of teaching.

Once outside the airport we met another representative from the university, who led us through the black night to two waiting taxis. We were separated again, with the children and me in one car and Daryl and our luggage in another, each of us accompanied by a university emissary.

Although I had not suffered from separation anxiety before entering China, I felt it now. I was traveling with my two young children in a country where I did not speak the language, hurtling through the strange streets of one of the most populated cities in the world, with a man whom we had met just minutes before.

What if we're whisked away to some secret place and never heard from again? I thought unreasonably, my fiction-writer's brain working overtime. I prayed again for strength and wisdom and for a sense of calmness.

The children and I pushed aside the black veil-like curtains on the back windows of the car to capture glimpses of Shanghai. As we wound through the shadowy streets, an occasional dim light cast a yellow glow around families and friends huddled in front of doorways. I suspected that the heat and humidity of the August night had driven them from their crowded homes, seeking fresh air and camaraderie.

Bicyclists jangled bells as they wove their way through the dark streets. Cars honked and flashed their lights on and off, as if signaling in some unknown code. Over the next year, as we visited many Chinese cities, these sights and sounds would become commonplace for us, but no less perplexing. (We would learn later that Chinese drivers were forbidden from driving at night with their headlights on. Instead, they would flash them on for a few seconds to get an overall view of the road conditions, then turn them off again. This was supposed to keep from "night-blinding" bicyclists. The incessant honking was to warn them that a car was approaching.)

Living in China, just six years after the end of the Cultural Revolution, there was still ample evidence of the destruction of that turbulent era. An era when workers fought one another in factories and students battled on campuses, trying to prove which of their factions were more loyal to Chairman Mao. During that devastating time, students were encouraged to report any suspicious behavior of their teachers, and children were rewarded for testifying against their parents. Suspicious behavior included having ties to anything western, such as reading a Bible, playing music written by composers like Beethoven and Bach, or receiving letters from abroad. Eventually schools were closed and whatever education took place was done by parents or by teachers taking a few students privately.

By 1982, when we arrived, China was slowly recovering from the effects of those years of neglect. A whole generation of children had been deprived of a formal education. Structures now were being repaired, but funds were limited. The six-story classroom building where we taught had gaping holes where windows had been broken out, probably during fighting.

Elevator shafts were devoid of their elevators, radiators no longer lined the hallways—torn out in that chaotic time as being materialistic and unnecessary. I certainly differed with that opinion in the middle of winter when the puddles of water on the floor beneath the broken windows of my English classroom turned to ice.

We knew from our earlier reading that some churches and temples were beginning to open for worship again. All had been closed in the 1950's after the Communist regime came into power. We were thrilled to know that Hefei had an open church, and not long after our arrival, we were invited to attend. Our joy turned bittersweet, though, when we discovered later that the young teacher who took us there got into trouble for being a Christian. His accompanying us to the worship service had been noted by the authorities. We knew that if we complained to the Office of Foreign Affairs and tried to take the blame it would make matters even worse for the young man.

Daily life for us was a study in contrasts. From our apartment window we could see the university's computer lab building, but in the grassy area in between, a water buffalo grazed nonchalantly. During our year on campus, we watched as the science building, a modern structure, was built from massive concrete blocks hauled uphill from the train station on carts pulled by men and women.

Living in China was difficult, but gratifying. We learned to dress in multiple layers of clothing during the winter, even when relaxing in our apartment. Although our apartment was heated, during the middle of winter when it was freezing outside we could expect the inside temperature to be no more than fifty degrees. We couldn't depend on having hot tap water. Sometimes we had only cold water, sometimes only boiling hot water. It became an adventure to see what was going to come out of the spigot. We thanked God for the heated rooms and running water. We knew our students and our Chinese colleagues had no heat or hot water in their apartments. Many had no running water at all. We learned to appreciate things that we had taken for granted in our comfortable home in America.

Throughout our year in China, we experienced repeatedly the grace and mercy of God. We had stepped out on faith, not knowing what to expect, and had grown in our understanding of how God can work in our lives when we trust Him. We were limited in speaking openly about religion, understanding that our classroom sessions, as well as more private times, were often monitored. However, we shared our beliefs in subtle ways with our students and colleagues. They had been taught that belief in God was a harmful superstition practiced by the ignorant. They were surprised to hear that their instructor, an American engineer with a Ph.D., was a Christian.

"How could you leave the comforts of living in America, to come here to teach?" they asked.

"We believe in God and believe He leads us when we ask for guidance. We feel this is the place God wants us to be at this time," Daryl replied, explaining our desire to live according to God's will.

Throughout the year, we experienced great family adventures traveling around China, as well as quiet times together in our apartment. After our return to the United States, we learned that our joy in being together and the love we showed to one another was noticed by those who worked on the compound where we lived.

"There's something special about the way they treat each other," a worker who saw us daily had said to one of our Chinese interpreters who visited us later in America.

Although we often felt we hadn't done enough to share our faith with those around us, we were grateful to know God had used our family as a means to show His love.

That first night in Shanghai was the beginning of an exciting journey of faith as we learned to trust God for all our needs. Ten months later, amid the cacophony of strings of crackling firecrackers celebrating our departure, we looked back on times of great joy and of occasional sadness.

With overflowing hearts we rejoiced, grateful that when God called, we said, "Here we are, Lord. Send us."

No More Do Overs
by Michael Anderson

"Could you hustle a little, Mike?" Mr. DeMars said. "We're running a bit late for church. Go ahead and get in the back seat with Lynn and Sherry."

"Mr. DeMars, sir? I think you ran over our neighbor's cat."

"What do mean, son?"

"Well, I saw something run under the car just as you were pulling in the driveway, and it didn't come out."

"Did you look under the car?"

"Yes sir."

"And what did you see?"

"Pink snow and a dead cat, sir."

"Oh that's just great," Mr. DeMars said with a scowl, "Let me think a second".

He rolled up his window while I continued to stand in our driveway, shivering in my snowsuit and parka. I watched their mouths move inside the car, as he discussed the situation with his wife.

The DeMars had always picked me up for church. My family didn't attend. Lynn DeMars and I were almost teenagers, and we were in BYF (Baptist Youth Fellowship) together. We enjoyed hot dogs, baseball cards, and comic books. We were discovering girls, but for now we were inseparable pals.

The window rolled down on the other side of the car.

"Here dear," Mrs. DeMars suggested, "Take this plastic litter bag and I'll pop the trunk. Take out the snow shovel, scoop up the cat, and slide it into the bag. Then just put everything back in the trunk and let's go. We'll deal with the cat later. We're going to be late, and we'll miss the missionaries."

Oh that's right, I thought, *the foreign missionaries were going to be in church this week. No Sunday school today. This was going to be an extra long and boring service with lots of praying and junk.*

We arrived late and the only seats left were down front. We crowded into a second-row pew. I thought I smelled cat, and I began sniffing myself hoping it wasn't from me.

The church was crowded and hot. The choir sounded off key. *Can't I just play outside in the snow?*

Lynn stood next to me as we lip-synced whatever song the congregation was singing. We could always anticipate lyrics with "holy", "glory", and "praise", and our mouths adjusted quickly, so no one knew that we didn't have a clue as to what we were singing

Sunday morning giggles were inevitable whenever Lynn and I were together. Today was no exception. Lynn had a bottomless pit of knock-knock jokes and keen recall ability. He would get me started and I couldn't stop. Stifling giggles only made my stomach sore. Mr. and Mrs. DeMars looked at me with stares of disapproval.

Then came prayer time. The huge sacred hall became still while the preacher agonized aloud. My mind drifted constantly from the moment I bowed my head. Visions of Sherry DeMars (Lynn's older sister) overpowered any righteous thoughts. I wondered if I would sit next to her on the ride home. She wore pretty dresses, and her hair smelled like a beach.

The music started again, but I didn't notice. People were squeezing by me towards the aisle, then to the altar in the front of the church. Mrs. DeMars leaned over and whispered, "Lynn's going down. Would you like to go with him Mike?"

My friend was starting down the aisle. I decided to catch up with him.

I wonder why you're going down front Lynn? Are you getting an award or something?

Lynn knelt beside several others at the steps to the altar. I knelt down next to him. He was quietly crying. *Maybe I stepped on Lynn's heel walking down here.* I thought.

The music stopped, the congregation stood up and applauded, and two men in suits gave us each a small Bible and welcomed us into the family of God. "You're a Christian now Mike. You just prayed and asked Jesus into your heart."

I did? Pure personal embarrassment prohibited me from letting on otherwise. I didn't know I'd just been born again. I was a good boy, but wasn't I supposed to be different now? I thought I was. I thought I smelled like dead cat.

Over the next five years, Lynn and I drifted apart and our friendship had become strained. Then I found new friends, Paul and Barbara, when I moved near Chicago after high school. I remember the night when the three of us were in Paul's car.

"Why are we stopping?" Barbara questioned, as the car slowly rolled to a stop.

"You'll see, my little Barbie doll," Paul quipped.

"Why are you turning off the engine? It's freezing outside. We need the heater on"

"I'll tell you about needs. I have needs, and right now I just need a little kiss".

Paul pulled the lever pushing the bench seat backwards. Then, twisting his body, he wrapped his arms around Barbara. Her glasses fell off onto the floorboard, as she began to struggle.

"Paul! What are you doing? I can't see. What's gotten' into you?"

"Aw, come on Barbie just give me a kiss"

Paul pulled his gloves off, tightened his grip, and pulled her close.

"Get away! Get your hands off me!" Barbara shouted.

"Just a kiss, girl. Just one kiss" Paul became more aggressive.

"Paul, no! Mike, do something!"

Until that moment, I had just sat there on the far-right front seat with my face pushed against the window and my eyes gazing outside. I was hoping Paul would start the car soon, as I was getting cold. I felt Barbara's body squirming next to me as Paul continued with his testosterone attack. I looked to the stars and I wondered about the craziness of this entire scene.

I didn't know Paul and Barbara well at all. They worked at the same factory I did, and, like me, were saving money for college. Paul was a big guy, jolly and loud. Barbara was petite, perky, and cute. They were considered by most of the "factory rats" as religious freaks, but I was the new kid in town and desperate for friends. So when they invited me to a special evening church event in Chicago, I was glad to just get out of the house.

Suddenly Barbara laughed as she scooted towards Paul's side. Both were now quiet and I glanced over and saw the two passionately embracing each other. Kissing sounds taunted my ears. I turned back, rolled my eyes, and leaned my face against the window one more time.

Was God looking down from Heaven at us? If so, he must have been disappointed observing the actions of three teens on a cold winter's night, all in the front seat of a rickety Ford. He probably shed a tear that wintry night looking at us bundled in winter coats, parked along a dark, deserted, and snow-covered road in Lake Zurich, Illinois with the car engine off. And him knowing we had just returned from a Billy Graham crusade an hour earlier, where Paul and Barbara had led me to Jesus Christ. I had been "saved" that miserable night, but now I felt stupid.

Is that all there is? Is this what being a Christian is? I recall wondering if my conversion was real. *Another dud,* I thought.

Another chunk of time passed (about 15 years). I had married the girl of my dreams (not Sherry DeMars), had two great sons, and resided in Marietta, Georgia, the buckle of the Bible belt. We attended Fellowship Bible Church, where I heard words like "saved" and "born again" often, but with a personal first-time perspective. My wife and children, in their own time, had accepted Christ as their savior and you could tell a difference in their daily lives, aspirations, and attitudes.

I ushered at the church and even helped set up the folding chairs. When the preacher prayed the invitation nearly every Sunday, I bowed and asked Jesus to come into my heart. My words were sincere, but when the prayer was over and I opened my eyes, I felt nothing. I began each new workweek without any real purpose for my life.

One Sunday, standing in the back of the church service by myself, I bowed like I had many times before, and I prayed the same old prayer for salvation. With my head down and the music playing I suddenly felt what seemed like a warm, thick, honey-like fluid flowing from the top of my head, around my skull, and onto my shoulders. I felt it on the inside too. Something was definitely different about that moment. It was like glowing volcanic lava moving down the mountain, melting all debris in its path.

The flow continued through my heart. I was frozen in time, not wanting to move from that place. The sensation subsided, but the music continued. I opened my eyes, looked up, and focused on the wooden cross on the wall behind the choir.

I remember that day as clearly as those special weird times of my youth. I heard Him knocking and I opened the door. And this time it took. No false starts. No more do overs.

My life from that day forward has had purpose and meaning. It has produced fruit beyond what I could imagine. I am walking with my Jesus daily as a new creation and a child of God and nothing but glorifying Him seems to make sense.

Suspended
by Jennifer Evans

My heart hung suspended on the edge of my frazzled nerves--
but with my body tightly belted into the window seat of the 747,
no one else noticed my confused grief. Gray asphalt bumped
beneath us and became a blur. We tilted gently and in the
sudden quiet, Manila had dropped away into my recent past.
Butterflies danced in my stomach. After four years, I was going
home.

Letters and fragments of ocean-wide phone
conversations scrambled together in my mind. Facing life alone,
Mom had taken a new job. Dad had remarried two years ago,
and had retired from his work. Sis had a fourth child, and her
family had recently moved to a new neighborhood. There was
so much to catch up on, and to top it all off, this weekend there
were two family reunions scheduled.

The evening sun stains the sky a deep orange as twilight
draws a curtain over the past four years in my adopted country.
Suspended between sunset and the bottomless blue ocean, my
mind returns to Maguisguis, the village that had been my home
for almost three years, and I silently mourn. Just fifteen miles
from Mount Pinatubo, our quiet hamlet had now become a
ghost town. Under a yellow tarpaulin, I still visualize wide-
eyed, dark-skinned children wondering what was happening to
their home. Melancholy, I relive scenes of a purgatory sky
raining mud onto our arms and eyelashes, and the gray pall of
volcanic ash settling over life as far as one's horizon could
stretch. Involuntarily, I replay the last few weeks in the village,
more real than the silent movie flashing on the airliner's screen
before me.

I could almost feel March's summer sun as I remembered climbing the steep hill to one of my favorite spots: the cemetery just outside the village. I recalled being sticky from my mid-afternoon walk and sitting on a boulder protruding from underneath a thorny Maguisguis tree, from which the village took its name. The neat bamboo and thatch houses looked like miniature baskets dotting the valley.

I moved to Maguisguis to implement a literacy project. Several years prior to my arrival in 1988, the New Testament had been published in the Botolan Sambal language for the very first time. It was useless to more than half of the population, the indigenous Ayta people. Only about ten percent of that ethnic community was literate. How could they know God loved them if they didn't hear Him speak to them in their mother tongue? Most of our Ayta neighbors believed in the Christian God they had heard of from their Catholic friends, but they also sacrificed chickens if their children were sick. They implored the spirits in rocks, trees and other objects with the help of shamans. For them, God was just one of the pantheon, and why worship Him? If He were good, He wouldn't hurt you... For the first six months, I had no American companion. Helen, a local friend, had become my housemate and language tutor. Even my nightmares were language-learning lessons. Helen woke me more than once and forced me, though half-asleep, to explain my terrible dream in Sambal. She was herself half Ayta, her mother being Ayta and her father Malay-Filipino. She had come to faith in Christ as a teen, and had a deep burden for the indigenous people to understand God's Word and be able to read it. I can still see her in my memory, silhouetted with bowed head in the middle her bed in dawn's shadows, whispering her prayers to God before she started her day. I was the missionary, but I knew I could learn more than just language from Helen.

Every experience was bathed in uncertainty. My first meal was something called *andolan*. In a chipped enamel bowl lay a dozen three-inch long slippery fish, complete with whiskers, skin and tiny fins. Helen set the bowl on the table, served the rice and called me to supper. The fish had already been boiled, and were ready for consumption. She laughed as I tried to follow her lead in eating with my fingers, poking my elbow into the air and looking unceremoniously foreign. After some practice, I finally developed proper table manners.

During the first week, I followed Helen to the river intending to help her wash clothes. She deftly wound a rag around her hand and set the donut-shaped wad on her head to cushion the bulky basin full of dirty laundry, and headed for the river. Squatting, she settled on a flat rock and dampened a blouse in the water. I found a nasty sock and began: first wet it and then add the soap, scrub, scrub, and rinse. I held up my prize and grinned. Helen smiled back and retrieved the sock, dipping it immediately for rewashing. I took out my notebook and proceeded to gather words and practice mimicking them, consoled by something I *could* do. The literacy work for which I had come seemed a far-away dream.

Stupidity was embarrassing. My helplessness was a blessing in disguise, though, because my absolute dependence won their hearts. After six months, I found I could communicate fairly well.

The following year, Vangie, a fellow American, came to work with me, and Helen moved back home to be with her aging mother. After several months, my new coworker and I were keeping busy with many kinds of literacy activities, including a children's class in which we used Bible stories with a flannel graph as well as a literacy primer. The stories were new and fresh to these young people and they were delighted to help us retell them with the flannel figures. They were learning the Bible stories, but reading was a different problem.

After one exceptionally long morning with our little class, we trudged down the hill to our cozy bamboo house. We dragged ourselves inside and closed the door. Sitting at the table with our chins in our hands, we stared at the revised primer materials we'd been testing with the kids. Syllables just didn't make sense to them. We needed flashcards for phonics, but neither of us could draw. Helpless again.

Laying aside our frustration, we had just set to work cooking lunch when we heard a vehicle stop in front of our house. Sliding open the bamboo door, we welcomed ten Filipino and Malaysian visitors. During lunch preparations, one young man spoke deliberately through the chatter.

"I am a professional artist," he began, "and have worked in child evangelism ministries in my country. I'd like to redeem the time while we are sitting here. Is there anything I could do to help you?"

In a matter of minutes, he had produced exactly the drawings we needed. I was still learning God's attention to detail in my helplessness.

One April morning, excited voices filled the dusty air. Clusters of ragged people, just returning from working in their hillside fields, shouted and pointed at something on the hazy horizon.

"What's going on?" I asked.

"Look at Mt. Pinatubo!" People were chattering in a terrified frenzy. "It's smoking!" I tried to calm their silly fears. I'd never even heard of an active volcano in our area. We just had mountains; lush, green, quiet, serene mountains.

"It's really true," one old woman said, "this morning, my brother was in his field and he saw white smoke coming out of Mt. Pinatubo. He would not make that up. He really saw it!"

Her aged face was lined with fear. I couldn't rule out an eyewitness testimony, but still I had my doubts.

"Let's go to the crossing," another suggested. Several women left their rice pots on smoldering fires and followed us to the fork in the powdery dirt road where the view was better. My heart sank and the roof of my mouth went suddenly dry. There on the horizon just fifteen miles away, a thin curl of white steam was rising into the blue above Mt. Pinatubo.

For the next two months, life went on as usual but the ominous cloud hovered, a constant reminder that trouble was brewing. June 2nd was to be the big day: graduation. The children would receive certificates for their diligence in learning to read. For Vangie and me, the week was a flurry of activity. We had planned an overnight field trip, which included a visit to the municipal buildings in town and the provincial capitol where our young students met the governor.

They had their first experience ordering from a menu in a restaurant, and then we overnighted at a small bamboo beach house. The kids were delighted with the light switches and flush toilet. A shower with running water was another new experience, providing quite a contrast to bathing in the river or dipping from a bucket.

We bought their graduation clothes: skirts and blouses for the girls that they could use later for school, and shorts and shirts for the boys. There were certificates, invitations, facilities and decorations to prepare. A special speaker was coming from Manila. Food was a crucial element: the whole village might turn out, and it would be improper and embarrassing to run out.

In the rush of our preparations, Pinatubo sputtered, hidden under a gray cumulus-like expanse. One by one, villages all around us were evacuated. People in Maguisguis did not want to go. This was home. Eight kilometers should be safe enough...right?

After the graduation ceremony, we packed our things and went to Manila, planning to stay there for one week. The TV news said that Pinatubo was getting ready for a major eruption. On an official scale of one to five, our mountain was still a two. On Tuesday, though, I arrived at the Manila office to find our regional director waiting. His face wore an uncharacteristically nervous expression.

"They have raised the public alert level for Pinatubo," he began. "They now expect an eruption within two weeks. I think we should move all of your things here to Manila today." My stomach churned as I struggled to find the right response. Again, I was overwhelmed with familiar helplessness.

Later that same morning, we drove into sleepy Maguisguis. Neighbors gathered around our porch as we loaded boxes of literacy materials and personal things into the waiting vehicle. I tried to hide my own confusion and internalized grief. We were scheduled to leave for a year of assignment in the U.S. within a month. What would happen to all of these people who had laughed with me, taught me how to speak their language and loved me into their lives? The van was finally loaded and the house was empty. My heart was torn between fullness and emptiness, ready to leave and begging to stay.

Only three days later, Maguisguis residents and their meager belongings were hauled by dump truck, ox cart, wagon and public vehicle to a safe camp about twenty miles away. Pinatubo began a series of dangerous eruptions just seven hours later. A seasonal typhoon brought bone-soaking mud-rain, adding insult to injury for the evacuees. From Manila, we watched heart-wrenching scenes on TV, scanning them for faces we knew, listening for news of the people we loved.

A week after the initial eruption, Vangie and I helped a group of volunteers gather blankets, food and extra tents for the evacuation center. To our great relief, we learned upon our arrival that no one from Maguisguis had been hurt or left behind.

A break in the clouds altered my gaze and my daydream faded. Most of the plane's other passengers had curled into their seats to sleep. Somewhere between east and west, I had to find a balance between grieving for the homeless children and celebrating as a child coming home. Picturing their faces on a background of dull gray ash, words from friends in the evacuation center still rang in my mind.

"This has happened to make people realize the power of God," one said.

"We were scared, but God got us out just in time!" another commented. I was awed and humbled by the depth of their faith. They were helpless, but they knew Who was in control. How many times had I been helpless among them? Had I really learned His sufficiency? It suddenly occurred to me that faith was going to have to be a deliberate choice. Isaiah's words that I had read the week before replayed through my mind:

The prophet records, "This is what God the Lord says – He who created the heavens and stretched them out, who spread out the earth and all that comes out of it, who gives breath to its people, and life to those who walk on it: I, the Lord, have called you in righteousness; I will take hold of your hand."

Sixteen sleepless hours and three meals passed. I breathed a sigh of relief as the wheels bumped onto solid ground and the blur of the San Francisco airport raced by. Seatbelts snapped and rumpled people stretched themselves to life. Nothing was different, but I was no longer suspended. Instead, I found that in His arms, I was being held.

The Double Portion
by Rose Wade-Schambach

"Instead of their shame my people will receive a double portion," Isaiah 61:7a (NIV)

The sunset had converted the sky into a tapestry of pinks and oranges that reflected on the water of the bay, but I hardly noticed the beauty before me as I drove the old van heavy with children over the long bridge that led us into an unknown future. The death knell had sounded in my marriage, and the children and I were leaving. For years my marriage had been precariously held together by broken promises, but the recent revelation of my husband's latest infidelity was more than I could bear. It had come to a final showdown, and we had reached an impasse: he had refused to leave, but would neither promise that anything would change. Seeing no other options, I made up my mind to make a new life for the children and me.

I called my friend Becky, who graciously offered to let the children and me move in with her until we could get on our feet. It was going to be hard to start again, especially since I only had a few dollars in my pocket. But what was even harder was recalling my children's tortured faces every time their father and I fought in front of them. I knew instinctively that this was the best decision for all of us, yet how do you explain to mere children that their Mommy and Daddy would no longer be living together? As I drove along the darkening streets, I thought back to the conversation between my oldest son and I, as we were getting ready to leave.

"Where are we going, Mom?" Nathan asked, his forehead knitted with worry.

"We're going on a little trip," I replied, feigning excitement.

"Are you leaving Dad?" he persisted.

"Daddy and I think it would be a good idea if we take some time away from each other. I know it's difficult for you to understand, but I'm really going to need your help. Now, no more questions right now. I promise everything will be okay."

But who was I kidding? What kind of promise was that to make to a child? How would I make it with no job or other resources to carry me through? My two older children were away at college, but I still had four more children depending on me with the youngest still in diapers. I felt the icy grip of fear creeping up the back of my neck as I drove to Becky's.

The further from home I drove, the more I wrestled with my decision. Maybe I had acted impetuously. Perhaps I should turn around and go back home and try to make my marriage work one more time. As much as I wanted to go back to my comfortable surroundings, I couldn't make myself turn the van around. As uncertain as the future seemed, anything would be better than the life I had just closed the door on. I had already been through some tough things since becoming a Christian, and the Lord had always been there for me. Even so, I couldn't help praying that the Lord would soon send some kind of sign that He would still take care of us in spite of all my mistakes and failures. All these thoughts filled my head as I drove into the apartment complex where Becky lived.

Becky was waiting outside when we arrived, and she rushed over to give me a needed hug. I sprang from the van, finally allowing the tears to flow as she held me close to her.

"It'll all work out," Becky whispered in my ear. "You'll see."

Becky continued to encourage me, even after days of fruitless job searching. "God takes care of His widows and orphans", she reminded me.

My heart wanted to believe her. She certainly was speaking from experience. Becky had left an abusive marriage herself years before and had raised her son alone. She had literally been in my shoes and had walked the rough terrain before me.

After a week or two, I was finally offered some jobs cleaning houses. Since it was summer, and the kids weren't in school, I was able take them with me. The older two boys, Nathan and Jonathan, helped with some of the cleaning tasks, and my daughter Hannah kept Ethan, who had just learned to walk, out of trouble. We were a rag-tag crew, but somehow we always managed to get the job done on time.

Every day we made a little more progress. Soon an apartment became vacant in the complex where Becky lived, and the manager allowed me to move in without paying a damage deposit if we painted the walls and cleaned up after the previous tenants ourselves. The apartment was dingy and only had two bedrooms, but we were glad to finally find a place we could afford.

We moved in with just some clothes, a few kitchen essentials, and a table with three wobbly chairs that someone in our church had given us. We had no television to entertain us, so I told the children stories at night until they fell asleep. Because we had no beds, we slept on sleeping bags on top of soiled carpet that smelled like sour milk.

I hoped that eventually the court would help me get my old house back and award me some kind of child support, even though I had been the one to leave. Until then, I would have to do the best I could to provide for the children.

My lowest point came one night as I tossed and turned on my sleeping bag and tried unsuccessfully to get some sleep. Through the thin walls of the apartment, I could hear the couple downstairs arguing over the sound of a blaring television. Out in the parking lot, people were coming and going, and their laughter floated up to mock me. To add to my predicament, the baby had been sick all week, and I had been unable to clean any houses. Soon the rent would be due, and I didn't see how I was going to be able to pay it. Self-pity wrapped around me like a heavy cloak as I struggled to pray.

"Is this the worst it is going to get, Lord?" I cried.

"Be still, my child, and wait," came the voice of the Gentle Shepherd.

The next day, my old friend Gayle called and invited me to lunch at her home. I needed some adult company, but I felt guilty for leaving Nathan, who was only thirteen, to supervise the younger ones when he should be out having fun like other kids his age. I finally made up my mind to go. Although I hadn't seen Gayle for quite some time, I knew that she, too, had been going through a divorce. I thought maybe our visit would give me the encouragement I so desperately needed.

She gave me directions to her new home. As I pulled into her driveway, I couldn't help but feel envious that her circumstances were so much better than mine. After lunch Gayle showed me around, and I felt another wave of jealousy surface. Her voice was bubbly as she shared how the Lord had opened the doors for her to own a home of her own. I noticed her beautiful furnishings, and inwardly cringed when I thought of how the children and I were living in comparison.

"Look," she said as she pointed to her mailbox as she walked me out to my old van when it was time for me to leave. "When I moved in, I didn't realize it, but my house number is 5008. That adds up to thirteen, which is the Biblical number for a double portion!" I hugged her good-bye and told her that I was sincerely glad for her. And strangely, as I uttered the words, I found I *was* glad for her.

"But what about me, Lord?" I cried in desperation as I drove home. "Have you forgotten me and the children?"

Tired and discouraged, I paused briefly to ask the Lord to forgive me for being so self-absorbed. I brushed away the tears as I trudged up the stairs to my apartment. As I rounded the corner, I stopped with my mouth wide open. For the first time I noticed the numbers on my own front door: 7694. Double thirteen! Did that mean what I thought it meant? Was I to be blessed with a double portion times two? In that one moment, I felt lighter than I had in a long time.

"I'm home!" I announced to my waiting children.

Epilogue: The years I spent as a single mother were difficult, but the Lord always proved Himself faithful to this widow and her orphans. Since those days, the Lord has truly blessed me with a double portion. He has given me a wonderful husband, a beautiful home, and six additional children for a total of twelve in all! I am doubly blessed indeed!

Issues of the Heart
by Jack Elder

Micky dreaded the Thanksgiving trip to Florida as his mother had passed away in the spring and that holiday would never be the same. This year would be especially difficult as his mother-in-law was in the last stages of bone cancer. He knew this would probably be the last Thanksgiving they would be with her.

As Rhonda, his wife, prepared for the trip, she relived a recent dream in which she saw herself riding through a tornado astride a wooden 2x4. *Tornados are destructive. Would something devastating happen or was this just a dream?* She wondered.

Micky went over in his mind the list of things they would need to pack. *Sure am grateful for the Chrysler Town and Country mom left us with everything we'll have to take,* he thought. *If we could get away first thing Wednesday morning, we could beat the traffic out of Atlanta and arrive early enough to have a nice dinner with dad.* He shook his head. *Yeah, right. The chance of that happening was between nil and zero.*

For the last week, He had been going to the doctor because of an aching leg. They tried different things, but so far, nothing helped. He had also picked up a nagging cough. *Probably the chill in the fall air,* he thought. *It should go away when I get out of this Georgia cold into the warm air of Florida.* Still, he wasn't feeling all that well either. With the restrictions on flu shots this year he hadn't gotten one.

They finally pulled out after eight a.m. and had to fight the Atlanta traffic. Micky was already getting that grumpy feeling that not everything was going as he wanted. He wished he could just jump in the car and drive until he arrived, but experience had taught him that there would be many pit stops. He would have to go with the flow if he wasn't going to get too frustrated.

By the time they reached their destination in Florida, he thought that maybe he had the flu. They decided he shouldn't go and see his mother-in law with the potential of giving her any flu bugs in her weakened condition. Rhonda spent the next few days with her mom and her husband spent his time at his dad's house where he had grown up. At least he felt at home there.

The next week it was time to return home. Micky was feeling poorly and didn't want to drive home. He was sick and his heart was beating very rapidly. Rhonda drove the van and the closer they got to home, the worse he felt. Instead of driving directly home, Rhonda drove straight to Emory Hospital where emergency personnel immediately placed her husband into intensive care.

He had been born with a heart chamber problem and had a Blalock shunt put in when he was 16 years old. Throughout his life, he had been in and out the hospital many times and even had each of his annual checkups at the hospital where they could thoroughly checkout his heart.

Now back at Emory hospital, Rhonda waited for word from the doctor on what might be wrong. Fear began to attack her mind. *Is this the end?* she thought. People with this kind of heart condition didn't normally live a long life. *No, Micky had gone through these attacks before and always came out okay.* Somehow, deep down in her spirit she knew this time was different.

Micky's cardio doctor finally came into the room. She had a somber look on her face. "He's a sick puppy, Rhonda," she said. "His blood pressure is really low so we've got to thin his blood and hydrate him. His oxygen saturation level is also low. The next 24 hours will be important. It appears to be a problem with his heart and not the flu. All the symptoms of the last few weeks all point to his heart."

Rhonda knew that this doctor was always upbeat and wouldn't say her husband's condition was critical, but Rhonda knew something was seriously wrong. She phoned some friends to requesting prayers. This was definitely a black Monday.

Rhonda walked to the little chapel and sat there in the solitude of the small room. She had been here before and was always amazed at how empty this room was. Wasn't anyone taking their needs to the Lord? She somehow knew instinctively that this would be the greatest battle of her life. *I think I'm about to ride through a tornado on a 2x4,* she thought. She prayed on her face and wept for quite some time.

She stayed by her husband's side through the long night reading her Bible and praying. About 2 a.m., a doctor came in to check him. Rhonda had never seen this person before or since. He looked at Micky and then turned to her and said, "He isn't going to make it to morning. His heart is barely beating and his kidneys have quit. It is just a matter of time."

He walked out the door leaving Rhonda alone. Fear began to attack her mind. *Wait a minute,* she thought. *That was from the devil or maybe it was the devil. I don't have to believe that. I believe the Word. Jesus is the healer and Micky is going to make it.* She continued to pray and intercede for her husband.

A few hours later, the day nurse came in. "Morning," she said startling Rhonda, who had dozed off. "Looks like he made it through the night. That's a good sign," she said too cheerfully for a morning like this. Rhonda felt a little more peaceful. She wasn't surprised he had made it through the night, but knew the battle was just beginning and she couldn't give an inch.

The doctor came in and looked at the monitor. "His kidneys have failed and we need to put him through a dialysis cycle to clean up the toxins in his blood; however, that is very dangerous with such low blood pressure."

Up to this point, Micky didn't remember much about what was going on. He knew this was the worse he had ever been and even questioned the Lord if he was going to make it. *I'm in your hands,* he prayed. *If you want to take me, I'm okay with that. But I'm not giving up without a fight.*

They ran the dialysis at night and very slowly to minimize the risks. By this time, they had poked and prodded him everywhere a person could be and them some. Thin blood means bruising very easily and he became one big bruise. His heart was still beating at a high speed and none of the drugs were helping.

Rhonda spent the next few days in a blur. One day, as she came back from the chapel, she walked past another room and saw a woman standing by her husband who was also in critical condition. As she walked by, she felt the Lord tell her to go and encourage that woman. *Lord I don't need to be encouraging others when I need so much. Okay I will.* She stopped and went back and spoke with the woman.

"Oh, thank you so much. I was just praying that someone would stop and encourage me. It doesn't look like my husband is going to make it. His heart has stopped twice already."

Rhonda prayed with her and two days later stood by her side as her husband slipped into eternity. She held the man's hand and quickly fired a prayer off to heaven. *Lord, you raised people from the dead, I will be your instrument if you want to do it again.* It was not to be this time.

Rhonda was thankful that Micky was still with her, even though the hospital staff constantly bombarded him with all sorts of tests. All the tests, including an echogram, showed that there was no damage to his heart. The kidneys, however, were a different story. For four nights, they would continue the dialysis.

Rhonda's church members and friends began visiting and calling her. One of her good friends called and said she just felt to give her Psalms 118:17 "He will not die, but live and give glory to the Lord."

Another friend called and told her the same thing. Rhonda thought, *out of the mouth of two witnesses a thing is established.* Before it was all over, two more people called and quoted the same verse. She knew it was the Lord confirming the Word to her. *Having done all, stand.* She would make her stand, even though all the medical statistics were against them.

She got a few hours sleep a day and never left her husband's side except for short periods of time. Tomorrow would be Sunday.

"Would you tell the nurses that I want to be left alone," Micky said to Rhonda. "I can't take any more. Just give me a day to rest." All the poking and prodding had reduced his strength to two notches below nonexistent.

Rhonda told the nursing staff that he would need to rest on Sunday, and they obliged.

In both of the Sunday morning church services, the pastor led the congregation at Mt. Paran Church of God in intercessory prayer on behalf of Micky. Those present said there was an unusually strong presence of God's power and many who didn't even know him wept in intercession.

Monday morning, a week after entering the hospital, they scheduled a shock treatment to bring Micky's heart into a normal beat. It worked and he could once more rest. When the doctor came in, she said, "We have some good news. It very seldom ever happens, but his kidneys are working. Are you going to tell me Rhonda, how that happened?"

"Yes, doctor, let me tell you how that happened."

They released Micky and he went home to recuperate. He still has much cardio strengthening to do. During his recovery, Rhonda's mother passed away. But in spite of it all both Micky and Rhonda are standing strong and continuing to give glory to the Lord for the good things He has done.

Throw It Away
by Cynthia L. Simmons

"Hello? Dad?" Debbie answered the phone in the hallway of her dormitory.

"Debbie, is that you?" her father asked. "How are you?" Debbie did not see her father much after her parents divorced.

"Yeah, it's me. I'm fine," she said.

"How is school? He asked.

"Classes are okay. I think I'm better at occupational therapy than art."

The year before Debbie had dropped out of the University of Colorado where she had studied art, and returned to Connecticut to live with her mother. Debbie had dropped out of college twice and had no sense of direction, so her mother insisted on career testing. A psychologist in New York administered the tests and recommended she study Occupational Therapy. The next fall, she entered Boston School of Occupational Therapy.

"Did you get the car working?" he asked.

"The car? No, I don't have it." Debbie sighed. "I left it in Colorado. It never worked." Debbie's father had given her a car when she started school in Colorado, but it did not run well in the high altitude of Colorado.

"I'd like to get that car fixed," he said, "but I'll need the keys."

"The keys? Let me see. I think I left them with the car. Can't remember." She closed her eyes and put her fingers up to her temple.

"I want the title too," he said.

"Title? Oh, dear! Where could it be?" she said frowning. "Do you need the title?" Her hand began to tremble as she adjusted her necklace.

"Yes, I need it. It proves I own the car," her father explained. "I'll bring it here and then repair it."

"How are you going to get the car to Texas?" Picturing her dad trying to drive the car, she rolled her eyes. "I parked the stupid thing at my boyfriend's house in Colorado, but I can't—I just can't remember where I put that stuff."

"Debbie, do you have a hard time keeping up with things?" He tried to make his voice sound calm. He did not want to upset her.

"Yeah, I lose everything." She closed her eyes and shook her head. "I keep losing my dorm key too."

"Well, I guess you're just a loser," he said chuckling.

"Ha!" Debbie said, "that is a good one." She laughed too. "I'm a loser."

The phone call ended and Debbie returned to her room. Thanksgiving break began the next day. Debbie tossed two books in her suitcase for the trip home. One taught meditation and the other covered the occult.

Maybe I'll get a chance to read some over break. What's life all about? There have to be answers to life out there somewhere. Her father had served in the military in World War II and had helped to shut down concentration camps. Horrified by the cruelty he saw, her father had rejected his Jewish heritage after the war. He did not make time for religion in their home. Instead of going to synagogue or church, her family often went skiing together on weekends.

Her mother, who was not Jewish, searched for meaning also. On occasion she visited various churches with Debbie and her brother. After the divorce, her mother took her to a congregational church for confirmation. However, Debbie had ruled out Christianity since she questioned how Adam and Eve fit into evolution.

The next day Debbie rode a bus to Connecticut for the Thanksgiving vacation. She expected rest from the pressures of classes and tests. Nothing prepared her for what she experienced.

She was greeted by her mother with, "Debbie, how is my 'blonde witch'?" Her mother had fondly labeled her the 'blonde witch' since she dressed like many of the hippies of the day. Debbie wore loose fitting clothes and long blonde hair. A peace medallion hung around her neck on a long chain.

Later in the day, Sue, her best friend from high school, came by to visit. Sue attended the University of Connecticut, and the girls had looked forward to seeing each other. Debbie curled up in an overstuffed chair across from her friend. Sitting together in the living room they could smell the aroma of baking from the kitchen where Debbie's mother prepared the Thanksgiving meal. Debbie and Sue sipped hot tea as they chatted and laughed. All at once Debbie's heart started racing. The room faded and her limbs started tingling.

"I'm going to die," Debbie yelled as she tried to stand. Her mother had heard her cry out and rushed into the room. Seeing Debbie's flushed skin, her mother got upset.

"What's wrong?" Her mother frowned as she reached out to touch Debbie's cheek.

"I'm dizzy!" Debbie clutched her chest and fell over in the chair gasping and wheezing. "I think I might faint. I'm scared!"

"Let's go to the hospital," her mother announced. Her eyes were big and her brow wrinkled.

Sue watched in silence. She was earning a degree in nursing and prided herself on staying calm in a crisis. *Debbie?*

What's going on? Hmm. Sweat is pouring off her skin and– she's trembling. She felt her own heart pounding too.

Leaving Sue behind, Debbie's mother bundled her terrified daughter into the car and drove to the hospital.

I'm not sick, Debbie thought to herself while the car raced to the hospital. *I'm reacting to what my father said yesterday. He was joking, but I know he's right. I am a loser.* Looking out the window, Debbie saw they were halfway to the hospital. *I can't believe I lost those keys. I can't keep up with anything. My life is a mess.* For the first time she saw how irresponsible she had been. *What if I die?*

At the hospital, nurses hooked her up to an EKG machine to check her heart.

"This reading is normal," the doctor said studying a strip of EKG paper the machine had printed. "I don't see a problem at all."

"I think I had a panic attack," Debbie explained. "I'm okay." Debbie had learned enough medical information studying occupational therapy to understand what had happened. Reviewing test results, the doctor agreed and sent her home with a prescription for Valium. The rest of the vacation her mother hovered around giving her anxious looks.

"Are you okay, Debbie?" Her mother asked again and again. "Can I get you anything?" She stayed nearby watching for the smallest sign of illness.

"I'm fine," Debbie answered. But she didn't tell her mother about the conversation with her father.

After the Thanksgiving vacation, Debbie's worried mother had her brother accompany her to the bus station.

"Take good care of your sis," her mother had said, trying to smile as they left.

Debbie renewed her efforts to find peace from New Age and occult books she had purchased. In class the material she studied kept her focused, but outside of school she could not concentrate. Bedtime was horrible.

I don't feel tired at all. The lights were out and she was in bed. She had adjusted her covers, turned over several times, and toyed with her pillow. *But what if I die? What then?* Alone in her bed she knew something was missing from her life, but she did not know what. Burning incense, using crystals, and meditating did not fill the emptiness in her soul. *I'm alone and afraid. Does anyone care?*

Walking around Boston, she often felt terror grip her heart. One of her occult books had suggested that Jesus was real and a troubled person could turn to Him for help.

I'm scared stiff. Debbie thought one night while walking. *That book said to reach out to Jesus.* She had memorized the Lord's Prayer for her confirmation. Desperate for relief, she decided to recite it and was amazed when her fear went away. She continued to quote the Lord's Prayer whenever she felt rising fear. It helped her survive college.

At twenty-four she completed school and an internship. Debbie worked for a short time in Massachusetts, but then found another job in Connecticut. In her new job she met a therapist named Karen, who was a Christian. One day Debbie noticed a book on Karen's desk.

Look at this book, Debbie thought. *Maybe I should get it. Karen seems so peaceful.* Debbie bought the book. The name of the book was *Beyond Ourselves* by Catherine Marshall.

One afternoon Debbie returned to her tiny room in the hospital dormitory. She picked up Catherine Marshall's book and started reading the chapter called 'How to Enter In.' Mrs. Marshall described how she grew up in church knowing about Jesus and His death, but she could never grasp the core of Christianity. Guilt haunted her each time she sinned, but she could not change. At last, exhausted by a long battle with tuberculosis, she knew she was too weak to try anymore. Listing all of the sins she could remember, she asked for God's forgiveness. After she put her trust in Jesus, she found peace with God. She realized later that she had been resting in her parent's faith. Instead, she had to receive Christ for herself.

I believe Jesus exists, Debbie thought, putting the book aside. *He helped me when I was terrified in Boston.* Inhaling the smell of the sandalwood incense burning on her dresser, she considered her life. *I've tried meditating and it left me empty.* Her eyes went to the bookcase over her single bed. It held books on metaphysics, astrol-projection, and the occult. *I've spent loads of money on books, but they had no answers.* She remembered holding crystals over people and chanting words to cure illness. *It never worked. I didn't cure anyone or get power. I've done it all, and I feel lost and alone. But–when I cried out to Jesus, He answered.* A verse Mrs. Marshall had quoted came to her mind, "Seek ye first the kingdom of God and all these things will be added to you." She stood and walked to the dresser to snuff out the incense. As the acrid smell of smoke filled the room, she continued to examine her heart. *None of this is worth the money I spent. The occult didn't give what it promised. Meditation is useless.*

Taking a deep breath, she made a decision. *I want Jesus.* Her mind went to the community bathroom down the hall. A large institutional type trash can stood beside the bathroom door. *It's big enough. This junk belongs in the trash.* She strode to the bookcase and filled her arms with books, then marched out of her room to the trash can. Opening the lid, she crammed the books inside and returned to her room for another armful of books. It took several trips, but she emptied her room of books and incense. She glanced back at the trash can once she was done. It was full.

The next Sunday she made up her mind to go to a church that a Christian friend from Ohio had recommended. However, the church, which had met in a theater, had changed locations. She found the building empty.

I won't give up, she thought to herself as she drove back to her dormitory. She called a church member the following week and got the new address. The next Sunday she got ready to leave for the service, but could not find her glasses. She hunted through each drawer of her antique dresser, under her bed, and even among the plants in the window. Determined to go anyway, she wore her prescription sunglasses to drive to church. Even after church she could not locate her glasses, so she bought a new pair. However, the following Sunday morning she could not locate her new glasses and wore her sunglasses again.

Several ladies gathered around her to greet her after the service, and she told them about losing her glasses.

"You lost two pairs of glasses?" one lady asked. "You need to ask the pastor to pray with you." The pastor did pray with her and in his prayer he quoted the verse "If therefore thine eye be single, thy whole body shall be full of light." As Debbie listened to him, she realized that she needed to keep her eyes on Jesus. The next week she found both pairs of missing glasses.

Once Debbie began to go to services each week, she heard about a Bible study written by the Navigators. Since she was eager for more scripture, she decided to attend. In those lessons, she began to understand how Jesus purchased her forgiveness by His death and began to grow in her faith. She learned to turn to God with her fears. Knowing she would go to heaven took away her fear of death. She slept better at night.

Years later Debbie realized she had to write her father a letter. *I have to tell Daddy I'm different–and why.* Gathering pen and paper, she sat down at her desk. Tears filled her eyes.

His opinion doesn't matter now. Pausing a moment, her mind went back to the conversation in college. It hurt to think about what her father had said, but she knew God had forgiven her past failures. *I'll give him the Gospel.* Brushing away her tears, she wrote and poured out her heart. At last she put the letter in an envelope and attached a stamp. *Dear God, you are my father now. You're the one who matters.*

Stalking Me
by Robert Graves

At age thirteen I took my first drink of alcohol, never imagining that I'd be an alcoholic at by age eighteen. We were at the lake, my friend and I—and the booze. I had never been drunk in my life, so when the dizziness came, I didn't even realize what was happening to me. I felt loose and as though every hair on my body was standing on end; my first feeling of drunkenness. I didn't get blasted that evening, but from that day on for six long years my need for alcohol grew stronger than all other desires. Day after day, night after night, drinking consumed me. My mother managed to keep me in school. At the time, I didn't know how, but now I know it was through persistent prayer. Still, she had to wait six years before her prayer was completely answered. By then I had been in and out of jail too many times to count.

I remember one particular time very well. I had bought a beat-up '56 Chevy for twenty-five dollars. It took about 20 cans of spray paint, but I painted the whole car flat black, mostly to cover up the skull and crossbones the previous owner had painted on the driver's door.

One Friday night, the money ran out before my desire for alcohol did. Being half drunk, still thirsty, and broke put me in a desperate predicament. I bumped into a friend in the same plight who had a place in mind where we might get some money.

"I'll go inside," Joe said (not his real name). "All you have to do is take me there and wait for me in the car."

"What have I got to lose?" I reasoned. It developed I had a lot to lose. The places he went into were not open.

The first two places proved unprofitable, despite the big canvas bag of tire chains that Joe came running to the car with, thinking that he had a bag of coins. Funny, now. As a matter of fact, it was hilarious to me then, too. Joe shouted a few choice words and heaved the bag out the window.

While we were stopped at the third place, a police car drove by. I started the car, Joe hopped in, and we sailed down Dallas Highway. Then came flashing lights in the mirror. The police had seen us and turned around. An attempt at evasion in my bucket of bolts would be futile, even though Joe tried to get me to at least turn a corner so he could jump out. I figured, like a drunk man figures, that I could talk my way out of it.

They had us. The first officer approached my window with his flashlight glaring. He pointed it down at the door. An impression was still visible. "Hey, look at this," he said to his partner, pointing at the skull and crossbones. "We got us some genuine pirates here." They took Joe and me to the Marietta city jail and booked us on two felony counts of burglary. We stayed there until Monday, when they transferred us to the Cobb County jail, where felons were kept for prosecution.

After a week in jail, the preacher and the Sunday school superintendent from mother's church bailed me out. Both signed a five-thousand-dollar bond, and the church lent me two hundred dollars to pay the fine. Why? I didn't know at the time.

I finally paid the two hundred dollars back. I also paid, not with money but the hard way, for five years' probation. But I would never be able to buy back the felony record that would follow me everywhere I would go for the rest of my life. It would be there for all time, for all men to see. Stalking me.

At first, when I got out of jail, I was cautious since, being on probation, I knew what would happen the next time I got caught for anything. I quit drinking—for three months, but then became worse when I returned to my old life, graduating from alcohol to pills, then pot. I experimented with amphetamines, orally and injected. It was the '60s and San Francisco had Haight-Ashbury; Atlanta had Fourteenth Street and The Catacombs. *The Great Speckled Bird*, Atlanta's alternative newspaper for the hip, reported all the happenings. I wasn't alone in my desperate search for meaning and acceptance (as the Jesus "freak" generation proved).

Finally, before it was too late, I realized that my life, like a story, would someday end. It could end in a tragedy or in happiness—the choice was mine. I began to search for meaning elsewhere. I longed for someone who could help me. Then I remembered something the preacher who had signed my five-thousand-dollar bond had said to me. He had talked of Jesus. I had already heard about Him. I knew of Him from Sunday school; I knew of Him from mother. But He didn't know me. I decided to introduce myself.

"Dear Jesus," I said, "I'm living a life not worth living."

"I know," He said. "I've been watching. Waiting. I've got a new life for you, you know."

"But I've done much wrong."

"I haven't kept a record."

"I need you," I said.

"And I want you," He replied.

"You do?"

"Oh, yes. I do."

That day I learned why things that could have ended my life in tragedy had not occurred., and why things too good for me kept popping up in my life. Since that day, I no longer worry about my past record, for now that I belong to Jesus, I know that nothing less than *goodness* and *mercy* will follow me all the days of my life. Stalking me.

Adventuring with God
by Judy Becker

The January issue of Biblical Archeology annually showcases the digs for the year that enlist volunteer workers. I had always wanted to do this. My husband of 46 years had died the previous year, and I was readjusting my life. *Why not have this wild adventure before I get any older?* I asked myself.

The six-week tour that appealed to me visited five Middle Eastern countries: Israel, Jordan, Syria, Lebanon, and Egypt. It included two short digs. Being a Bible teacher, a chance to see the geography of the land would enhance my understanding. The problem was where to find the money for such an extended stay.

After Harvey died our old RV was becoming a money pit. I was never going to drive it by myself, so I decided that was the biggest part of my answer. I set about fixing what I could and put it on the market. When it finally sold I danced around the kitchen praising the Lord as I watched it go down the driveway.

Because it was not a Christian tour, I began praying weeks before I left that it would not just be an adventure, but that the Lord would use me for his glory. It soon became evident that he had heard my prayer.

After arriving that first evening, Kevin, a young ministerial student tried to witness to me in the cab on the way to the hotel. I explained to him that I had been a Christian for forty years. That was my first opportunity to declare Christ as my savior. Two other young people, Andrea and Chris overheard our testimony to each other. Kevin and I quickly established a Christian relationship.

The second chance to witness came a few days later after visiting the garden tomb that day. At the dinner table Kevin and I were discussing Christ's amazing death when my roommate, Marie, interrupted to state, "Jesus *was only* a historical figure." After a short discussion the battle lines were drawn: Two argued against Christ being the only way to heaven. Kevin and I took the positive side, while three remained neutral.

Cathy, a worldly-wise business woman in her thirties argued, "But Judy, you are saying that Jesus is the only way to God. There are many ways to God. He has several names." The argument continued as Kevin countered with John 14:6 quoting "…no man comes unto the Father but by me." Finally, I got in the last word flatly stating, "Cathy, there is only *one* way." After that the subject of conversation changed.

The next evening another opportunity arose. Our Jerusalem based Jewish guide and archeology teacher, Kathryn, took us to Ein Karim (John the Baptist's home) where we had a traditional Jewish meal like Jesus might have had. After riding the city bus back to the center of town she singled out Kevin and me and told all the rest to seek his own diversion because she wanted to talk to us. She said she had heard that we were strong Christians. Unbeknownst to us the others had told her about our confrontation. In spite of her dismissal of the others, Chris and Andrea tagged along. We spent the rest of the evening witnessing to her, while our two neutral comrades listened.

Still another opportunity to witness came on Saturday. Earlier I had seen a sign in a bookstore announcing charismatic services in the church next door on Saturday night. It stood across the plaza from the short alleyway to our hotel in the Old City at the Jaffa Gate. I planned to attend that evening after we returned from an outing to the Dead Sea and Ein Gedi. We were starting an archeological dig on Sunday and I feared I would not be able to attend church if I didn't take advantage of that service.

My hair was dreadful after swimming in the Dead Sea. After washing it, I discovered that my dryer wouldn't work. Time was short. Undaunted, I put on a dress, slapped a headscarf on my wet head, grabbed my Bible, and headed out. At the bookstore, when I asked about the church meeting I discovered it would be in Armenian and I wouldn't understand a word.

Disappointed, I started back across the Square when a woman in a shiny blue dress, head covered and carrying a black book, which I took for a Bible, caught my eye. I thought *I bet she's going to church. I'll just follow her.* As I turned to do so a man tapped me on the shoulder and asked, "Excuse me, but do you believe in God?"

It was a young bearded Orthodox Jew possibly thirty years old dressed in his black suit, and hat, with a prayer shawl hanging out of his pockets. I replied, " Why yes, and I believe in Jesus, too, and have for forty years."

He spoke in a raspy whisper, "I want to talk to you." I told him that my hotel was just up the alleyway. We could talk in the lobby. He had noticed me because of my attention to the other woman and because I also had my head covered. (Was that why my dryer stopped working? It was fine the rest of the trip.)

He refused to walk with me but followed ten or fifteen feet behind, quarreling with himself as he went as to whether he should do this. After we climbed the steps to the lobby he refused to stay there. Someone might see him talking to me, even an Arab, and tell on him. Since I knew my roommate was in the room, I asked her permission for us to talk in there.

"My name is Judy," I began.

"You may call me Morty," he replied. *Was that short, for Mordecai?* I wondered.

We sat down on the end of my bed. I began to tell him about Jesus being God and the Jewish Messiah while Marie listened in. I offered to pull up the Hebrew Scriptures on my laptop. But he refused. "It's Sabbath," he said. After a while he asked, "Why do the Rabbis not tell us these things?"

"They don't know them." I replied. I kept trying to get him to make a decision, but he was afraid.

At one point he pulled his prayer shawl out of his pockets and said. "I have been an Orthodox Jew all my life. I—don't want to be—an Orthodox Jew." He then told that he had been at the Wailing Wall all day crying out to God to show him the way. I felt honored to be God's answer to show him the "way."

By this time he had loosened up considerably. He asked, "Would you pray for me?" Then he slapped my hands down upon his thighs just above the knees. Nervously, I removed them. But he slapped them down again saying, "No, you have power." Later I learned that he had a physical problem with his legs. After praying all I knew to pray, I implored the Holy Spirit to pray for him, then I began to sing in the Spirit. He was excited about that.

It didn't look like he was going to accept Christ, but he would not leave either. I tried to think of some way to get rid of him. I suggested we have Kevin pray for him. He liked that idea. We went to Kevin and Chris's room. But even when Kevin prayed he still wouldn't leave. After Kevin closed his door while we were standing in the hallway, he grabbed me in a big exuberant hug and cried, "My mommy, my mommy."

I was really getting wary at this point and explained to him that I was recently widowed and very sensitive toward a man touching me. Suddenly he drew himself up in a huff and demanded, "You think this is something sexual?"

"Well, no," I said, not wanting to appear afraid. I couldn't get over the change in him. Finally, I remembered we had another Christian join our group that week. I suggested we talk to her.

We found Melissa in the lobby. I beckoned to her and we went to her room. After explaining the situation she proceeded to tell him the exact things I had told him even using the same words. This assured me that God was working. I guess it's true that a Jew needs two witnesses to establish truth. By this time he was beside himself with joy. We finally sent him off with the instructions to get himself a New Testament and read the book of *Yochanan,* Hebrew for John. We also told him there were Messianic Jews in Jerusalem who believed on Jesus. He should find them. Although Morty made no verbal commitment, his attitude of joy showed a change of heart.

That week during the day we dug up an aqueduct in Eastern Jerusalem. At night I worked at proving to my roommate, Marie (one year older than me), that Jesus was God. She finally said, "You have given me much to think about."

I arrived late to the second dig since I had opted for an extra week in Jerusalem. Again the Lord blessed me. Though the rest of the team now reduced to six had been digging for a whole week just outside Amman, Jordan. Only Kevin had found anything significant. The first day I unearthed two small jugs and a piece of the ceiling of a room adjoined to a mud brick. The Professor in charge asked. "How can you come in here and find something the first day when all these others have been digging for a week?"

"Have you never heard the parable of the eleventh hour workman?" I laughed.

We were digging in the ancient city of Jogbehah, the city to which Gideon chased the Midianites. Each day we arrived at the dig shortly after 5:00 AM. The site was in the sun and very dirty work. Shortly after noon we walked down a four-lane highway, and crossed over to a school where we washed out our pottery shards to be classified and counted. Each bucketful came from a designated section marked off by strings at the site. These would be recorded and studied later by the archeologists.

After four days of digging we toured the rest of Jordan. As we traveled to Petra, I marveled at the terrain of ancient Moab and the current cities that were so old they were mentioned in the Bible. In Petra, I separated from the rest of the group to visit one of Petra's significant buildings, the Monastery. No one else wanted to make the climb up the 1000 intermittent steps to the top of a mountain. At one point the path was a narrow passageway right next to a sheer drop off of several hundred feet. Even though the path was about five feet wide, I hugged the rock face wall on that one. The building was not much more impressive than the Treasury at the entrance to the city, but it was a setting that I was using in a fictional work, and I wanted firsthand observation and pictures. The view from the top looked first into the caldera of an ancient volcano and beyond you could see for miles and miles. It was well worth the climb. I was especially interested in seeing Petra not only because it was in the ancient land of Edom, Esau's dwelling place, but also because it is the favored hiding place for the "woman" of Revelation 12 for prophecy buffs like me.

The next leg of our journey took us to Syria. Only three of us had signed for this part of the tour, twenty year old, Andrea, and thirty year plus, Chris, and me. Each time we had entered a new country the young people were hassled by passport authorities while I sailed through. In Syria it was they who sailed through while my passport was pulled and I was told to wait outside this ominous door. As each person came and went through that door I asked, "What is wrong with my passport?" Everyone replied in Arabic. They revealed nothing. Finally, I went through customs without a word. I demanded to know what had happened. The official spoke to a man in line who spoke English and he explained to me: "You look like someone on their list who is dangerous."

Me? Dangerous? A white haired sixty-six year old woman? Chris said afterward that if that had been him, he would have called for me shouting "Mommy, Mommy, help!"

We toured Damascus seeing the famous mosque, walked down Strait street to where Paul received his sight from Annanias, saw the church meeting place in Annanias' basement and the window in the wall where Paul was let down in a basket.

Syria as a country was a surprise. Not all desert at all, but it had a fertile agricultural plain in the center of the country from Hama to Alleppo, two ancient cities mentioned in the Bible. However, crossing Eastern Syria, with its burning desert, was not pleasant. It was so hot that our nostrils burned with every breath in spite of the air-conditioning going full blast. The desert was barren of everything green except military uniforms. We passed maneuvers time after time. Eventually, we came to the oasis. Palmyra, a city of palms, was built originally by Solomon, but ruled by Queen Zenobia during the Roman era. Though we arrived early in the afternoon we were told to rest in the air-conditioned hotel until 6:00 PM, when it would be cool enough to walk the ruins of the queen's city.

The next day we retraced our route back to Damascus and headed for the Bekaa Valley in Lebanon and the multi-temple ruins at Baalbek. Some believe Solomon started this complex toward the end of his reign. It was an ancient example of wickedness and idolatry. That evening we arrived in Beirut, a half rebuilt city. As we toured the next day we saw ruined, bullet ridden, buildings left over from the Christian/Islamic Civil War, but we also saw more newly built commercial banks than you can imagine. Beirut, once the Wall Street of the Middle East seems destined to be so again.

This was especially interesting to me because as a prophecy student I believe the Anti-Christ will arise from Lebanon's financial enterprises according to Ezekiel 28. Not only was God giving me opportunities to witness for him to Andrea and Chris, but also to soak up the culture and feel the lay of the land, which has enhanced my gift of teaching ever since.

We were reunited with our tour group in Egypt where we saw the usual sights. Egypt is a lush agricultural band on either side of the river Nile, but it is also obvious as you fly over it that the green stops short beyond the influence of the river and it's canals. Absolutely *nothing* grows in the Egyptian desert except at the Oases. Because it almost never rains in this country, they are wholly dependent on the river.

The Nile is the swiftest flowing large river that I have ever seen, not at all like our large sluggish rivers in the US. Ruins with structures of mud bricks abound on its banks reminiscent of the Exodus story.

From Karnak we cruised up the Nile for several days to Lake Aswan. Then we exchanged our boat for a train and traveled overland all night back to Cairo. From there as weary travelers, we headed back home on our flight to the US.

Determined not to waste my last chance to witness I opened the conversation with my seat companion, a little Greek fellow from the island of Cypress who delighted in not having to sit beside a fat lady. He was flatly uninterested in the gospel.

But I believe the Lord rewarded me for being faithful. During the refueling in Amsterdam, the steward asked if we would like to sit up front in first class. We ended up in the luxurious number one and two seats. I was the first to disembark the plane.

Although my last effort to witness was a failure I believe I will see Morty in heaven and maybe even Andrea, Chris, Marie, and Kathryn. It was a great adventure and I know God answered my prayer to let me be his witness over and over. Although I never saw a harvest, I planted and watered the word of God and His word never returns void.

If He Leads He Will Provide
by Brenda Thompson Ward

By the time a person is thirty years old, been married ten years, has three children, and a job that means security in the future, one would usually think his or her life is settled. However, if that person is a Christian, God can turn their life around.

My husband, John, always felt that he should go into some sort of ministry. We married at an early age, and while he never forgot that desire, he shelved it because he felt his obligations to take care of his family would not permit us to pick up and go off to a Christian college. The problem with that attitude is that God will not allow you to forget something that you are definitely meant to do.

We were living in Hartselle, Alabama, and we were active in our church. Every year the church had a missions conference, and without fail, John and I would talk about the tugging of our hearts to give in the urge to surrender our will over to the Lord.

As each missions conference approached, we would both get nervous. We knew we should be in a full time church ministry, but, putting future financial security and moving the children out of the familiar before anything else, we would go hear the missionaries and go home and discuss what we should do. I did not realize that John was waiting for me to say I would be willing to uproot and go, while, at the same time, I was waiting for him to say, "Let's go."

Finally, one night one of the missionaries was talking to us, and John said, "I know the Lord wants me to serve Him in a ministry. I'm not exactly sure what, but I'm waiting for Him to open the door."

The missionary smiled and said, "John, you're going about this the wrong way. You go until He closes the door."

That was all that was needed. That night John and I went forward. When we knelt at the altar, we told God we would do whatever He wanted us to do. When we prayed, we were both a little fearful, yet peaceful at finally making the decision to follow and accept what the Lord had for us.

I enjoy the adventures of living and the surprises that we run into as we walk through our life. Some are pleasant and some are not. Everyday life experiences can bring such heavy burdens that you feel the only way to get through the rough times is to lean completely on the Lord. My most valuable lessons have been learned those times.

That missions conference was in October 1975. By January we had sold our home, packed up, and moved to Chattanooga, Tennessee where John enrolled in Tennessee Temple University.

Until that time in my life, I had never thought about what I would do in a ministry. In my deepest imaginations I did not feel it was meant for me to be a pastor's wife. I could not envision doing anything that would be useful to a ministry. I felt I had no worthy talents. John would get his education and training, and I would take care of the children. We knew I would have to go to work, but that would have to wait until our youngest was in kindergarten. Until then we would live use our equity money from the house for expenses.

The first challenge we faced was being in a small, two bedroom, basement apartment with three children. The apartment had a hall down one side and rooms on the other side. It is an amazing experience to watch how people adapt to surroundings when you know that is the home the Lord provided for you at that moment. We were cramped to some extent, but we were happier that we had ever been.

Highland Park Baptist Church, the campus church for Tennessee Temple, was much larger than our small church in Alabama with its two hundred members. Highland Park four thousand attending each Sunday and Wednesday. It could have been frightening, except that people were so friendly and gracious.

There was one woman I had admired from reading her books and articles. She taught a Sunday school class and I wanted to hear her. I did not meet her the first thing, instead, a sweet, white haired woman came up to me and said, "Hello, I'm Mary Cravens. We're so glad you came today. Why are you here at Tennessee Temple?"

"My husband is training for a ministry. We're not certain yet but he is leaning toward the field of Christian education."

"And what are you going to do?" Mrs. Cravens asked.

"Me? I don't know. I'm sort of dumb."

Mrs. Cravens eyes popped open wide and she said, "I beg your pardon?"

I did not realize it at that time, but one of Mrs. Cravens' ministries was helping women to see who they are in the eyes of God. That day she told me to go home and read Psalm 139 everyday until she said to stop. That would have been easy, but she added another assignment. "Whenever I run into you at church or on campus, I want you to tell me what you've learned about Brenda and God. He made you for a reason and He does not make junk. You're important to Him, and He has special plans for you."

By the time we had finished that conversation it was time for Sunday school to start and the woman I wanted to hear got up to speak. I already knew that Jessie Sandberg was a wife, mother, teacher, and a writer. I read her articles and wished that I could be like the women she wrote about.

Without getting a degree, I still received an education. Mrs. Cravens taught me to accept me as I was, to work on those things that needed improvement. She showed me that I could do things I never thought I could do. I never would envision myself teaching or speaking before ladies, but I do now.

Jessie taught me not to doubt God when circumstances were not what I wanted them to be. I remember one incident in particular. I was hired to work for a man that was difficult to get along with. I was the bookkeeper, and one of my duties was to prepare the bank deposit at the end of each workday.

One day I forgot to place the deposit book in the money bag, and the carrier returned it. My boss was furious and threw it almost hitting my head. I was terrified.

That was a Wednesday night and we would be going to church. So, I called Jessie and asked if I could meet with her before the service. I was sure she would tell me to turn in my resignation and never see that awful man again.

When I arrived at her office, I shared what had happened that day. Jessie let me talk until I had finally reached the end the story of terrible my ordeal. For a few seconds there was silence, and then she asked, "Brenda, did you pray for this job?"

"Yes."

"Do you feel God gave you this job?"

Suddenly I had this feeling in the pit of my stomach that this was not going to head in the direction I wanted to go. However, I knew I had to be honest so I replied, "Yes."

"Then why are you doubting in the dark what God has shown you in the light?"

I knew I would not be resigning from my job, but I did not know what to do. Through my tears, I asked, "He hates me. What am I going to do?"

Jessie smiled as she replied, "I doubt he hates you. You made a mistake and he was upset. Tomorrow you go to work and talk with him."

"What do I say?"

"Apologize to him. Tell him you prayed for this job and you need this job. Also, tell him that you will do your best not to disappoint him like that again." Even after we had prayed, I went away nervous.

Next morning, my boss opened the door and greeted me with a smile, as if nothing had ever happened. I arrived earlier than the other employees, so I had some time alone to talk to him. I did just as Jessie had advised me to do. I was amazed at the results. This man looked at me and said, "I'm sorry, Ms. Brenda. I have a terrible temper and I've never tried to control it. Don't worry about anything, we'll get along fine and I'm sure you'll do a good job for us."

Following that conversation, our relationship was different from before. My boss treated me as a friend, and we were able to have a joke between us. The bookkeeper before me had gone to lunch one day and never returned, so when he would get angry about anything, I would ask if he wanted me to take an extended lunch break.

Strange as it may seem, harsh experiences are not the worse things that can happen. Ignoring God's voice and not surrendering to His will for your life is far worse. Had my husband and I refused to go to school and make the sacrifices we did, we would probably financially be secure today, but many lessons would not have been learned.

My children saw their parents pray for food, clothes, and tuition. God always provided without our having to ask anyone for help. One summer I got to go to classes when my tuition was provided. I asked Mrs. Cravens who provided the money, she replied, "God did. That's all you need to know."

My husband worked a full-time job while he attended school. I worked at an exclusive men's clothing store forty hours a week. We never had to hire a babysitter or use a daycare because we had work schedules that made it possible for one of us to be with the children at all times. That was important to me and God worked all that out.

Sometimes, even if we did not share our need with anyone but the Lord, still wonderful things happened. One month our home church back in Alabama send a truck full of groceries. There was so much we ended up sharing with every family in our small apartment complex.

When John and I announced we were selling our home, uprooting the kids, and going away without a job or a place to live, our families thought we were losing our minds. We had never done anything so daring. I hadn't been taught to view life according to eternal values. God, in His infinite wisdom, knew I needed to be at a place to learn and to grow as a Christian.

Mrs. Cravens is gone now, but I'm sure that she is in heaven still wearing her sweet smile. She taught that I am not dumb and that God can use anyone who is willing.

I contact Jessie occasionally. She was the great example of a quiet and meek spirit, from whom I learned to accept people. She told me, "When you see that person walking toward you, stop and quickly pray, Lord, help me to see her through Your eyes," when I needed help dealing with difficult people. It is tough to be contrary if you pray that prayer.

I'm thankful that God shook up my little world and sent us out to work for Him. I had thought we had been headed to the mission field, but that was not His plan. God led John into Christian education and he is the administrator of a Christian school in Georgia. I, a woman who felt she was too dumb to do anything, am now teaching a ladies' Bible study and is writing.

The Bible tells us that God will supply our needs. Usually, we interpret that to mean material needs. I firmly believe that if we had not surrendered to the urging of our hearts and traveled that road toward the unknown, I would not be where I am today. At the time, it was all about John getting the training he needed to fulfill the desire of his heart. I had not thought about the desire of my heart.

I still read Psalm 139 frequently. Mrs. Cravens never told me I could stop. Still, if I began to feel like I'm not important to anyone or I feel to inadequate to do what I know I should, I read that chapter and I realize that God knows me and I may not be important to anyone else, but I am important to Him. After all, he made me for a reason.

God has such an exact timing we are not conscious of. He sent two wonderful women to teach me how the Lord wanted a Christian woman to live. I had been in church almost all my life. But, I was never taught that God has a reason for each of us being here.

I consider Jessie Sandberg and Mary Cravens to be a great representation of the woman mentioned in the book of Titus. They taught by example. We could look to them for love, encouragement, prayer, and a pattern by which we could live our lives. They had a tremendous impact on my life and I will always remember them both as models of a Christian woman.

We all have heroes and Jessie and Mary are two of mine. I hope that I can be positive Christian influence the lives of young women. The world around us is filled with people seeking answers. I know I was back in 1975. I'll be sixty my next birthday and I look back on my life and I see more than one example where God sent the right person at the right time to encourage, teach, and befriend. I have found that where He leads He will provide what is needed.

The Awakening
by Judy Parrott

I know how I would feel if I had sent my precious children to Sunday school, thinking they were getting exposed to God, and finding the teacher was not even a Christian. At least *now* I know. At one time, however, I was that teacher, and was no more an advocate of Jesus Christ that any other non-believer. I was simply a willing soul who walked into church and blended with the saints. The worst part was, I was unaware that I was a tare (a weed that looks like the real thing). I looked like wheat, I even talked like wheat when I hung around with the wheat, but if you asked me who Jesus was, my answer would be, "How the heck do I know?"

Martha, the person involved in my awakening, was a little Catholic freshman with a big conscience. We were in college together, and she needed a place to live, so I took her home with me. She knew a real Christian didn't swear and yell at her kids over every incident, even if she did wear a big old cross around her neck. This picture she saw in my home was black and white, while the Christian life was Technicolor.

Martha began to entice me to attend the Protestant church down the street. A few weeks later, the pastor announced that nobody was available to teach the eight-year-olds in Sunday school, so Martha generously offered my services.

"It will do you good, Jude. You are a born teacher. Besides, your kids need to go to church and learn about God." Little did I know how the color of my life was about to change.

It was November, the Sunday before Thanksgiving 1973, in Holland, Michigan. I had been teaching a third grade Sunday school class about six months when a new director took over. He decided the teachers needed some training, so we all met every evening for a week of classes. He apparently heard about the subjects I was teaching; *A little evolution stuff won't hurt anybody,* and the book*, "Chariots of the Gods."*

The first evening the leader asked some pertinent questions. "Would you like to have been on earth before Jesus came, during His life on earth, or now?"

The second night the question was, "Do you consider yourself a sinner?" I certainly didn't think *I* was one.

Saturday night at the end of a session, we were each told simply to say, "Jesus is Lord", one at a time. *That's silly*, I thought. However, when it came my turn I was unable to say it! The words refused to form in my mouth. I was terribly embarrassed and confused. Finally, determined, I blurted them out, jumped up from my chair and ran. I got in the car trembling, and began to sob as though my heart would break, for no apparent reason. It was very unnerving.

Sunday morning, the pastor was ill at home, so the elders decided to play an audiotape for us by Dr. James Kennedy with the message of salvation. I had never recalled hearing how to become a Christian before; maybe I had never listened. When challenged by Dr. Kennedy to reach up, in my mind or with my hand, and expect Jesus to grab it, he said this was the leap of faith required to be born again.

I took the challenge, closed my eyes, and put my hand in the air, and I really did expect Jesus to respond. I felt no physical touch, but a spiritual person was definitely revealing Himself to me. I knew in that moment that Jesus was alive and was right there with me. No words can describe this revelation. Nobody could ever talk me out of it. It was an appointment with God, planned and initiated I am certain, by Him, and because I responded, He revealed Himself to me.

That morning *half the congregation* accepted Christ as their Savior. In awe, we came forward for the first altar call this church ever had, to ask Jesus for salvation and forgiveness of our sins.

Soon after I prayed that little prayer of faith, I suddenly felt spiritually naked and aware of the sin in my life, but before the shame overwhelmed me, I felt this 'monkey of sin' climb off my back, and a cloak or covering drape over me. I learned later it was a cloak of righteousness that had come from Jesus. There was a physical release from emotional burdens that seemed to weigh a ton. I didn't see them leave, but I felt like my body was floating! We were each handed a small metal cross. I clung tightly to that little cross, finally beginning to comprehend that it stood for something more precious than all the gold in the world.

I had buried my guilt under tons of denial, because I had no place to go with it. Now I understood Jesus was willing to carry it for me, and set me free. This was a realm much deeper than mind or body stuff; it was spiritual. This was about a spirit, which for thirty-two years, I didn't even know I had. I drove home feeling like a bright light had been passed into my chest, and that others could see it at a glance. It was not symbolic, but a very real experience.

My husband was away hunting for the weekend, and I was free to study my Bible all afternoon. For the first time, the words became clear to me, like watching a three dimensional movie with the special glasses on. In Corinthians I read, "The man without the Spirit does not accept the things that come from the Spirit of God, for they are foolishness to him, and he cannot understand them, because they are spiritually discerned." The truth, then, had been hidden from me until I invited Jesus into my life. Until that moment, I had functioned with only five senses, and now I possessed a sixth.

In the evening, the church had a testimonial meeting. The members whose lives I admired most shared how they had been reborn by God's Spirit. One said life was like puzzle pieces she could not assemble until she invited Jesus to forgive her sins. All of a sudden, the pieces came together and she saw the purpose for her life. I could relate to that analogy.

I was shaking my head in agreement, smiling widely, enjoying all the great stories that now made such sense, when a strange phenomenon occurred. Radical new thoughts started creeping in; I thought they were mine. Nobody warned me this might happen. I had become a traitor to my old master, and he bombarded me with thoughts in the first person but I didn't recognize him. *These people are inducing me to join them so they can extort money from me!* I began to fear they would coerce me to Africa to work in the jungles. *This is a cult, and they are trying to brainwash me!* Anger poured in like a hot flame; I jumped up, incensed, and for the second time, ran out of church.

The devil tried his best to drag me into hell that night. It had been sleeting and freezing, and the roads were covered with a clear glaze of black ice. I started the car, stomped on the gas, spun in a couple circles getting out of the parking lot, and soon I was going a hundred miles an hour on a treacherous piece of highway.

Seeing the speedometer cleared my brain; I began pumping the brakes as the intersection raced to meet me. The car responded by spinning like a top, pressing me hard against the door. God had to be helping, because miraculously, there were no vehicles at the intersection. Head reeling, I stopped, frantically clinging to the wheel, wondering what had gotten into me. Satan was obviously urging me to take my life, but God intervened. I had not yet read the warning, *Be sober, be vigilant, because your adversary the devil, as a roaring lion, walks about, seeking whom he may devour.*

About ten that evening, the doorbell startled me. I saw an elder and his wife at the door. "What do you want?" I asked warily.

Marilyn said, "We need to talk to you just for a minute. We know what is happening to you."

How could they know? I thought. *I didn't tell anyone.*

I reluctantly let them in, still presuming my suspicions in church were correct. She made small talk, but she realized I was too distraught to be visiting. I was very uneasy and just wanted her to leave. It was a bizarre feeling. I had always been at ease around them before. They sat on the couch, and she asked if she could pray. I just glared at her but she began anyway.

"Satan," she said, "you will leave now. Judy is God's property. She has chosen to follow Jesus Christ, and you have no authority over her. Loose her in Jesus' name!"

That command was so powerful, the irrepressible feelings of hatred and anger dissolved instantly, and the wonderful peace I had in the morning returned. The outlandish ideas now seemed so absurd, I could not imagine having believed they were true. I started pouring out my heart to her about secrets I had carried for years, and experienced a tremendous release of pressure.

Marilyn became my precious mentor, calling me every day for at least a year, giving me one verse a day to strengthen my faith, like daily bread. She brought me to visit other Christians and share my new birth experience, which built up my faith and provided support to other believers.

One evening soon after my conversion, I was lying awake praying in bed, and a brilliant light entered the room! It was so peaceful; it didn't hurt my eyes; but I could see nothing in the room except that wonderful light. It stayed for about ten minutes and submerged me in a love I never knew, and a sense of being valued and precious to this light. Then it faded away, and I was alone in the dark. I think of that night often, wishing it would happen again. Jesus, I know, was the light.

About a year later, I had been studying about the Holy Spirit, and one night asked Jesus to fill me with His Spirit. I cannot express this intimate encounter in earthly terms, except to say I felt certain to die from the ecstasy of being so filled with part of God Himself. My life took on a new meaning and depth from then on.

Many miracles have occurred in my family since then as a daily way of life as God promised. He healed my children when they got sick, and even our animals experienced His healing power. I know God cares for us all so much more than we can understand. God is love. He can be nothing else.

Recording even some of the wonders would take several books, which I may write some day. I am convinced nothing is impossible with God, and when we seek Him with all our hearts, He will be sure to let us find Him.

Our Becky's Missing!
by Charlene C. Elder

Her car wasn't in the driveway and there were no voice mail messages on our home phone.

"Honey, have you heard from Becky?" I asked my husband when I came home from work. He shook his head no.

"I'm really concerned about her. She acted rather strange the other night and then went off with her new friends." My mind replayed the incident. Becky had come in from school and asked to go shopping for some new clothes. That in itself wasn't unusual for Becky. Her choice of clothes had always been unique. It wasn't unusual for Becky to dress as the individual she was. This time was no different, but the clothes she wanted were a bit unusual: army-type boots and pants.

"Mom, don't you want me to dress better? All the girls are wearing this now...can we go and get them tonight?" She begged as she presented her case.

"If I'm not too tired when I get home from work, we'll go look for some."

"Great," Becky responded as she ran out the door to meet her friends.

After I got home from work and we had eaten dinner, Becky and I drove to the only shoe store within a ten-mile radius that carried the type of boots she wanted. She found her size. "Don't they look good, Mom?" she asked me as she stood in front of the floor mirror seeing how they looked on her.

"I guess so," I responded with hesitation. "But I don't think they'll go with everything."

"Oh, yes," she said with such conviction. "They'll go with anything. All the girls are wearing them with dresses and pants. I'll fit in better, Mom."

"Okay," I said to her as we approached the cashier and purchased the boots.

From the shoe store we went to the store that carried the pants she wanted. The next morning, dressed in her new pants and boots, Becky looked like she was ready to enter the army. She had also cut her hair extremely short and bleached it. That wasn't unusual for Becky either; she loved changing hair colors and styles. She informed us that there were others at her school that were also lightening their hair color. "It's the latest thing," Becky told us.

The following evening I returned from work and was preparing dinner when Becky and her new girlfriend, Sharon, came into the kitchen. "Mom, this is Sharon. She's in some of my classes."

I smiled politely at Sharon, noticing she was dressed the same way as Becky and had the same hairdo and hair color. They headed upstairs to Becky's bedroom to do their school work, and a few hours later Becky drove Sharon home.

As the days passed, Becky spent more time with Sharon and other mutual friends and less time at home. She had been good in keeping her curfew and was doing very well at school, until she met Sharon.

"Mom," Becky said as I walked in from work a few days later, "I need some money because my friends and I are all going out to eat tonight. Do you have ten or twenty dollars you can give me?"

I checked my wallet. "No, I don't have but a couple of dollars. I'd have to go to the ATM and get some cash, but I won't be able to do that for an hour or so."

"They're waiting for me now," Becky complained. "Can you just give me your ATM card and I'll bring it back to you?"

Because I was in the middle of cooking and had several other things scheduled to do that night, I didn't want to take the time to leave and get cash from the ATM.

"All right," I told her. "Here's my ATM card. You can get $20 out and bring back the receipt. Understand?"

"I promise," she said as she took the ATM card, grabbed her purse and headed to the garage. I remember she paused as she opened the door, looked at me, and said "I love you, Mom."

I finished making dinner, and was putting it on the table when my husband came home. After we had eaten, I cleaned off the table, did the dishes, and proceeded upstairs to our office to work on the other items on my evening agenda. The hours passed. Becky wasn't home yet by the time we went to bed. The following morning we noticed Becky's car wasn't in the driveway and she wasn't in her room. I thought perhaps she had stayed over at one of her friend's which she had done from time to time. I knew she'd call me sometime during the day at work.

A couple hours after I'd gotten to work, my husband called and asked me why I had taken $500 dollars from the ATM.

I gasped. "Five hundred dollars?" I thought for sure there must be a mistake. "I gave Becky the ATM card last night so she'd have $20 for eating out with her friends. She's supposed to get it back to me today and give me the receipt."

My husband said he'd check again with the bank and we hung up. It wasn't but a few minutes later that he called back, and confirmed that someone had taken $500 out of our checking account. We still hadn't heard from our daughter.

The day passed. Still no word from Becky. I called her cell phone. No answer. I continued calling every hour or so. Still no answer. There were no messages on our voice mail at home. Now I was getting concerned. *Had something happened to Becky? Had someone robbed her and left her somewhere? Where was she? Was she okay?*

The hours went by slowly. Minutes seemed like hours; hours seemed like days. We called Becky's friends, but no one had heard from her. I wanted to know *where* my daughter was and that she was all right.

Throughout the long hours of not knowing I had to trust the Lord. I prayed for Becky, for her safety and protection; calling for His angels to guard and protect her and bring her home safely. The uncertainty of Becky's whereabouts wore on both my husband and I, yet we had to continue working each day as though nothing was wrong. Inside I was torn to pieces as the enemy of man's souls tried to convince my mind that she was dead. I had to fight hard to keep from giving into fear and despair. I spent many hours in prayer, in reading the Word of God, and in learning to trust the Lord no matter what my senses told me. Many hours of sleep were lost but many hours were spent in prayer.

Another day passed, and we still hadn't received any word from Becky. Sharon's mother called us to see if we knew where Sharon might be. We shared what we both knew and concluded the girls must be together. Sharon's family had not heard anything from Sharon either. We promised to stay in contact with each other, especially when we knew something further. My husband I weren't sure what to do next. We had always given Becky room to be herself. She was a strong-willed child but for the most part she stayed within the boundaries we established.

Finally I told my husband I couldn't wait any longer; I had to know what was going on and where Becky was. I was going to call the police and give them a missing person's report. It was not like Becky to wait so long to contact us if she was going to be gone. Just as I reached for the phone to call the police, it rang. I nearly jumped out of my skin. I grabbed the phone. "Hello?"

"Hi, Mom, it's Becky," the voice on the other end said.

"Becky, *where* are you? Are you okay?"

"I'm fine. I'm in Florida, and I have a lot of new friends."

"Oh, Becky," I started. "Why didn't you tell us where you were going and what you were doing? I was just minutes away from calling the police and giving them a missing person's report."

"Oh, Mom, don't do that!" Becky cried. Her voice was frantic. "Please don't do that! Whatever you do, don't call the police. I can't talk a whole lot right now. I'm at a pay phone. Promise me you won't call the police."

"Becky, what's going on?" I asked.

"I can't talk right now, but you can't call the police, Mom," Becky said. "They might hurt me if you do. Please don't call the police."

"Who might hurt you?" I asked. "If you're in danger, I need to call the police."

"No, please don't. This group wouldn't like it if you called the police, so please don't call them."

"I don't know if I can promise that. I want to know where you are and what's going on."

"I can't talk about it any more now. But I'll call you again soon. Please don't call the police!"

"All right," I hesitated. "But you have to promise you'll call me tomorrow and then every couple of days and let me know you're okay. Otherwise, I *will* call the police and they'll come and find you!"

"I promise, Mom, but please don't call the police! I love you."

"I love you...." The phone line went dead. Caller ID only showed that the call was out of area. There was no way to call her back.

I informed my husband of Becky's whereabouts as best I knew from what she told me. He agreed to wait a little longer on involving the police as long as we'd hear from Becky. What could they do? She was eighteen. What could we do other than pray?

I called Sharon's mom and relayed to her what we knew. She still hadn't heard anything directly from Sharon, but had contacted the police. Because Sharon was also eighteen years old, they could not pursue a runaway report, especially since Sharon had left on her own volition. I told Sharon's mom when I heard from Becky again I'd let her know.

The battle was on. Wherever my daughter was in Florida, she was in potential danger. She might have left on her own volition, but I wasn't about to stand by and let her life be destroyed.

My husband and I continued praying. I don't think I slept much that night. My mind replayed the incidents from the past weeks. *Was there something we had missed? Could we have stopped this from happening?* Some answers were clear; others weren't. The only thing I knew to do at this point was to pray and ask the Lord for His help.

At night after work when I got on the treadmill and opened my Bible, I read and prayed the promises of God - praying for my daughter, for her safety and protection. God's Word became a greater tool and support to me because of it's promises of return of the captives, of safety, protection, *and* deliverance. I read the Word with great eagerness, taking those promises as mine. Without God's promises and His peace throughout this situation I wouldn't have made it.

The one verse that gave me ammunition against the forces of darkness was from the book of Jeremiah. I knew the Lord had that particular verse just for me. It told me to *"refrain thy voice from weeping and thine eyes from tears... thy children shall again come unto their own borders...there is hope in thine end saith the Lord."* What comfort those words gave my heart and mind. I quoted that verse out loud day in and day out. I fought for my daughter's life as I wielded the 'sword' of the Word of God.

My daughter was diligent in calling every two days. We wouldn't talk long, but I continued to let her know we loved her, and we wanted her back home. I sensed from how she spoke that she didn't want to be where she was.

One night, several weeks later Becky called again. This time it was from a pizza place where she had been allowed to get a part-time job. She said the group she was with didn't allow you to be by yourself much, so she had to be very careful. They were constantly watching her, controlling the groups' actions, but interestingly enough, she was the only one they allowed to get a part-time job. They were unaware of her personal telephones calls from work.

"Mom," she started. "I really want to come home."

"You *can* come home, Becky," I told her. "Just come. You've still got your car. Right?"

"Yes, but it's not that easy, Mom," she said. "But I want to go back to school."

"You come home, and you can go to school."

We talked about her going back to school and what she wanted to study. She couldn't go into detail on what the group was or what they were doing. If they found out she was talking to anyone, she would be dead she told me. I knew God had allowed her to get that pizza job. Even Sharon hadn't been able to do that. Becky's break was over, but she said she'd call again the next evening that she worked.

When Becky called a few days later, she said she planned to be home in two weeks. I was encouraged. I continued praying for her safety and protection. I knew God was going to deliver my daughter.

She was due home on a Tuesday evening. I planned her favorite dinner. Monday night the doorbell rang, and I opened the door.

"Becky," I exclaimed. "You're home earlier than you thought."

I hugged her as she came in with her bags. I asked how she was.

"I'm tired but I'm okay," she said as she put her bags down. "But they threatened to kill me, Mom, if I left. Even as Sharon and I were driving out, they smashed my car window in!"

"I'm so glad you're okay!" I told her as I hugged her tightly. "We'll get your window fixed."

Tears flooded my eyes. I couldn't help it. The tears I shed were of joy and thankfulness for God's mercy and grace. My daughter was back home just as the Lord promised in his Word!

It was several days after Becky was safely back home that my husband I learned more details about where she had been and what she had done. The group she became involved with was a skinhead, white supremacist group. They demanded total adherence to their rules and their ways, no exceptions. They were ready to fight law enforcement, if needed; and each member was instructed in how to handle various types of weapons. All members received strict teaching in their beliefs and nothing else was allowed. Because she couldn't share any of this information with us, we didn't know how dangerous it had been for Becky.

The Lord had brought my daughter through a difficult time in her life. He had taught me how to stand on the promises of His Word and trust Him no matter what the situation looked like to my natural eyes. I knew with certainty that no weapon formed against us would prosper.

Sharon was also reunited with her family but still posed a threat to Becky as an informant for the group. For the next 2 months Becky was continually looking over her shoulder. She knew they were watching her. But the Lord's angels were protecting Becky, and I knew the Lord would continue to keep her safe.

The journey of my daughter some ten years ago brought her to where she is today. Becky is now married to a great man. They have a beautiful two-year-old daughter, and is expecting their second child this year. God has been faithful just as He promised.

Not Looking
by David Beck

I dropped out of high school in March 1980 during the third quarter of the school year, with four English classes and one elective uncompleted. I had only smoked marijuana on an occasional basis until the summer of 1978, but once school began that fall, I made that a full-time endeavor. Staying out with my friends and constantly watching television at home over the next eighteen months had lowered my grades.

The principal explained that since I had not passed any two English courses taken in a given quarter up to this point, it followed that I could not be trusted to take twice that amount. Without those courses, I would be unable to graduate on time with my class. Further, the principal announced that anyone not able to make graduation would be required to attend summer school. Not being the type of person who liked school in the first place, I decided to quit and join the military if my parents would allow me to. Both agreed, and that's when I stopped attending.

I already had a part-time time job at a dialysis clinic, which evolved into full-time employment upon leaving school. Having chosen a delayed enlistment, I would not have to report for duty until late October, almost an eternity away for a teenager. More time to party and live it up was the general idea.

God had a plan for me and knew exactly what it would take to change my life. My paternal grandmother, a person very dear to me, died in August 1980 as I awaited my impending military service. After the funeral, my father and cousin, one mildly religious, the other an agnostic of sorts, were discussing a book about the end of the world. I'm not sure what brought up this subject between the two, but I was so struck by the interesting topic that I joined in the conversation and learned about the book, *The Late Great Planet Earth*, by Hal Lindsey.

I went straight from my uncle's home to Zondervan's, a religious bookstore at a local mall, bought the book, and went home to pursue what I thought would be the next fad in my life. How could I have known that *The Late Great Planet Earth* would change me in every way that I could imagine?

Before I finished the book, I was convinced that the Bible was God's Word and that Jesus was the Son of God. The subject of Lindsey's book was eschatology: the end of the world as predicted in several books of the Bible, with *Revelation* being his primary resource. What convicted me most of all was not the future predictions, but those that had already been fulfilled concerning Christ and his earthly mission 2000 years ago. If those prophecies had come true, then if follows that the ones pertaining to the future are also valid and will come to pass.

Although my eyes were opened to God's truth in late August of 1980, I wasn't saved until March 1983. Foolishly, after receiving the information that God had given me, I still did not immediately change my lifestyle. Instead, I lingered in the wrong path, failing in my military service, which resulted in my early separation, albeit with an honorable discharge. I returned home and resumed partying with anyone that I could.

Through one of my buddies, I was reintroduced to a person I had casually known in high school. He partied just as I did, but wanted a better life. After a disappointing date with a young lady who was upper class and religious, he and another friend showed up on my doorstep the next day.

"We're going to church," they announced.

"Okay, so am I," I said, without really thinking about it, but confession is made with the mouth, and God made the most of that opportunity.

My life began to take a turn for the better. In spite of having earlier dropped out of high school, I earned my GED and went on to graduate from college with a bachelor's degree in political science. I was nearly burned out after only fourteen consecutive quarters of college in my race to graduate before my father passed away from a terminal brain tumor. Thankfully, I earned my degree just three weeks before his death in 1989.

Formerly a hard-rock music lover, I served in a gospel music group for most of the 90s, only leaving after we failed to successfully transition into a full-time capacity. I then studied computers, receiving a Microsoft Certified Systems Engineer certification. I also began writing, having been blessed with a vivid imagination and a passionate sense of humor.

As I look back, I can see God's hand in everything positive in my life. I had failed in so many things: dropping out of high school, my use of drugs, and my less than satisfactory military service. After finding Him, I earned a college degree, found joy in Christian fellowship and music, and am pursuing my love of writing and being published.

Gently, but firmly, God picked me up, and placed my feet on His path. My ministry will be to use my gifts to witness to others who find themselves in the same downward spiral, and to let them know that rescue is "only a prayer away."

Nothing Short of A Miracle
by Lloyd Blackwell

I thought the host pastor had stood up to make announcements and then to preach. I heard my name mentioned several times so I smiled back at the crowd as they looked at me. There was more talking and I heard my name mentioned again. Then the pastor looked at me and sat down.

My interpreter suddenly leaned over to me and said with an excited voice, "You are supposed to preach." Well, this was news to me for I was totally unprepared. Whispering a quiet quick prayer, I stepped to the lectern, opened my Bible to a random New Testament page, smiled at the congregation as if I knew what I was doing, and began to preach.

Participating in many local and foreign mission projects for thirty-five years has involved me in many situations that I was not trained nor equipped to adequately handle in my own ability. Like most mortals, I have felt inadequate, unprepared, unqualified, fearful, overburdened or under-equipped to take on certain mission projects. As a result, I have had to overcome a reluctance to participate in an area outside of my comfort zone, especially in a foreign country. These limitations are sometimes overwhelming to all of us and have kept many voluntary missionaries sidelined and out of the mission field.

The Bible speaks of this many times, especially in the New Testament. Nowhere does it record that God calls qualified, trained or certified people to do his bidding in spreading the gospel around the earth. Jesus did not use that logic in selecting his disciples either as those chosen were very ordinary people. In fact, the Bible clearly indicates that God would never ask about my ability or inability—just my availability. That's what makes a person like me qualified for mission involvement.

Anxiety, fear and dread of failure are all components of entering into new areas of responsibility—missions being no exception. Commitment and faith is a part of the necessary mix of ingredients to make it successful. Faith is a gift of God but requires a personal decision. It took me many years to gain enough Christian maturity to trust in a complete faith, a faith where I turned all over to God, in a given situation. This is the kind of faith where I had to develop a complete peace in my decisions, no anxiety and no fear of the end result; only follow with confidence where God leads.

I had always prayed for the blessings and leadership of God in my mission involvement and felt confident that I was doing what was pleasing to Him. However, in retrospect, I don't believe I had turned my life over to Him completely, always reserving a degree of self-direction. I had felt equipped enough to personally handle that responsibility. With God's help I had always managed, which had given me confidence.

All of that changed in 1999 when I agreed to participate in a February 2000 winter mission trip to Romania. There was usually two or three feet of snow during this period, giving the farmers some unusual free time. My major assignment was to teach the men and preach to the farming families.

I knew absolutely nothing about preaching but I committed immediately, without reservation, because I had previously made a commitment to God that I would go where He sent me. The commitment alone was a step of faith. Little did I know how much more faith would be required of me over the next three years.

All of Romania was struggling with a poor economy. It had been just a few short years since they had overthrown their Communist dictator and kicked the occupying Russians out of the country. Life was especially difficult in the rural areas where farming was simply an existence.

Communism and religion were not compatible. Only the Eastern Orthodox Church was allowed to exist under the 45-year reign of Communism. Most of the new Christian church buildings were converted homes, using one or two rooms for worship. These churches would have a membership of four or five to perhaps thirty persons.

Our trip to Bucharest, Romania in 2000 went smoothly. The real journey would begin the next day when we would go by bus across the Transylvanian Alps to Tirgu Mures and beyond into the countryside. My destination was the last stop in the remote rural area. Here I would be met by a local pastor and transported by automobile through the snow to my farmer-family host, who spoke no English.

Our bus trip took about eight hours and we kept a reasonable schedule as we dropped off various segments of our voluntary missionary group. We had picked up several interpreters earlier, one for each of our small groups, and they were departing the bus with the proper people. We were on the final leg of the bus journey when my interpreter suddenly had a seizure a couple of miles from the last stop, our destination. A quick decision was made to leave me without an interpreter and rush our sick friend to a hospital. I was left with my host pastor (George) who could only speak a little broken English.

As the bus left, George and I loaded my luggage into his car for the three-mile trip through the snow to my rural host home. We traveled on a dirt road you could only visualize through the snow and hope you stayed between the two shallow ditches. We made very slow progress for the first couple of miles before we finally became stuck in the snow. Fortunately for me, my host and another man were watching for us about a mile further down the road and they trudged through the snow to our disabled car. My host took my luggage from the trunk and we both walked back to the farm while George and the other man decided what to do about the car.

The following afternoon our leader brought another interpreter for me to use in a preaching service the next day. We had been praying for a healthy recovery of my first interpreter while he was ill. I was happy and relieved when he returned in decent health the day following my first preaching service. Now I had two interpreters.

I did lots of praying for my four preaching services, but never turned everything over to the Lord in full faith. As in the past, I depended on my own strength to a small degree; still, God blessed all of us in the services. The first service produced no immediate fruit, but the remaining three services produced four professions of faith. God is faithful, even with a not-so-good amateur preacher.

I returned to Romania a second time in 2001 and was blessed beyond measure. Never have I seen the Lord work in lives as He did in our group. I went out into the same general rural area as previously but worked with a different group of churches. My small team was composed of a youthful schoolteacher, who taught the ladies, and a young high school senior who taught the children's Awanas program to the Romanian youth. My charge was to preach and to teach a couple of classes for men. George remained our host pastor.

On this occasion I had an entirely different approach to our mission activity. I had decided God could do a better job using me without my interference. After much prayer and thought, I turned *everything* unconditionally over to God and asked him to use me for His purpose and will. In all sincerity and honesty, I admit that I felt such a complete confidence and peace as I have never experienced in my entire life. I no longer had a single worry or concern. Never before or since have I felt such assurance that wonderful things were going to happen and that it would involve me.

Things started off with a bang from the very start. My first preaching service yielded five new Christians. A second and third preaching service at other churches produced even more converts of men, women and children. Our classes were extremely well attended and successful. The program training for Awanas (Approved Workman Are Not Ashamed) was going well. God was blessing all of us together in large numbers.

George, our host pastor, decided to rent a community center in a village of 300 residents for a special Saturday evening service. We would teach some adult classes in the morning and I was to preach that night. This would be our greatest effort, and in a village of no known Christians.

We had experienced a wonderful week, with God blessing right and left. The early afternoon was utilized for further training for the Awanas and that had been well attended. Before that program was over, George set up a rented PA system and placed a speaker out front near the road and started making loud announcements over and over.

A Christian leader, a school principal, had come from another village to help us, and he could speak decent English. I kept hearing George repeat my name often over the PA system, so I asked our visitor what he was saying. He responded, "He is saying 'Come to a revival tonight and hear evangelist Lloyd Blackwell preach.' " And come they did, an estimated 150 men, women and children came, about half of the entire village.

I preached with full confidence that God would use me, and He blessed beyond comprehension. I first gave an invitation to the youth, with a warning not to come forward unless they were serious about accepting Jesus into their heart and lives. They came forward in droves. I next gave an invitation to the "mamas" with the same warning, and many stepped forward.

Finally I invited the "papas" to come forward, if they were man enough to accept Christ into their lives, and more came forward. Overwhelmed, we could not record the personal information for everyone that night because of the huge response.

Never have I seen God bless so much. More than 70 converts gave their personal information that evening and the others returned to give theirs the following week. An unbelievable 105 men, women and children accepted Christ into their lives that night. God was at work overtime. I cannot claim any of the credit and am keenly aware that I could not have done this through my own ability. I made myself available, but God delivered on His promise of equipping the unequipped. God even had further plans as 11 of the 105 made a request for me to personally baptize them the next day.

When I awoke early that Sunday morning, I noticed it had snowed again during the night and the temperature had dropped considerably. There was concern that we might have difficulty getting to the remote country church. Fortunately we had departed early enough to allow additional time for the trip. It was a slow drive through the snow to within 600 feet of our destination where we walked the remaining distance. The church, a converted house, was the largest and most modern in the area. However, as with the others, it had no indoor plumbing or bathroom. It did have a well and an outhouse.

Upon our arrival at the church that Sunday morning, I was asked to pose outside in the snow for pictures with the new Christians I was to baptize later in the service. As we were doing this, I noticed everyone coming through the snow and mud was bringing a bucket of steaming hot water with them for the just-completed baptismal pool. Some of them had walked several miles with the buckets of water they had heated on their wood-burning stoves. I grew a little emotional as I realized how difficult it must have been for many of them.

Afterwards, we went inside for some more pictures before the morning worship service was to begin. I also got a first look at the steaming new baptismal pool, the only one within a 50-mile radius. After a couple of photographs were made, I walked to the podium and sat down by the pastor just as the service began. The pastor sat to the right of the podium. I sat to the left with my interpreter sitting next to me, the usual arrangement.

I thought the host pastor stood to make announcements and to preach. I heard my name mentioned several times, so I smiled at the crowd as they looked at me. There was more talking, and I heard my name mentioned again – as the pastor looked at me and sat down. My interpreter suddenly leaned over to me and said with an excited voice, "You are supposed to preach." Well, this was news to me. I was totally unprepared.

I breathed a quick prayer, stepped to the podium, placed my Bible on the lectern and casually opened it to the New Testament—no place in particular. Without turning to any other page, I looked out at the congregation, smiled as if I knew what I was doing, and began to preach.

I was uninformed, unprepared and unequipped, but I exuded a heart-felt confidence as I preached from the page of the Bible before me. I did not panic, stumble or falter during the entire unprepared sermon. In fact, seven men, women and children came forward to receive Christ during that service. Not because of me, for I was in a fog the entire time. Whatever rationalization one might make, I will always be convinced that God orchestrated the five preaching services and the results.

As we concluded the service, I retreated to the back to prepare for my first ever baptisms. The water in the baptismal pool no longer gave off steam, but was still pleasantly warm. As I looked at the water I was reminded again of the love, devotion and determination required of these people to lug this hot water by hand as they walked through the snow and mud for this special occasion. I wondered if most of our complacent American Christians would have made the extra effort.

The entire congregation stayed to watch the baptism in their just-completed baptismal pool. I doubt if over one or two in the group had ever seen a baptism in a baptismal pool. This was truly a special occasion. I stepped into the pool and held out my hand to help the first one to be baptized, a lady of sizable proportions, into the pool. I knew if I could handle this one, the rest would be a pushover! I braced myself as we positioned ourselves for the immersion. She relaxed a little as I brought her down and across my extended supporting knee. God blessed us both and everything went extremely well, I survived and so did she. There were even a few sighs of relief in the observing audience. God continued blessing as all eight of the new converts were baptized into a new life with Christ. Unfortunately, a family of three that were to be baptized could not be there because of the snow.

I have never been involved in a mission trip that went off as well as this one. The numbers were staggering to me, 129 souls saved in five services, and eight baptisms. If I didn't have supporting witnesses and pictures, I would find it impossible to believe myself. In fact, it *seemed* like a dream to me.

I will declare it again—this was something far beyond my ability and it had to be a "God thing." Only He could have made this happen through me. I am living proof that God can equip the unequipped to be used in His purpose, if they will only make themselves available. To me, this was a gift, and *nothing short of a miracle.*

Increasing Light
by Marcus Beavers

If then the light within you is darkness, how great is that darkness!

December 30, 1966: Nolan Russet jumped out of bed, slapped his alarm clock, and got ready. He locked his apartment door, and drove his car to the Huddlehouse, went in and ordered a late night 'breakfast' of two eggs (sunny side up), sausage, toast and coffee. He ate alone, studied his watch, paid and walked out.

Next he rolled along empty streets downtown. The large shadowy bank building stood tall in the dark sky. He saw bright lights on the sixth and seventh floors. In the security garage of the bank, he slammed his car door and glanced at his watch. *Ah good... forty minutes to spare.*

Outside the garage he strolled up and down the lonely Atlanta streets, looking in store-front windows. They were full of illumination. He admired displays of men's clothing, the textures of the cloth, and dozens of shoes. The street air smelled dusty.

A little before midnight he headed for the bank building. The humming elevator took him to the seventh floor. He got off and entered the large cold room and heard the low roar of huge mainframe computers. Several employees looked up at him as he opened the door, and looked down again at their tasks.

He checked with his supervisor and began his work of computer operations. During the next eight hour shift he worked quickly and efficiently. He sang sad songs, felt depressed, joked with fellow employees, and followed his instructions. He worried about school.

The next morning after work Noland shuffled into the Georgia State classroom. He sat down, and heard the ridiculous squeak of his wooden desk. Some attractive bright-eyed co-eds were chattering nearby, looking rested and sharply dressed. The rest of the class came sauntering in, and the professor last. It was an accounting class. Noland hated this class, its homework, and he could barely stay awake.

After several slow classes he went to the school snack bar, consumed a tasteless sandwich and glanced at the school newspaper. In a few moments he would meander over to the library and attempt to do repairs on his homework. Usually he fell asleep.

Noland's first attempt at college, years ago, had gone up in flames. Now he was backpedaling to complete his education, in the major of business which he found uninteresting.

For relief he sampled books on psychology, and believed books on positive thinking. He bought a yoga book and tried its exercises. He tapped into religious radio stations, and read more religious books. All these things failed him.

Three changes came at the beginning of 1967. First, one bank officer gave him a dayshift job. Second, he signed up for night courses. Third, he moved home because of finances.

Noland brooded over his past and present. *My grades are lousy, I don't like my classes, and I'm miserable in my new job.* So he dropped out of school and was promptly drafted.

"Dad, I'm sorry," he said in dull tones. "I wasn't sure I'd pass the physical. After that, they loaded us on a bus and brought us straight to Benning." He paused and sighed deeply. He then explained about his car parked on an Atlanta side street.

"Yes son, we will get the car," his father said.

"And finally Dad . . . would you please call my boss, Mr. Simms at the bank, and tell him what's happened?"

"Yes, son, I will. You couldn't help being drafted." His father's voice now faltered. "And Noland, please send us your address, when you know it."

Russet forgot all his past troubles as he went through Army basic and advanced training. At Fort Sill, Oklahoma he liked being in the field artillery. His first four months of military life had zipped by. His next challenge was upon him— artillery officer candidate school. He endured its ups and downs, took the harassment and stress, and absorbed vast amounts of military training. He got through it, but had self-doubts along the way. When the school ended, he was among the glad survivors and graduates.

He was shocked to read military orders sending him to Germany, and *not* Vietnam. After a short time of leave at home he was flown overseas. He arrived in Germany and learned that his unit was less than twelve kilometers from the East German border. The Russians were the bad guys next door.

His battalion had a steady round of training, inspections and weapon firing exercises. Battle alerts and potential attacks were a regular part of the Cold War.

In 1968 Noland was sent to an Honest John Rocket Battalion. His commander liked him and gave him tough jobs. After running an artillery survey school, locating benchmarks for his unit's battle firing field positions and managing a group of German target operators for tank gunnery, Russet felt tired.

In the meantime, his mother wrote him long letters about her Christian renewal. She wanted her son to read his Bible and go to chapel. So Noland did. He met a U.S. Army Chaplain that he liked named Roger Parks.

Parks was different. He was enthusiastic but not gushy. He gave short sermons that were interesting. Noland soon found himself talking to him after chapel services.

The young chaplain took the young man under his wing, and invited him to his home for meals with his family. It was a Sunday afternoon. The lunch dishes had been cleaned. The two little girls, Chaplain Parks pride and joy, asked their mother to take them for a walk. Mrs. Parks said yes.

They left the chaplain and his young friend lounging in the living room. Parks was talking excitedly about something he had read recently. He rummaged about noisily in a desk drawer. "Ah, here it is," he said, pulling out a magazine. "An article by Francis Schaeffer called 'The Universe in Two Chairs.' I find it very interesting." He raised an eyebrow as he said this, and gave the magazine to Noland. "Please take a look while I make us some coffee." Parks went into the kitchen.

The aroma of fresh coffee soon wafted into the room. By then young Russet felt sleepy. He read slowly about two chairs, two guys, God and a clock. He shook his head, not getting it. The smiling chaplain returned, carrying a small silver tray with two cups of steaming coffee upon it.

He placed the tray gently on the coffee table, and asked with a smile, "Well? Isn't that a great article?" Noland mumbled it was. "I have this grand idea," Parks continued, eyes sparkling, "Schaeffer, the author, is not very far from us, just down in Switzerland. We could drive there together. I've heard good things about him and his ministry."

Russet gave a befuddled smile, and a nod of his head. "Yes," the chaplain explained, "I sure could use a break." So they talked over possible plans.

But that bright Sunday became a painful memory for the young lieutenant. Chaplain Parks was soon sent to Vietnam.

Within a month Russet received a frightening letter from his friend. The words seemed to scream off the page. The letter was written in a nervous scrawl. He described battle scenes, of men dying and of fierce bombardments by enemy mortar fire.

Noland cursed bitterly as he thought about gooks attacking his friend. He deciphered the last few sentences of the letter.

These bothered him most—"Noland, please find my family, still living in Germany, and comfort them. Don't tell them how bad I'm having it here," the chaplain had written.

It sounded to Noland like a last request. But he did not honor it. Instead he was busy preparing for a pleasurable time of travel. His European discharge was less than 30 days away.

In December 1969 Russet was out of the military. He had saved his money for many months. He carried a book in his bag called *Europe on Five Dollars a Day* to help him find cheap food and lodging. He traveled to many places by train and car.

But during one painful stay in Vienna he found in his bag a scrap of paper. On it was the address of Francis Schaeffer with a note that read "if you need this?" It was in Parks' handwriting.

Noland composed a short letter and mailed it to the home of Francis Schaeffer in Switzerland. He put his old return address of Kitzingen, Germany on the envelope.

Two weeks later in Germany, he returned to the little town of Kitzingen and visited his friends, the Blasals. They gave him a letter from Switzerland.

After reading it, Noland awkwardly explained, as well as he could in German, what the letter was about. His friends were alarmed, thinking he was going to an ashram. But he calmed their fears by saying, "My Army chaplain friend wanted to go there, but couldn't. So now I'm going."

The next day he drove through storms. After getting past the towns of Lausanne, Montreux and Ollon, the rain ceased. He rolled down his window and breathed deeply the fresh Swiss air. Then he turned up a narrow winding mountain road that led to Huemoz and Villars.

It was late afternoon when he arrived in Huemoz. He found the home of Mr. Schaeffer, and showed his letter to a young Englishman named Os who made him feel welcome.

It was in May 1970 when he arrived. The mountain weather was marvelous: crisp cool nights and bright sunny days. The air was exhilarating. The village of Huemoz was very old, from the 1500's, and now contained about 25 Swiss chalets, a town fountain, an old stone church, a small French dairy and bakery. The smell of evergreen trees filtered through the air.

The Schaeffer's work was called L'Abri, French for 'the shelter.' The ministry began in 1955 when Francis and Edith Schaeffer (with their children) opened their home to strangers who came to stay and ask their questions. Now there were at least seven or more chalets associated with L'Abri, and in each one a family or head person assisted with the work.

Noland's host, a tall soft-spoken German named Udo, on his first day, explained the routine and rules of L'Abri. Students were to study half a day, and work the other half. Work included cleaning of chalets, or outdoor chores as assigned. There would be 'breaks' for tea. After meals students or guests were asked to volunteer to wash the dishes.

The study involved listening to taped lectures by Francis Schaeffer (and other L'Abri speakers), and there were hundreds of subjects to choose from. Each student or guest was rotated to different chalets for meals, as assigned. Discussion times were in the chapel once or twice each week. Usually Schaeffer lectured and then opened it up for questions or comments.

Noland sprayed fruit trees that morning and listened to tapes in the afternoon. At meal times he met some of the students visiting there. They came from many countries of Europe and from Britain, Japan, China, Australia, Africa,

United States, New Zealand, South America, Malaysia, and other places.

The preparation of meals was a by a small number of dedicated persons, and the food was good. The meal times lasted longer so students could get to know each other and the families of L'Abri. But after ten days of attending all that was offered at L'Abri, Noland left in discouragement and went to Spain.

In Barcelona and Madrid he watched the day's bullfights and walked the lonely streets at night. He stared into store-front windows at shoes. His thoughts were eventually drawn back to L'Abri and he loaded his car and headed back to Switzerland.

Udo did not welcome him back, but was irritated with him. "You go off and then you come back, expecting us to find a place for you," he said. When Noland asked if he might study longer at L'Abri, Udo just said, "You can order the tapes when you are back in the states and hear them at home."

After a few more sharp questions, Udo finally relented. "Okay," he said, "your old room has one bed available; you may stay there until it's needed. Then you must leave." Noland, from that time on studied with new seriousness.

He studied Schaeffer's teaching on the book of Romans. The Bible became interesting to him. For two months he studied, listened to tapes, did chores, talked with more students; took part in discussions, observed painful struggles in others. Serious drug users were there and found a basis for hope. Noland was glad.

He finally understood the world's abnormality, a world in rebellion and in contempt for the One True God: a world of men (male and female) which 'neither glorified him as God nor gave thanks to him,' as the Bible has said.

Noland, through the years, had accepted ignorance and blindness, not caring what the world was. He saw now that he had been wrong, and was under God's wrath, because of his sin. He had broken God's laws and was guilty before the Living God who is the Creator, Sustainer, and Disposer of all things.

During those eight weeks of study, Noland learned that the Jesus Christ of time, space and history, is God the eternal Son. Now, for Christ's sake, his debt before the holy God was paid in full.

The problem of 'split thinking' was no longer his. The fallacy of believing that only the seen world is real, and the unseen world is not, is a lie he rejected totally. Such a lie was no longer worthy of belief.

That last day on the mountainside, Noland had true light of understanding and knowledge he had never had before; and he thanked the Infinite Personal God for it. He also praised him for his Savior and his time at L'Abri, for the Schaeffer's and Parks (and others) who had helped him along the way.

In subsequent days and years, Noland Russet found out the Christian life is not easy. But it is the only way of peace, and of eternal life.

Still Has a Purpose
by Michael Anderson

I wasn't there the day they took my grandfather to the assisted living home. My boss strongly suggested I be elsewhere and I yielded to his pressure. There were bills to pay.

My visit to the Sunshine Care Center was awkward. I carefully entered the main door, checked in with the receptionist, and nearly tiptoed down the freshly mopped hallway. There was an eerie quietness and smell of disinfectant. *I've been in noisier libraries,* I thought, as I passed patients in wheelchairs with looks of hopelessness oozing from their hollow eyes. My forced smile and greeting nods went unanswered.

I had never seen my Granddad in a gown. I'd never seen him without hair. The cancer treatments had taken their toll, and while he tried to be of good cheer when he saw me, he winced with pain.

Two nurses entered the sterile, darkened room to assist him. Did he feel resentment when the nurses talked to him like he was a baby? I did. Granddad was stronger than Roy Rogers and more courageous than Davy Crockett in his younger days. They didn't know him then. *You shouldn't talk to him that way,* I thought.

Our visiting time together was brief and often interrupted by hallway commotion. We talked about the weather, baseball, and my late grandmother. The conversations were shallow, never really connecting. I think we wanted to embrace, but the oxygen tubes and IVs in his arms barricaded any opportunity for a hug. He asked if we could pray together. I bowed my head straining to hear every breathy word he spoke.

Just then a large nurse stood at the doorway loudly announcing visiting hours were over. She added that it was time for my Granddad's bath, and I had to leave. I picked up my jacket, patted granddad's shoulder and wished him well.

"Y'know son, there's not much he can do with the time he has left," the nurse whispered to me on my way out. I barely made it to the car before my eyes filled with tears. *Why would she say such a thing?*

My youth had absorbed the fingerprints of my handlers. While some left smudges, my Granddad always treated me with care. There was no neglect from him. No judging. No silence. He had encouraged me and had often told me he was praying for me. I needed some of that encouragement now.

Grandparents rarely let go of their grandchildren, but grandchildren let go of them. Grandchildren grow up. They move on. They move away.

My new apartment was three hours away from home and next to the university where I just completed my business degree. Now I was working at the only job I could find – installing gutters on houses. *What was all that college for?*

Since I couldn't visit Granddad often, I tried to call him every other day. I wanted to encourage him, like he had always done to me growing up. Sometimes, when feelings of despair poisoned my heart, I would call him, but often more out of duty than desire. Granddad didn't need my problems. He had his share of troubles and loneliness. I felt selfish when I called him and guilty when I didn't.

Things were not going well at work. The crew I worked with knew I was a Christian and agitated me daily just to see my reaction. I prayed God would rescue me from this continual persecution.

Late one night, just before I was going to bed, the phone rang. *Who'd be calling me at this time?* It was Granddad. *Why was he was calling me?*

At first I thought something terrible was wrong. He quickly put my mind at ease. Then I felt a guilt surge, as I had not called him for nearly a week. He seemed especially alert this time and his memory particularly keen. Usually Granddad is too tired to talk more than five minutes, but this was a 15-minute call, the longest we've had in a long time.

He remembered about my new job. What's more, he told me that he'd been praying that the Lord would help me be a witness for Him on the job. *How could I do that? Witness? These guys were mean.*

Like most construction jobs, it was "a man's world" in every sense of the term. Their attitudes and profanity grated on me. It would take a lot a prayer to ever get me to witness to my coworkers.

The next day, something was different at the job site. I was afforded not one, but two extensive opportunities to witness to a couple of the men I worked with. And they seemed sincerely receptive. The guys responded with questions, and my words flowed with a confidence I had never experienced. They were seeking truth from me. I was actually aware of what Granddad had reminded me - that my job was also a mission field.

I called him that night, and after I told him how the Lord was already answering his prayer, he told me that that same morning, a nurse that he didn't even know had come to him to talk about Heaven. She wanted to make sure she was saved. I asked for her name but he didn't recall. He asked that I pray for her and said, "the Lord knows who she is." He can seldom remember what he ate for dinner, but whenever someone comes to my Granddad to talk about eternal matters, his memory and alertness are so much better.

Before we said our goodbyes, Granddad had more encouraging thoughts for me, including nuggets from Scripture. *His strength is made perfect in our weakness. He will never leave or forsake us.* He reminded me of how easily I had become concerned about other things more than about Christ's kingdom. I thanked him for that and he consoled me.

As I hung up the phone it occurred to me. Granddad indeed was still doing something special with the time he had left. The Lord still has a purpose for him here.

God Is Not a Trivial Pursuit
by Bonnie Greenwood Grant

"So you think that I got my job with Price, Price and Preston because you prayed?" My youngest daughter asked incredulously. Rebecca's beautiful face was marred by the angry frown and the glare from her icy blue eyes. "I got that job through my own effort," she said.

Besides the look of anger, I thought I heard a little desperation in her voice. She was in a scary situation. She was out of work and her unemployment was rapidly running out.

Rebecca was up for partner in a Seattle law firm, when the terrorists brought down the Twin Towers. Her cases generally involved the legal aspects of establishing Initial Public Offerings [IPO's] for Dotcom clients, whose industry was already becoming somewhat shaky by April of 2000. Its collapse accelerated in September 2001 with the fall of the Twin Towers. Rebecca was the first to be let go because her salary was the highest of all the associates-who would soon follow her into the unemployment line.

Rebecca has been angry with God and angry with me for my association with Him for a long time. I'm not sure why. God has been very good to her. He gave her brains, beauty and a free law degree from Georgia State. She had wanted to get her degree from the University of Washington in Seattle where she had received her Bachelor's degree. To offset the *disgrace* of attending a red neck school, she applied to Georgetown in Wash DC for her Master's degree. Georgetown wasn't as prestigious as NYU but she loved it. She was caught up in the excitement of the city and the school.

In the process she discovered that her law education at Georgia State had been quite good. She went to Georgetown because she wanted to be hired by a Seattle firm. Georgetown was a resume maker.

When it came interview time she called us to ask for prayer. I believe that at the time, there was an element of faith, rather than an attitude of *covering all bases* or *leaving no stone unturned.*

The Seattle firm had set aside only thirty minutes to interview at Georgetown, whereas they spent several days at NYU. My daughter moaned about the unjustness of the situation.

My husband and I prayed for her to get the position. I prayed for her to get the job even if it were *not* in His will so that she would know that it was God who got her the job. I wanted Him to orchestrate things in such a way that there could be no doubt in her mind that God is Lord of the universe and jobs.

A girl from NYU got the job. Rebecca was crushed. "So much for prayer." She mumbled angrily.

Shortly thereafter, the firm called back and told her she was hired. The other girl had turned the job down. She got her Seattle law firm. It immediately became evident that it is much better to go with God's plan than our own. She hated the job from the beginning and moved to another law firm in the same building two floors below. She was working seventy hours a week and was next in line for partnership. Her salary was in the six figures but her world came crashing down on 9-11.

My daughter repeated her question. "Do you think I got my job because you prayed?"

I looked up from my reflections. She was waiting for an answer. I knew if I told her the truth that she'd start berating me. I nodded. *Yes, I do believe that God gave you the job because of prayer.*

Her voice rose, " But I'm the one who got the job and I'm the one who saved so I'd have the money to get me through the hard times."

Who gave you the talents? Who gave you the opportunity to earn lots of money so that you could save? Who gave you the inclination?

"Well, is that what you're saying? I wouldn't be here if you hadn't prayed?" I felt like a Christian staring into the jaws of a salivating lion. I nodded.

"You don't know how embarrassed I am by you. When I tell my friends that you talk to God, they roll their eyes." She said.

I felt like saying, *Well, that's their problem* but I didn't. My child was searching and I wanted her to understand. I want her to have a personal relationship with her creator.

"Rebecca, when you came home from work did you talk to Kaze?" Kaze is my son Jeremy's cat. My son and his Lilac point Siamese cat stayed with Rebecca for a year. Every one talked to Kaze. Rebecca adored Kaze. If Rebecca and Jeremy had to be gone, their friends would come over and cat sit. Kaze was an integral part of my children's lives.

"You don't think God tries to communicate with us? Do you think He cares less about us than you care about Kaze?" I asked.

"Mom, people feel uncomfortable around religious people. My friend, Carolyn has a friend that "found God". All that friend does now is talk about God and how her life has been changed. She makes Carolyn very uncomfortable because Carolyn doesn't know how to act around her."

That evening we gathered at *George and the Dragon*, a neighborhood tavern for trivia. My husband is a trivia buff who loves the thrill of competition. Rebecca and several of her friends joined us for an evening of fierce rivalry. I was a little nervous about sharing the evening with Rebecca's friends, especially when I was *an embarrassment* to my youngest daughter.

Her friends didn't treat me like a freak. Quite the reverse- I was treated with great respect. When a question came up concerning health or the Bible, my area of expertise, one friend leaned forward, pointed toward me and said, "You're on." The others looked at me in expectation.

The health question was, "Niacin is a B vitamin. Which B vitamin is it?"

"B3"

My husband was the only one who challenged my answer. The others had no idea but they were sure I was right. They looked toward the DJ and nodded expectantly.

"Niacin is vitamin B3." Cheers went up from our table.

The next question was "Which animal is mentioned most in the Bible?" The group, once again looked at me expectantly.

Sheep was the first thing that came to my mind. But then, pictures started flooding through my brain, Sampson with the jawbone of an ass in his hand, Joseph and Mary riding on a donkey to Bethlehem. *Sheep or donkey, oh, Lord please help me guess right.* I thought about Nahum and the talking donkey and Jesus riding the donkey into Jerusalem.

"Donkey"

"The animal most mentioned in the Bible is the donkey or ass," came the DJ's response. The table went wild and they patted me on the back.

"Way to go Mom." Rebecca hugged me. My daughter was proud of me.

When I started writing this story, I pulled out the concordance and counted the number of times asses and sheep were mentioned. I realized again that God is sovereign. Sheep are mentioned 40 times more in the Bible than donkeys. If I had guessed the "right" answer I would have been wrong.

I'm sure some people would say, "Who cares? "or "So what?"

The outcome was important to me and because we have a God who loves us, it was important to Him.

When God Has a Plan
by Judy Parrott

Scrawny George weakly shuffled into the prayer room, clutched the back of a seat and dragged his emaciated body onto the soft cushion, panting. Big swollen wart-like blobs all over his face revealed that death was trying to steal his body. The desperate homosexual visitor, at only thirty-one, was dying of AIDS.

Gloria introduced herself to this backslidden Christian at Landmark church, with amazing results. She was the first to confirm to George that God would heal him. The healing team at Landmark met daily to teach George the basic principles of Christianity, especially about healing and deliverance. George studied diligently and sought God's will for his life.

One Sunday morning he found it impossible to drag himself out of bed, when God spoke, *If you will go to church today, I will heal you.* George was just waiting to die when God spoke the words, *Your faith will heal you.* His will and God's power got him there.

George received his miracle that day as well as a powerful deliverance from a spirit of homosexuality. He said it felt like the spirit rose from his stomach and out the top of his head. He bounded joyfully home from church that day, free of bondage for the first time in many years. From then on George began to improve. His face cleared up, he gained weight, and went happily to work every day. Soon his viral count dropped from 102,820 to 613. Months later, the doctor's comment was, "Either you are extremely lucky from this medication, or this was an act of God." His doctor knew no one that had ever survived AIDS. He had put George on a medication called AZT, but the longer he was on it, the sicker he got, so he had stopped taking it on his own some time before.

Meanwhile, his faith was growing stronger every day. George's unique testimony was written up in *Charisma* magazine. He accepted an invitation to speak in Ohio to a group with AIDS, and was an effective and encouraging speaker.

Later he was interviewed on Atlanta Alive TV. A Christian woman in England read *Charisma* and it stirred up hope for her son, who was also a homosexual living with a man. She got George's address through the magazine editor, and invited him to England to share his wonderful healing story with her community and hopefully with her son.

George had never been out of the country before, but he was excitedly looking forward to sharing what God had done for him. He was inspired to ask Gloria, his adopted spiritual mom, to accompany him, but she couldn't afford it on such short notice. The plane was to leave on October 12, 1999, two years after George's search for a cure began.

Gloria began praying about going along, and one day a woman, out of the blue, handed her a hundred dollars and simply told her it was for England. *Maybe I am in this plan of God's, after all,* she thought. She eagerly began looking for her passport, scouring every possible area, sorting through every paper in the house. She wondered if it might have been stolen, and had no choice but to presume it was God's sign she was not to go, even with the hundred dollars in hand.

Gloria worked as a volunteer for a man that claimed to be an atheist who had a bus tour business. The morning of October 12 at 10:30, the day George was to leave, signs suddenly started appearing. Her boss unexpectedly gave her three hundred dollars for her trip. He said it was for helping him with his tours, but he never paid her anything before. He had a daughter who was dying from AIDS. Quite possibly, her story about George was flickering a tiny flame of hope. Gloria decided God was again opening a door at the last moment. It must have taken Him a while to touch the boss's heart. She called George to tell him the news.

"Is there a place I can stay if I come?"

George said, "I will be staying in a home where they have only one extra bed. Let me see what I can do." He called back shortly with an offer for Gloria to stay in the home of another English family.

She called the travel agent, who shocked her with; "The cheapest ticket available is eight hundred dollars."

A few minutes later, however, Gloria's daughter Lynn called back with exciting news. "I found you a ticket for only four hundred."

What next? Gloria again tore the house apart for the passport, confused over what obviously appeared to be God's plan. *I wish He would just talk to me,* she thought. She purposely put the concern aside, trying to force herself to trust Him to reveal it, and kept her lunch date with her friend Jeannie. It was now noon on the day of departure.

As they visited, she mentioned some item in her safe, and a bell went off. The passport was in the safe! Now her heart was racing. Catching the plane was still possible, but barely. She suddenly remembered her medicines were at the pharmacy, and she had to pick up the passport, but if it was God's plan, she would make it. If not, she surely didn't want to be in England without Him. The plane was leaving at seven, so she had to be there by five, the rule for international flights.

Jeannie went to fill prescriptions. Gloria showered, dressed and packed several outfits she had considered, quickly stuffing them into her worn suitcase. At the last possible moment, the girls returned as the pastor drove up the driveway with George. He delivered them to the airport through the bumper-to-bumper Friday traffic of downtown Atlanta, arriving miraculously on time!

George was thankful the flight to Manchester airport was uneventful for his first overseas flight. For the next ten days, Gloria introduced him in several churches and a college, sharing how God's plan led her to join him in England. She had lots of great stories, and brought the house down- even in the staunch Church of England. The presence of God was manifested in mighty ways neither of them had ever experienced, and had only seen on TV.

Audiences began sharing scores of healing testimonies, which always results in a crescendo of faith. Many fell on the floor from the power of God's Spirit without even being touched by human hands. A woman with crippling arthritis could painlessly walk around after prayer. George recalled, "I remember the anointing (outpouring of God's power) being so strong I was perspiring. It was truly an awesome experience. Gloria and I prayed for a young man who had visions of Satan, and was babbling and speaking incoherently."

The man whose mind was severely damaged by drug abuse was suddenly able to speak clearly after prayer. He started running around hugging those around him, laughing and thanking God. His mother was beside herself with excitement and said she would never forget them. "I've got my son back!"

"The last church we spoke in," said George, "had one hundred fifty members, the pastor told us, but he didn't expect many to attend because of college break. When I looked behind me, the church was packed. I really couldn't believe it."

The family where Gloria was staying asked if she and George would visit a friend in a nursing home. Paralyzed from a stroke, the middle-aged man seemed very agitated when they came into the room. His frantic eyes darted around the room, perhaps in fear or agitation over his helpless state. Gloria took his hand and began telling him about Jesus and His love. After visiting a bit, she asked him to squeeze her hand if he would like to accept Jesus into his life. The nurse had said he could move one hand just a little. He jerked his hand from hers the best he could with his infirmity.

Gloria then talked about the possibility he had family members in heaven, and if he would like to see them again. She took his hand again. "Would you like Jesus to forgive your sins and give you eternal life to be with your family some day?"

This time he pressed lightly but perceptibly on her hand with all his strength, gluing his eyes firmly onto hers, so she took it as a yes. She explained he could repeat her words in his mind and God would respond to him. When she finished praying, "Dear Jesus, forgive my sins, and come to be the Lord of my life," she asked if Jesus had come into his heart. He clutched her hand as tightly as he was able, staring peacefully into her eyes, obviously no longer upset. Then his eyes closed gently and remained shut.

The guests looked intently at him several minutes, wondering if the man might possibly have died; he was so still. Then his wife appeared outside the window and knocked, as was her habit. In the past, he had always lifted up a couple of weak fingers from the blanket, but this time he opened his eyes wide, and lifted his whole hand for her, which paralysis kept him from doing before. The change was dramatic for him, and very obvious to the nurse standing by that something special had just transpired.

The great commission God sent them on bonded Gloria and George to the people of England. Many believed on the Lord Jesus and saw His delivering power and love. George was on fire, looking forward to God's next mission, but never got a chance to discover it. He was killed in a car accident a year after his return from England. Gloria decided that must have been God's next assignment for George. He graduated to glory.

Hazel The Bear
by Nancy Weber

God has amazing ways to restore our hearts. Many years ago, my heart was filled with doubt after growing up in an alcoholic home. God showed His love for this new Christian in a most unusual way, and taught me how to trust Him.

It all started early one spring morning, the phone rang waking my husband and I from a peaceful sleep. "Hazel the bear has escaped. Had we heard it on the news?" That call got our attention.

We listened to the radio as we were dressing. The bear had escaped at the Masterpiece Gardens tourist attraction in Lake Wales, Florida and the tourists were hiding in the gift shop.

We hopped on our motorcycles and headed out for Lake Wales, as we did every day. Today, however, our adrenalin was surging. Many thoughts raced through my head as I rode behind my husband those 35 miles.

Ken and I had married three months prior to this crisis, and I believed we would have a nice, quiet, stable, low-key, mature and relaxing life together even though we now had eight teenagers in our blended family. It is amazing how denial can blind someone to reality. I was ignoring the problems in our lives and in those of our children.

I didn't understand how much our relationship was keyed to my programming to be a rescuer and a crisis dependant person. I was an adrenalin junkie.

Ken's attraction, Masterpiece Gardens, which housed the famous beautiful mosaic of the Last Supper, was in Chapter XI bankruptcy. He also was losing his house because of the financial situation. His children had problems because they grew up, like mine did, in a dysfunctional family.

Ken had been divorced for 10 years when I met him, and he had custody of his three children. They started working at the tourist attraction when they were little—doing bird shows, (the first trained bird and duck show in the state of Florida), train tours, getting the tourists safely onto the sky ride, and operating the snack bar.

At one time the Great Masterpiece was one of the big three attractions in Florida. In those days, before Disney, it was Cypress Gardens, Masterpiece Gardens, and Silver Springs. Then the interstate system came in and finally the big blow, Disney World. The gas shortage in the late 70's dealt the crushing blow and Ken couldn't stay above water.

While riding toward the bear escape crisis that day, I was hoping that this publicity would be just what was needed to get people to notice that this pretty theme park was still on the map. Ken had tried desperately to borrow money to pay his bills but no one would give him a loan, so he filed for bankruptcy. One morning, about 2 months prior to this, we thought we had found the answer to the financial crisis. We both had awakened with the same vision. Use the attraction as a Christian camp and retirement center.

We believed it was from God, so we had set out to see the vision fulfilled. The gift shop in which the tourists were now hiding had been converted to a Christian bookstore. We were hoping to take all the money we would make that summer and start renovating the rest of the theme park.

What was Hazel's escaping going to do to our plans? I wondered. We were about to find out a lot more about how God's kingdom operates very shortly.

As we rode up the beautiful winding road toward the entrance I could see a helicopter hovering over the jungle. They were trying to track the bear. In the parking lot were the news reporters, television crews, sheriff's department personnel, and the Florida game and Fish Commission. I had never seen so many important people in one place before in my life. And, of course, the tourists were still in the gift shop.

We were told that Hazel was last seen ambling along the edge of the lawn near the sky-ride base before disappearing into the jungle. I walked around the park hoping to spot her. It was weird, a tourist attraction with no people in it. I could hear the helicopter, the monkeys, and the birds, but no people.

The Tampa Tribune featured the escape as if it were a hostage crisis similar to the Iranian hostage situation that was occurring during that same time. Hazel the bear, in cartoon form, was front page news, and they counted each day of her freedom.

The Game and Fish Commission were very unhappy with Ken and the job they had ahead of catching the bear. They tried to trap her with raccoon snares, which she escaped. Some neighbors, near a garbage dump, saw Hazel. We were really praying because I didn't want to see anyone hurt. Ken had confided to me that another park gave to him because of Hazel's bad disposition

For an adrenalin junkie, this was a perfect fix.

Ken gave me a short course on how to handle the media. I did live and taped reports for the various radio stations that called. There seemed to be a lot of interest in this event. I hadn't realized what a public figure Ken was until this. Even my son, who was stationed in the army in Germany, read about this in the army newspaper.

On the second day of the bear's freedom, some wild boar hunters who said they had dogs that could hunt Hazel down contacted us. Meanwhile, the Game and Fish Commission had bought in their dogs. By the third day, I was so concerned that I called our church's prayer line and asked people to pray that the bear could be captured.

That day I walked along the jungle before dawn with Ken, carrying a loaded gun for the first time in my life, planning to shoot the bear if she jumped out of the jungle. I could hear the dogs barking in the distance.

The officers from the Game and Fish Commission were in their truck with their dogs and a gun loaded with tranquilizer darts. Suddenly, as if in answer to our prayers, Hazel walked out of the woods on her hind legs right up to the truck and stood next to them. The officer fired his gun and the tranquilizer dart merely dribbled out of the end of the muzzle. He reloaded, but by then she had again taken off for the woods with the dogs on her trail.

By now, I was manning the phones and giving progress reports. Suddenly the officer ran into my office and shouted, "Go get the vet. We got Hazel, but we need to know if we can shoot her again with more drugs. Will she wake up if we don't, or will more tranquilizers kill her?"

The decision was made—no more drugs.

Soon the procession approached the newly repaired cage. The fellows who had volunteered to help were carrying her, each gripping one of Hazel's legs while Ken held her head. She began waking up 100 yards from her cage, so Ken reassured her in a soft voice to let her know that she would be okay.

After she was back in her cage we thought the crisis had ended. As we happily returned to our motorcycles, the Game and Fish Commissioner apprehended Ken in front of the Channel 13 news camera. Ken was cited on two counts of letting a bear escape and endangering the public. Ken was arrested in front of the TV camera! We were shocked.

The charges each carried a $500.00 fine or 90 days in jail. We couldn't face the fine or the possibility of him going to jail.

What was happening to the vision God had given us? Actually, God was teaching me to depend on Him. I would soon begin to understand another aspect of God's love.

The thought of a trial scared me more than the loose bear had. Ken had pleaded not guilty to the charges because the first judge had recommended he do so. He said the Game and Fish Commission would drop the charges because the charges were ridiculous and he couldn't even find them in the books.

That wasn't to be, though. Why? I found out that, years earlier, Ken had hundreds of squirrel monkeys loose on the grounds. Then Florida passed a law that the monkeys had to be on an island or caged—separated from the tourists. Ken couldn't catch them to do it. The officer, the same one who arrested Ken for Hazel's escape, said that if Ken didn't catch and cage the monkeys, he would have to shoot them. So Ken had told the officer to let him know when he was coming to shoot the monkeys, because he would have the press, radio and television stations there so the whole world could watch him kill the monkeys. It never came to pass.

Now, apparently, was the opportunity for revenge. Hazel had escaped and Ken was not at fault. She had chewed the chain link fence while she was in heat. There are wild bears in the surrounding woods. Now the officer from the Game and Fish Commission could get even. A trial date was set.

Without God's intervention, an adrenalin addict will create a crisis when life gets too peaceful. But the Lord showed me, through what was to happen, that I could experience peace instead of anxiety, even though the circumstances (the trial) were remaining the same.

In desperation, before I knew what God was trying to do, I went to a prayer meeting. Joyce, our pastor's wife, led it. That morning three different people opened their Bibles to Psalm 37 and one of them helped me to understand it. In the scriptures, God was saying the evildoer would snare himself with his own words. It was prophesied that morning that Ken would not have to utter a word in his own defense, but his accuser would talk too much and his own words would pierce his own heart. With this reassurance, newfound peace, and with a new attitude of absolute trust in the Scriptures, I raced home on my motorcycle to tell Ken the good news.

We opened the Bible and read Psalm 37 together. With confidence, I told Ken we didn't have to worry about the trial, and that he would be acquitted without having to defend himself.

The trial was still two months away and Ken wanted the protection of an attorney. Four of them said they didn't want to tackle a "Ken Curtis vs. the State of Florida" case. Finally, we found one, a criminal lawyer who was my former history teacher in nursing school.

As the date approached, I felt no apprehension. That amazed me because the thought of courtrooms would normally have intimidated me, even though I had never been in one.

On the day of the trial every defendant that was tried before Ken was booked, handcuffed, and taken to jail. They were rapists and armed robbers. What was Ken doing in a room full of felons?

The State of Florida had sent all of their Game and Fish Commission experts and they filled the front row. I sat in the fifth row next to Ken with a big grin on my face as I confidently waited our turn. Then Ken's attorneys approached me and said I had to leave the courtroom because the smile on my face made them think that we had a trick up our sleeve!

During the next hours in the hallway, I could see Ken's accuser through a little window in the door. He spent almost two hours on the stand using all that time to hurl charges at Ken.

But, just like God said it would happen, after hearing the accusations, the Judge called Ken to the bench, and without Ken having to utter a word in his defense, the Judge acquitted him.

Praise the Lord!

When the newspapers approached me in the hallway after the trial, I only quoted the first lines of Psalm 37. They printed their story starting with the Bible quote.

I realized that my personality had been contaminated by the mechanisms I had adopted to cope with my chaotic upbringing in a dysfunctional family. Yet, all along, God's help was mine for the asking. Now I have the reassurance that the Word of God is my shield and sword in combating fear and in giving me His peace that passes all understanding.

The Night I Cried Unto the Lord
by Donald S. Conkey

It now seems like a long time ago, and it was, nearly 50 years ago. It was a night I have never forgotten, a night I will never forget. Even today, if I close my eyes and think back, I am able to return to that one bedroom apartment on a university campus and relive that evening as if it were only yesterday; it was the night I cried unto the Lord, and He opened His door and let me in. He then supped with me and I with Him. It was the night I would come to personally know Jesus as my Lord, my Savior, and my Friend, an experience that changed my life forever.

My faith in Jesus Christ, however, had its beginnings many years before on a small Michigan farm. I was born to goodly parents. They loved me and wanted the best for me by teaching and preparing me for life according to their family customs. These customs included the expectation their oldest son would carry on the family tradition of farming the 320-acre family farm purchased and cleared by my grandfather in 1890.

Because my parents lived on an isolated farm, far from the city, and grew most of their own food, I was a child sheltered from the deep Depression that gripped the nation in the thirties. I knew nothing of the soup lines that fed the lonely and unemployed in America's cities.

Pleasant memories of living this sheltered life still linger in my mind. I remember working in the fields on hot summer days—planting and harvesting crops, milking cows by hand, separating the milk and feeding the skim milk to the calves and pigs and churning the cream into butter, and feeding the chickens and gathering eggs. I also remember caring for the sheep docking the lamb's tails, shearing them each spring, then spinning and weaving the wool into warm winter clothes. Even the family church brings back tender memories, for it was there I earned my first Bible by naming the Old Testament books,

It was a good life. Everyone, including myself, expected I would follow in the footsteps of my fathers, living and dying on that family farm. But the Lord had other plans for me, and many singular and accumulative events would take place before I finally broke this protective family culture and developed the faith and courage to knock on Christ's door to find Him, and develop a personal relationship with Him. Leaving the land I loved so dearly was hard, even when orchestrated by the Lord.

God's orchestration of my life began in 1947 when mother, an active and powerful woman in Michigan politics, through her connections, arranged for me to get the last seat on a bus filled with active Junior Farm Bureau farm youth who were going to study agriculture for two weeks in several southern states. At nineteen, I was the youngest member of this tour. My new companions, nearly forty would-be future farmers, were considered to be the best of Michigan's up and coming agricultural generation.

These young farmers taught me a powerful lesson, a lesson I could never have learned anywhere else. I learned that one does not have to be an ordained minister to pray. For me this was a revelation, something I have never forgotten. I learned that all people can pray to God, even young farmers, and that He listens to and hears individual prayers – of all ages. All I had to do was to acknowledge Him, stand at His door and knock, and ask to be let in, there to talk with Him as one person to another. But it was nearly ten years later before I would completely understand just how powerful an influence this trip was to be in helping me find my Savior.

It was a lesson learned by listening to and observing those young people offer up their nightly prayers after completing our daily travels. They knew God, I didn't. They were able to converse with Him in prayer, I couldn't. This was a powerful testimony to a nineteen year-old who came from a home where personal and family prayers were never practiced. This was something I wanted for myself.

I have forgotten most of what I learned during that trip to the southern states, but I have never forgotten that a listening and caring God answers sincere prayers.

The Korean War began in 1950. It was the war that broke up our family-farming tradition. The army sent me to Camp Gordon, in Augusta, Georgia for my military training. Georgia was one of the southern states I traveled through in 1947. Here I met and fell in love with a girl from Florida, the girl I would marry following my military discharge in 1954.

Even though I had learned to love the south while in the army I still had a strong desire to return to farming, which I did after being discharged.

My crops were looking good in the early summer of 1955. Then a powerful rainstorm cut my ties with the farm forever. That storm, which began at noon on July 15, 1955, a date I have remembered for fifty years, came in off Saginaw Bay and in thirty minutes it had totally flooded my fields. By 12:30 p.m. I was frantically draining water off the farm. But there was too much water and by 1:00 p.m. my crops had been destroyed. I had been financially ruined.

In retrospect, fifty years later, it is easy to see the hand of the Lord in that storm, but at the time I could not see His hand. What I saw was ruined crops and financial ruin. The storm that financially destroyed me in one hour provided four neighbors with a gentle much needed rain. I cried that night knowing I could never recover.

That was the night I made the decision to leave farming, enroll at the university and get a degree in something, anything where I could make a better living, and I did. I enrolled at

Michigan State University in Agricultural Economics, determined to go nonstop through to graduation. I borrowed $300 to get through my first semester, until my GI Bill of $160 a month payment came through. Finances were tight.

Once again the Lord stepped in, this time to support me. At the end of the spring quarter I applied for and obtained the best student job available in Lansing, Michigan – mopping floors at an Lansing Power and Light electric power plant in downtown Lansing. It was the choicest job in town because it paid $1.75 an hour, while jobs on campus paid only 75 cents an hour, and I could choose my own hours, up to 40 hours a week. I had been one of 156 applicants for this coveted job. I felt blessed when the job was offered to me, with one condition, I had to work full time, no school during that first summer. I agreed and went to work mopping floors. No power plant ever had cleaner floors.

This good news, however, was tempered with new challenges. My wife, carrying our second child, became seriously ill. Money was still scarce, but arrangements were made for her to visit her family in Florida. However, before she left we discussed me changing majors from a three-year course in agriculture, to an eight-year course in medicine.

Alone for two weeks I pondered this potential change of majors, so much that it began to consume much of my thinking. It became obsessive. My age was still a factor. At thirty there were reservations about changing majors, especially to one requiring so many additional years of schooling.

It was then I remembered my 1947 trip and the lessons I had learned about receiving answers to personal prayers. These thoughts triggered a desire in me to pray for an answer regarding my future profession. I still didn't know how to pray, and I needed divine help that could come only from God.

Then memories of my family's rural church surfaced. They were a reminder that I needed to go to church where I could commune with God. I located one near the campus and attended it the following Sunday. It was a much larger church than my parents' church and it had a huge balcony. I entered and went up to the balcony. As I looked out over the congregation I felt like I had just returned home. It was a good warm feeling.

I heard the minister's voice but I wasn't listening. I was thinking about what my Farm Bureau friends had taught me in 1947, about receiving answers to personal prayers. One thought kept going through my mind . . . *if those young people could get answers to their prayers, I can get an answer to my question – do I stay in agriculture or do I enroll in medical school?*

It was during this quiet period in the balcony that I made a life-changing decision. I would ask God in prayer for the answer to my question. I don't remember what the minister's message was that day, but I do remember the Lord's spirit touched my spirit, and told me to come to Him in prayer.

I felt spiritually ignorant, not knowing how to pray. But by now I was determined to pray even if had to learn how to pray. I focused on my prayer, and a plan began to emerge. I would ponder my question all week and on Friday, after the sun went down, I would kneel by my bed and pray until my prayer was answered. It was that simple. My faith was strong. I had no doubt the Lord would answer my question...*would I continue to study agriculture or would I enroll in medical school?*

As the sun set and the apartment darkened I knelt beside my bed. I had no idea a major life changing-event was about to take place. I began by reciting the Lord's prayer, the only prayer I knew. Then I found the courage to ask the Lord what I should do, *stay in agriculture or go into medicine?* Silence followed. I prayed more earnestly. More silence. I began to plead with the

Lord. More silence. I continued to pray, and to plead. I rolled on the bed, pleading and crying unto the Lord. Still silence.

I was determined. My inner spirit told me to continue praying. I did. All night long I prayed, I pleaded, I begged for an answer, and then, shortly before daylight, it happened! A light came into my mind. It was so bright that to this day I can still see it. There were no loud trumpets, only a bright peaceful light. I was not prepared for what I saw, or would feel. It surprised me. The closest description of this powerful life-changing event is Paul's testimony to Agrippa in Acts 26:13 where he said "At midday, O king, I saw in the way a light from heaven, above the brightness of the sun, shining round about me and them which journeyed with me." Never had I seen such brilliance. It flooded into my soul.

Then I slept. Hours later I woke up. My mind was clear. My prayer had been answered, and His answer was clear and unmistakable. I would stay in agriculture.

I completed my studies, left the university with a Bachelor of Science in Agricultural Economics and accepted a job in Florida as a lobbyist for the dairy industry.

Equally important to receiving an answer to my question was the inner peace that filled my soul. I now knew God lived and answered prayers. He had answered my prayer. My faith had been vindicated, and I knew without any doubt there was a God in Heaven who hears prayers from insignificant individuals like me, and who answers sincere prayers offered in simple faith.

I had stood at His door and knocked. He had opened his door and invited me in to sup with Him. I have never forgotten that night in July of 1956. It changed my professional life as well as my spiritual life. Now knowing He was real, I began to study the Bible more intently, reading it from cover to cover several times in the next four years. I became a student of the

Apostle Paul and learned much from his writings and life, yet there were questions that still bothered me. These were important questions, at least to me, that my ministers told me were still mysteries, mysteries that would be revealed at some future date.

I didn't give up. My search for those answers continued. I kept hoping I could again see and feel that life-changing power that came from that light seen in my university apartment in 1956. But it wasn't to be. Yet, like Paul, I would soon be led to my own Ananias who would remove the darkness from my eyes of understanding, baptize me, as was Paul, and bestow the Holy Ghost upon me.

I had progressed precept upon precept and line upon line from the faith of a child earning his first Bible, to learning for myself that God does indeed live, and that He was concerned enough about me to answer my prayer. I would never be the same again.

After graduation we moved to Florida and our family continued to grow. We purchased our first home, attended church as a family and found life was good.

Still, I was missing something I couldn't put my finger on until one evening in September of 1960 when there was a knock at our front door. I opened it and found two young men standing there. "Yes," I said, "what can I do for you?" "We are here to share a message with you," they said. By now, with four years of tutoring and Bible study from well-trained ministers, I felt I could discuss the scriptures with anyone, so I invited them in. I asked them the questions that had been bothering me and surprisingly they provided me answers I could understand.

As I listened I said to myself, *why couldn't I see that before.* My life was about to change again. But that is another story, a story for another time.

The Anointing
by R.T. Byrum

I left the Pasadena television studio at five o'clock for the thirty-minute trip home on my motorcycle, a Honda 175. It was my third anniversary as a producer and director of a worldwide evangelistic program, and my family and I were going to celebrate.

My wife, Karen, had made me promise to be on time to sit down for supper with her and my three sons. Afterwards, we planned to take the boys to the mall to let them pick out a few favorite toys. I dared not be late.

Less than four blocks from home, a young Latino couple in an approaching car turned in front of me at the intersection. Time seem to shift into low gear. I heard the drawn out screeching of my tires, saw the bending of my front wheel as my bike slammed into the passenger door, and felt a massive blow that took my breath and my consciousness away. Witnesses reported that I had been catapulted ten feet above the car landing nearly fifty feet away on the other side of the four-way junction.

Gradually the darkness began to clear away like clouds after a storm, and I realized that I was lying on my stomach staring through the cracked visor of my helmet at a hand bent backward across a wrist, and a ragged bone protruding from a damaged arm. It was my hand, my wrist, my arm. Strange. There was no pain, no fear—only wonder at the sight. I heard the voice of an onlooker, "The lady in the car is hurt really bad, and so is her baby, but the guy on the motorcycle, they say, is dead."

I'm dead? Is this what the end is like? Then, a stabbing pain like I'd never known before. An EMT was placing a splint to immobilize my arm. Again, blackness drifted over me like a feathered comforter. Later, my doctor will tell me about my fractured ankle, the broken toes, and the sixty stitches he used to close up various other wounds.

At home, my wife heard the sirens, and, with that intuition that no man understands, urged the boys to go ahead and eat after the prayer, because, "Daddy's going to be late." Dutifully, they bowed their heads, and she pleaded with God to be merciful to me, her husband, knowing somehow that I was the reason police and ambulance vehicles were rushing to an accident scene.

I awoke in the emergency ward as a doctor was taking my vitals. My wrist, on the X-ray film, appeared as a bag of misshapen marbles. My ankle was fractured in four places. The blackness returned.

Eight hours after the grinding crash I woke in recovery, my foot and ankle encased in a heavy cast, and my arm suspended in a lightweight contrivance made of fiberglass. My wife was holding my uninjured right hand, and the doctor was speaking to me. "Your wrist has been badly shattered and hasn't been set. I have a hard question to ask you."

I blinked back the tears that had begun forming. *What question? How do you feel about being a cripple? Is it all right if we amputate?* Numbly, I nodded as I heard Karen's breath catch in her throat. *Please, Lord, don't let me be a burden to my family. I need my hands in my work, my ministry.* Then, my heart slowed and peace replaced fear.

The doctor continued. "Because of the damage to the multiple bones in your wrist, I need to fuse them, and you will lose most of your range of motion. That means you must decide the position of your wrist and hand that you can best live with. Do you need some time to consider?"

I remembered the many programs I had directed about God's healing power, and the importance of having faith in His mercy. "Can't you just set them without fusing them?" I asked. "When I'm playing my violin or guitar, my wrist needs to bend one way, but when I'm typing or composing on the piano, I hold my hands differently. How can I give up either?"

The doctor smiled patiently. "Sometimes we don't have a choice in the matter."

"Well, I do," I said with faith in God's power to repair his wounded creature. "If it doesn't work out, you'll have to rebreak my wrist and fuse it. But I promise it won't come to that."

The next day, my wrist newly set in a plaster cast, my foot cast suspended by pulley and cable, and with bandages around my chest, leg and stomach to protect the stitches, I was permitted to have other visitors.

My pastor closed the curtains around my bed and sat in the chair next to my plaster of Paris arm. "Do you want me to anoint you and pray for God's mercy and healing?"

"More than anything," I said.

He unscrewed the cap on the small vial of oil, tipped several drops onto his fingertip and stroked across my forehead. His firm, warm hands were laid on my head at each temple, and he bowed his head in silence for a few moments before speaking.

"Lord, God of all creation. You made man of the dust of the earth, a miracle that no science could ever duplicate. Mr. Byrum is one of your precious children, and he is broken through no fault of his own. You know his heart, and you know his needs. He has placed his faith in you to restore him to wholeness that he may do your work. Your firstborn son, Jesus Christ, promised that whatsoever we ask in His name, if it is

Your will, it shall be done. Today, we claim that promise in the Holy Name of Jesus. Amen."

The third day after the accident, I was becoming restless. I explained to my doctor, "I have two television programs that I've recorded, which have to be edited and ready for distribution within ten days. I must get back to the studio to finish them this week." My doctor was not sympathetic.

"Son," he said in his sternest voice, "frankly, you are lucky to be alive. It'll be at least four weeks before we can even think about therapy, and even that depends on how well your bones have healed in your wrist and ankle."

"Doctor, I will walk out of here this week and I will finish my work on time. That's a guarantee."

His exiting smile was one of sadness with, perhaps, a mixture of exasperation reserved for similar hardheaded patients.

The fifth day, the staff rolled in the portable machine and X-rayed my wrist through the cast. Twenty minutes later, they rolled it in again and took a second series. "What's the matter?" I asked. "Did I forget to smile?" I was the only one who found that amusing, and my heart began to thump loudly enough that they must have heard it. *Something was wrong!*

Within the hour, the doctor removed the wrist cast, for a physical therapist who took my wrist in his hand. Gently he palpitated the area of the break. "That painful?"

Amazed, I said, "No."

"That?" he asked.

"Not at all."

Slowly he began to manipulate my wrist, moving it in ever larger arcs, swings, and rotations. All the time he watched my face for pain—and found none.

"Where did you say you worked?"

I told him the name of the evangelistic program that I directed.

"I watch that program all the time," he said with smile of understanding. Turning to the doctor who had treated me, he said, "You might want to give him a set of crutches and let him return to work. There's nothing more that you or I can do for him. I'll prescribe a week or two of therapy, but as far as I'm concerned, this man has been placed under the care of a higher power, and he will be—no, he *has* been healed."

The next morning, I was driven home by my wife, my sons in the back seat taking turns hugging my neck. When the garage door opened, I saw my mangled motorcycle lying where the wrecker had dropped it. At the sight of twisted bike, the extent of my miraculous healing became strikingly apparent.

As soon as we were back in the house, my wife, my sons and I bowed our heads and thanked God, not only for the blessing of my healing, but also for the witness of the miracle that took place before the doctors and nurses in the hospital.

Two days later, I sat with my postproduction editor and began the process of finishing both programs on time. I believe it was my best work—a grateful offering to the Master Physician.

Drama King
by Robert W. Ellis

It was July 1994 in Georgia. July is not kind to people who live in this southern state. It is hot and humid and people seek out air-conditioning after a short time out of doors. July in Georgia does have redeeming value, however. Every July our church would host a great Fourth of July service honoring our armed forces and our country.

During this particular July, I was a member of a praise team from our choir (more about that later). We had chosen a song entitled *We Believe* for the service. The song touched on the Christian values on which the country was founded. Even though it was a great song, the creative side of me kicked in and I wrote a short narrative to introduce the song. I thought that it needed a little something to give the song even more punch. Even though it was somewhat pretentious of me, I gave it to our team leader who read it, approved it and let me do it.

After the service, our choir director accosted me with a questioning look on his face. *Uh-oh, I am in trouble,* I thought. "Did you write that lead-in?" he asked. "Well...yes, I did."

"That's good. I'm glad to know that we have a writer in the choir." He said as he hurried off to his office.

*A writer...*that was only two spoken lines...*I'm not really a writer,* I thought. Yet that short encounter would prove to set the stage for much of my Christian service in years to come—but I am getting ahead of myself

Shortly after the director's comments, a lady approached me who had been working on our upcoming Christmas pageant. "Scott tells me that you are a writer and we need some help"

There is that term again, I thought. "How so?" I asked.

"Well, we have purchased a program for our upcoming Christmas pageant. We love the music but don't like the dialogue and our director would like for you to take a shot at rewriting it"

I don't really remember anything else she said after she handed me a large paperback volume with all the music and the dialogue. I *do* remember her walking away and looking back to see if she could detect the reason for my silence.

There are some aspects of my earlier life that were to influence me from that point on. Since I was about eight, I might have been referred to as a Drama King. That didn't meant that I was overly dramatic a bad thing happened, but anytime there was a drama to be a part of, I would leap to the forefront.

I had played Scrooge, Uncle Remus, a Ringmaster and other assorted parts in elementary school plays. I had played the disciple John in a church play and discovered that chicks loved men with beards. In my Senior high school play, *A Connecticut Yankee in King Arthur's Court,* I played the lead.

Later in college I would write and direct several skits performed by my fraternity. Somewhat bawdy things they were too. After college I entered the real world of responsibilities and had to forsake this love of drama and all that was associated with it.

So here I was, given the opportunity to be a part of that world again, only this time it was connected to something that could make an everlasting difference in peoples lives. *Could I do it?* I wondered. I didn't know, but I could not wait to give it a try even 30 years after my last endeavor in the drama arena.

I read the dialogue and looked at the music. Images and scenes entered my mind that I felt should accompany the music and I began to write down what the people in the scenes were saying. Most of the time that I was writing, I was also weeping. It was as though another person was sitting beside me telling me what to write, and I knew when a scene or line of dialogue would be touching to an audience...because it first touched me.

The most amazing thing about the opportunity was how it came about in the first place. First, I should not have been in that praise team. I loved music but my voice was not very good. The talented guy who had led the praise team had picked me over several people with much better voices than mine. My tryout had been a fluke. I had performed above and beyond my ability while others must have suffered laryngitis.

Thinking back, if I had never been on the praise team, or had not written the short narrative, or if the choir director had not asked me if I had authored it, nothing would have happened.

Over the next few weeks I rewrote much of the dialogue and showed it to the choir director. He liked what I had done and encouraged me to keep it up.

With the help of several other people, I put the dialogue in the proper format and copies were run off to begin casting the speaking parts. In addition, Drama King time returned. I read for the main narrator and was given the part.

Christmas was an even more special time that year. The program was well received and well attended that year. Many people accepted the Lord after each presentation. The choir director was thrilled and told me that I had a permanent (although unpaid) position on his staff.

Planning for the next pageant began a few months later. We were going to pick the music and write our own scripts from scratch from then on. That activity continued for eight more years, and the process of producing the pageants year after year never got old or arduous.

Other opportunities arose. Our drama troupe visited other states to present dramas in different churches. The group traveled to mission conferences in Brazil and Thailand to encourage the missionaries there. We wrote and performed sketches for the adults and hosted drama camps for the kids.

We were given the task to produce what we called a Heaven and Hell drama for presentation around Halloween. The real title of the play was *The Journey* and we performed it many times throughout several years and even gave permission to a large church in Tennessee to present it to their congregation.

A number times during these years I would get, what I would call *God pat's,* that is when someone would tell me how something in one of the productions had touched them deeply.

In 2002, my family and I were moved to join another church in the area—one that had a wonderful program for our grandchildren, a good music program for my wife and a drama ministry for me. Soon after we had joined, however, the pastor was transferred to another, bigger church.

While he left behind some Godly people at this church, much of the vitality seemed to leave the church with the pastor. It seemed like a cruel joke was being played. I had served in a drama program for many years and wished to continue in that area but the drama presentations came to a halt except for a few special occasions. Nevertheless, it seemed that God had other ideas in mind.

A staff member knew of my previous drama endeavors and gave my phone number to a lady in our new church. "I need some help," said the voice on the other end of the phone.

"Sure," I responded, "what sort of help?"

"Well, Jill tells me that you are a writer" *That term again.* "A missionary in Nicaragua has asked a team of us here at the church to produce a drama to be used for non-literate people there. I have only recently started on the project and the other members of the team have moved on."

She explained that the concept was to portray scenes and characters in the Bible in such a way that the drama could help people understand how much God loved them and how he gave his Son as a sacrifice for them.

"How far along have you gotten?" I asked.

"A short way into Genesis," came the response.

Over the next few months we divided up various sections of the Bible to be depicted and set out to finish the drama. It was a series of long presentations that would be given over six nights. She took the Old Testament and I worked on the New Testament, getting in a lot of Bible study during those writing times.

After finishing the first draft, the missionary himself arrived to meet with us, and we sat around my kitchen table for nearly three days editing the script. The working title was *The Drama of Redemption*. We also wrote a production manual for the people working with him in Nicaragua. Soon after he returned home, we received a note from him indicating that translation into Spanish had already begun.

Later, when I mentioned the drama to a missions director in another church, he became very excited and asked if he could get permission to send the script to other missionaries. Our missionary in Nicaragua gave his assent, and the drama is now used by missions in India and South Africa.

Only God knows how extensively the work will be given, but I believe that it will be used to lead lost people to Christ. We are now members of a third church in as many years. It may be that God only led us to the second church to help in the writing of the *Drama of Redemption*—we will know someday.

Oh, one more thing, our newest church has an incredible drama ministry.

Jailed In Dakar
by Robert Graves

But Peter continued knocking: and when they had opened the door, and saw him, they were astonished. ... he declared unto them how the Lord had brought him out of the prison. Acts 12:16

It isn't often that a missionary finds himself a prisoner of the people he was sent by God to help, but on the night of January 18, 1973, Missionary Robert Creel was being held in the city jail of Dakar, Senegal, charged with the hit-and-run death of a Senegalese child.

When Creel, Director of Senegal Bible Institute, left for the school the morning of January 18th, the day seemed no different from any other. Early that morning, as usual, he cranked his bus and began his trip to the school, stopping now and then to pick up students. He had, however, overlooked one small, but significant detail as he stepped outside that Thursday morning—the Renault van that he had parked in his yard the night before was missing.

During the early morning hours someone had forced his way into the van, cranked it, and quietly driven it out of the yard and down the street. Unfortunately, the driver lost control of the speeding van, veered off the street, passed under a tree and crashed into one of the many barrack-like Senegalese houses. The thief leaped out of the van and fled into the shadows. In the house lay a child, lifeless, and two others, injured. The police traced the van to the mission's field chairman, who normally drove the van, but he had loaned it to Creel to haul building materials. The chairman was summoned to the police station, where, after questioning, he was asked to find Creel.

"Brother Creel gets home from school by one o'clock," he explained. "His wife will tell him what has happened and he'll waste no time getting here. He should be here no later than one-thirty." However, at 1:30, Creel wasn't there; ten minutes passed, then twenty minutes. Two o'clock came and went—Creel still hadn't shown up. Unknown to the chairman, Creel had stayed at the school longer than usual that day to settle a disciplinary matter. When he arrived home, his and the chairman's wife ran out of the house and met him at the truck.

"Where's the van?" they asked, thinking perhaps he had given someone permission to use it.

"I don't know," he answered. "Maybe Ernie has it. He has the other key."

"No," they said. Then they told him what had happened. He left immediately for the police station, arriving there forty minutes later than expected.

On arrival, Creel was immediately taken into custody and questioned by the Chief of Police and several inspectors, but he was unable to satisfy his questioners. "You mean to tell us that you walked by the spot where you parked the van, and you didn't miss it? A large van worth several thousand dollars, and you didn't miss it?"

They listened skeptically as he explained that it was unusual for the van to be at his house in the first place, so it was quite understandable that he might walk out of his house and not notice its absence. The officers stared in disbelief.

Unknown to Creel at the time, the officers' disbelief may have been a reaction to an incident that occurred earlier that month where a white man was involved in a hit-and-run accident that left an African child dead. The police had found the man as he was changing his automobile license plate.

When the questioning stopped, the Chief gave orders to place Creel under arrest, and he was locked up in a cell. Friday morning, the police followed-up another lead they had that might further implicate Creel. When the thief fled the scene, he left behind in the van three items: a bag of rice, a piece of cloth, and a pair of sandals. *All we need to do*, the police reasoned, *is find the man whose feet these shoes fit.* This method of investigation disturbed Creel since African sandals (similar to flip-flops) could fit just about anyone. but the police determined that the sandals did not belong to Creel or anyone at the Institute.

Later that day, as the police were taking Creel to his home to pick up his key to the van, they decided to stop at the scene of the accident, thinking that someone would recognize Creel and offer information. Hundreds of angry Senegalese of the Wolof tribe were encountered milling around the scene when they drove up. "Stay in the car," one of the officers warned Creel.

While the missionary remained in the car, several natives questioned him. "Is this your van?"

"What happened?" Creel replied, hoping to deflect their questions. "Was anyone hurt?" His own questions served their purpose. Thinking that he knew nothing about the accident, the natives continued milling around the wrecked van.

After picking up Creel's key, they returned to the police station. By this time Creel and everyone at the mission and the school began to realize the seriousness of the situation. Under French law, the law of Senegal, the accused must be able to prove his innocence, compared to English common law, which requires the state to prove the guilt of the accused.

Can I prove my innocence? Creel asked himself. *Who are my witnesses? My wife and my children were asleep.* Such thoughts filled his mind...and rightly so, for without a witness to attest to his innocence, prospects for justice were scant. Fortunately, Creel didn't have to depend on some abstract principle such as "Justice Will Prevail" or "Truth Will Win Out." Such proverbs were meaningless to him as he sat in jail. But there was something he *could* depend on—God's Word.

Creel's fellow missionaries and the students of the Bible Institute had united in prayer Thursday night. The scripture verse on everyone's mind was Acts 12:5: "Peter therefore was kept in prison: but prayer was made without ceasing of the church unto God for him." Other Christians, stateside, were also praying for Creel. During a revival at the First Assembly of God in Savannah, Georgia, a lady felt prompted by the Spirit to stand and request prayer for the Creels. After the service another lady sought out the one who had requested prayer and told her that she, too, had felt the Spirit's prompting to pray for the Creels and she was about to request prayer when the first lady stood.

Creel learned about this Spirit-prompted prayer through a letter he received ten days after his arrest. Using the date and time mentioned in the letter, he determined that at the time the prayer request was made, he was in jail in Senegal. This precise timing on the Lord's part reminded Creel that God had His eye on him all along the way. Friday evening, twenty-seven hours after the accident, the police had a signed affidavit of a man who testified that he had seen an African man running from the scene of the accident. This and the lack of evidence was enough to secure Creel's release. The thief was never found, but the charges against Creel were dropped. Prayer went up, heaven opened—and the case was closed.

The Homecoming
by Jennifer Evans

Her face was thin and colorless like the sheet that covered her emaciated body. In spite of that, she focused a brave smile in my direction as I opened the massive door and stepped into the sterile room that still smelled of disinfectant.

"How are you, Hon?" she said, struggling against the IV tubing that was pumping poison into her leukemia-ridden body. She finally rearranged her frail frame to her satisfaction so she could face me.

"I'm fine, " I smiled back, wanting to weep. She never complained. No matter how much misery she was in, she always asked first about me. My mind wandered from 1981 back to better times in the early 60's and remembered my grandmother as I knew her then...

When I was a child, we lived away from my parents' families. It was a special treat those Christmases and summer vacations when we got to travel to Georgia to visit for holidays. Grandmommy's was a house that fairies could live in: a two story white frame built in the old days even before TV. The fireplace had been replaced with a huge gas stove, which was almost as novel for a kid from the suburbs who grew up with central heat.

Closets and pantries offered hours of entertainment to my sister and me, since we were avid explorers and never missed a chance to pretend some adventure we hadn't had opportunity to live out yet. The yard, too, was a fascination: pecan trees spilled nuts all over the place for any detective diligent enough to search for them under layers of fallen foliage. Grandmommy knew the names of every plant and tree for miles around. Nothing made me happier during those precious vacation days than to follow her through the flower beds with a sprinkling can in hand, helping her water the plants. There was a glider on the end of the porch, too, where we spent many hours squeaking the swinging couch and investing love in each other's lives.

Granddaddy was a big man, strong and quiet. He had been a butcher, a grocery storeowner, and an insurance salesman. But by the time I knew him Alzheimer's disease had already taken its toll, along with his voice and much of his memory. Grandmommy fed, bathed, and treated him as gently as she would a child. Her love for him touched me with a sense of reverence. Humility and quiet tenderness made her a saint in my eyes.

In 1969 during my eighth grade year, my father retired from the Air Force and we moved back to Georgia where both my parents had grown up. They had arranged to buy Mom's old home place. Cindy and I would actually be living in the house that had, until then, been reserved for vacations and Christmas wishes. Grandmommy was more than happy to share the big house with us since she had already been a widow for several years. Later, she bought a lot nearby and had a smaller home built for herself.

We arrived before Christmas, and the giant gas stove with its chimney flue was just where it had always been. Her house smelled familiar and scrumptious: like pine needles, biscuits, and apple pie all at once. The welcome hugs and kisses felt good when we walked in the door. But this time would be different. This was now to be home, not just vacation.

Grandmommy readjusted her furniture and moved things into her bedroom to make room for our lives. She patiently accommodated two teenagers, never complaining about the wooden floor upstairs shaking to the loud rhythms of our stereo as we practiced for the days when we dreamed of dancing with real partners. She listened with enthusiasm when I practiced the piano, encouraging me, and never wavering in her devoted attention. Along with our mother who, mercifully, had a hearing deficiency, Grandmommy endured trumpet and French horn duets of much less than professional quality.

I am sure she wondered throughout my high school years about my spirituality. When Grandmommy was a child, her minister-father was very determined to keep the Sabbath day holy. In carrying out that conviction, he restricted his offspring from any kind of childish or chore-related activity on the first day of the week. It was reserved for rest, for visiting with family, for meditation, and for religious pursuits. My Sundays, on the other hand, were days of recreating. After I became a Christian, I spent every opportunity in church, and was a devoted believer. I usually spent all my free time, including Sunday afternoons, sewing. Grandmommy worked at a clothing factory. My recreation was her life's work. When Granddaddy had gotten sick and was beyond the ability to support them, she had been hired there in order to provide their basic needs. It was tiring and tedious, but she never grumbled. Neither did she criticize my stubborn insistence on doing what to her was labor on Sunday, since for me it was relaxing. She pulled out many a zipper or pocket that I couldn't get to fit and sometimes even restitched them too.

In time, her two-bedroom brick house was completed just across the street from our big one and Grandmommy moved. Often I found her at her sewing machine, an early electric model in a mahogany cabinet. Everything she wore - coats, suits, dresses - found its way first between her scissors and then under the needle of that little black Singer. I almost considered that machine part of her, like a companion or a friend. In the winter of my tenth grade year, she made a double-breasted wool coat for me. I was so stylish in that midi-length frock, brown like my eyes and hair. I was sure I looked like a million dollars, thanks to Grandmommy's hard work.

The metal glider swing had been shifted to her cement front porch facing the busy street. It was a new house and different scenery but the same squeaky rocker where we could sit together and talk for hours. Hardly a day passed without my visiting her, just to chat. She told me stories of her childhood: about working in the cotton fields, cooking on a wood stove, playing hide and seek in the hollow tree trunk ash hopper from which lye - an ingredient for bath soap - was made, how to can pickles and make fresh applesauce... I pictured a quaint cottage, obedient children, and wholesome fun.

We watched the traffic pass and heard the glider squeak while Grandmommy listened to me. I told her I'd like to be a writer. We discussed crafts and sewing projects. She cared about my struggles at school, my challenges with homework, my first boyfriend. She waited until I asked before giving me any advice. My heart could be bared before her and I never felt condemned. She wouldn't wear slacks; she just wasn't raised that way. But she always welcomed me: jeans, T-shirt, bare feet and all. One day, an airplane caught our attention.

"When they send the first woman astronaut to the moon," she said, "I'd like to go."

I laughed. "Why?"

"Just because I'd love to fly, and I'd like to see what everything looks like from up there."

Sometimes we played a traveling game. Grandmommy had a big atlas, and we delighted in finding out of the way places in various countries and talking about what life must be like there. For our private game, we would pretend we could take a trip there and make our plans for a fabulous vacation...

The heavy hospital door creaked and a small shaft of light poured in through the crack.

"Mrs. White? I need to take your vital signs." Grandmommy's smile was weak but welcoming as the nurse entered. I realized that my cheeks were damp and reached for a tissue. It didn't seem real, watching her lie there, entangled in tubing. I remember thinking, *I can't give her up yet, Lord. It isn't time; she's barely retired, and there is still so much love and richness in her life to share.*

My memory sees the picture; I am standing at her bedside. She is resting now, not seeing the tears that tissues refuse to hold flowing in silent rivulets over my cheeks. I study the motionless figure. Even in the midst of pain, there is a peace in her face. I can't blame God; I am sure He has been anticipating her arrival. I am being selfish, wanting my Grandmother's presence as an assurance of stability and security. I drop my head. *No human can give me that,* I realize with sudden conviction, *not even this confidant and friend who is ready to go home.*

I read the Bible to Grandmommy as she rests. She requests her favorite chapters, and we talk more before she sleeps. I find a cot in the corner and settle, staring at shadows on the ceiling. Heaven is closer in this dark hospital room tonight because someone I love is soon to move there. Smiling with the thought, I realize I will again have the chance to live with Grandmommy in a big house. The cot becomes a cloud and I fade into my dreams.....

My Lord and My God
by Bonnie Grant

I was not raised Christian. I knew there was a God and that He loved me, but Jesus was just a picture I saw on the walls of my Catholic friends' homes. My mother did teach me the Lord's prayer but Jesus' name was never mentioned.

While attending the University of Washington in Seattle, I met an obnoxious young Catholic man in Chemistry class. He eventually became less obnoxious and after two and a half years, we became engaged. The Catholic Church insisted that I go to inquiry classes, in order to prevent religion from being a divisive agent in our marriage. I read the materials and had long intellectual discussions with the priest. I learned more about this Jesus fellow and thought I could accept or at least tolerate the beliefs so I decided to become Catholic.

On the day of my baptism I called Father Ambrose and told him that I wasn't coming. I could hear his sigh. He finally said gently, "Bonnie, Jesus loves you very much." How could I refuse after that comment?

At Sacred Heart Cathedral I climbed the great stairs up to the church with some trepidation. The huge church was empty except for the echo of footsteps, the priest and my future mother in law. She was the only Catholic available and she had been excited at the chance to be my sponsor. She had reminded me of the little kid who jumped up and down yelling,

"Me, me, please pick me."

I knelt in the confessional. It was dark, smelling of leather and old wood. I understood that I was confessing to God and that the priest was the representative of the community. "Confess your sins to one another," but his questions were

257

annoying because he pried into my life like a dentist after a diseased molar.

"Let me hear all the bad things you've ever done. Is this all? What about this?" I found out later that he wasn't really prying, but if a sin isn't recognized as a sin it won't be confessed and therefore not forgiven. At the time, I found the priest to be extremely offensive. I thought *I'm done.* I stood up and started to push open the door to the confessional. I had always thought of myself as 'good', but in that moment a spirit so profoundly pure and loving surrounded me. I fell back on my knees. I felt so unworthy of this love and started crying uncontrollably. I rose to my feet, turned, flung myself through the doorway and raced across the marble floor and out the big double doors. Standing at the top of the stairs with tears running down my face, I didn't even notice the beauty of the autumn leaves in the city spread out below me. Fr. Ambrose came rushing out looking for me.

"Are you all right?" I thought about it for a minute then nodded. *How often do you get to have the Creator of the universe hold you in His* loving arms? I knew God was real and that He loved me. Okay, I had known that before, but now I knew that for some mysterious reason, *He wanted me in the Catholic Church. What was next?*

For over ten years, I searched for Jesus. I went to church, I read my Bible, I taught Children's Sunday School, and talked to people but still no Jesus. About that time we moved from Seattle to a new parish.

One afternoon, I knelt in my prayer corner and said,

"Jesus, if you are real, I want you to be the Lord of my life. I give you my life and all that I have." "All that I have" included my children, husband and parents, and that was scary because I was afraid He might take my family from me. The following night we went to an Ultreya, the monthly meeting of all the people who had made a Cursillo weekend. The word Cursillo means a short course in Christianity. It is also called a *Walk to Emmaus* or *Tres Dias*, depending on denomination of the church. The month before my husband had made a Cursillo weekend. The men went first, then the ladies. He came home on an emotional high that I found irritating.

"Oh, you have to go. You'll love it," He kept repeating as he did his little Snoopy dance around the room, arms raised, feet skipping. My reaction, of course, was to dig my heels into the gold shag carpet, and mentally shout, *No I won't go.*

In the end, I agreed to go to the Ultreya, but I was not going on some silly weekend. The meeting was held in the church hall and the people were loving and caring. They shared scripture and one person shared his or her 'close moment to Christ.' At the end of the meeting, I was asked if I were excited about going on the upcoming weekend. This was Monday and the weekend started Thursday.

"I'm not going," I said.

They all looked concerned. "Why not?" I couldn't very well tell them that I was being a stubborn jackass, so I said that I wasn't registered.

Diana Koob, a young, blond, perfectly dressed, soft spoken woman with a zany sense of humor, just happened to have a registration form at her house. She'd never had one before and she would never have one again, but just to irritate me, she had one that Monday night. We all drove over to Diana and Richard's house and converged around a large coffee table. Diana filled the form out for me and said if I made the Curissillo weekend, and she had a feeling I would, she would sponsor me.

The weekend was already filled and there were three ladies on the waiting list ahead of me. I signed the registration form, thinking I was pretty safe. *Yippee, no weekend for me,* I thought.

Wednesday night, Diana called me.

"You made it. I'll pick you up at 5:00 PM tomorrow."

What? I was not happy. The weekend was held in an old school. It was right downtown by the Space Needle. There were no showers and no hot water. The "dorms" were two large rooms with small air mattresses laid on the floor. We brought our things into the room and put our sheet, pillow and blanket on our mattress. They prayed, and then prayed the rosary. If I had trouble with Jesus, I really couldn't relate to His mother. If I had driven myself, I would have slipped out and gone home. They started the talks.

"By now you all know that you were meant to be on this weekend. Many of you have almost miraculous stories of how God moved mountains to get you here. Jesus asked you to come on this weekend so that you could get to know Him better." That got my attention.

I fell asleep that night with everyone gathered around a woman with a zither, singing songs about Jesus. When I woke up, I ached all over because the air had leaked out of my mattress and I was lying on the hard wood floor.

From that point, the weekend got better. There were eight people at my table. We drew posters, talked and shared and became bosom buddies. I grew to love all of them. This was becoming a really *great* weekend. The spirit of God swooped, twirled, glided, soared, danced, sang and embraced everyone in the whole building.

Saturday afternoon we had a quiet time. I wandered into an empty room and knelt in a quiet corner.

"I just need some time alone with you, Lord."

He was there. Jesus Christ was standing in front of me with love and light streaming from his face and body. I knelt transfixed, staring at Him. I don't know how long I knelt in His presence. I kept thinking, *Oh, my God, you are real. You are real. You are real.* As He faded away, I thought *but wait, it doesn't make any sense. Why did you come? Why did you go through all that?* A line from a song that I had yet to hear until the next day, went through my head.

"To share his love is why I came." People later have asked me, "What did He look like?" I can't honestly say. He had long hair and a beard and He was dressed in white. When I see a picture someone else has drawn of Jesus, I will say, "That's not my Jesus," or "Hi, Jesus," depending on their accuracy.

I haven't seen Him since, but when I stay in prayer and in the scriptures, I do hear His voice- His small quiet voice-or he'll speak through scripture or other people and that's as it should be. Each of us encounters Jesus differently, my Jesus experience was up close, personal and dramatic, but more blessed are those "who have not seen and believed."

Jesus is mentioned frequently in our house. Maybe too frequently if our children are to be believed, but when you know a truth especially one as great as Jesus is real, it's very hard not to shout it.

Too Responsible
by Cynthia L. Simmons

Charlene was in bed and almost asleep, but she sprang up when she heard the phone.

Oh, no! Is it Mom? She jumped out of bed and covered her gown with a housecoat. Straightening her short hair, she scurried through the house until she reached her parent's bedroom. Her father had answered the phone, and he wore a serious look on his face.

"It was the hospital," he whispered, hanging up the phone. "Your mother just died." Charlene took a gulp of air, and then let out a long sigh. For a moment, time stopped, and she felt alone in her grief. Her mother had entered the hospital for removal of a cancerous tumor on the brain. However, she had not awakened from the anesthesia. For five days she had been in the intensive care unit in a coma.

It's all up to me now, she thought to herself. *I am responsible.* Her whole body felt numb, and a weight descended on her heart. *There is so much to do.*

Although Charlene was sixteen, she looked much younger. She had a petite figure and a sweet pixie-like face framed by dark brown hair. However, she had been married six months and had just given birth to a baby boy. She and her husband, Jerry, lived with her parents. Using all her will power, she pumped herself full of energy so she could manage the household. Over the next few weeks Charlene pushed aside grief to fill every moment of her day with work.

Mom is not here to manage things. I'll do it. I don't know how, but I will. Charlene's mother grew up in a family that did not display affection. As a result, she and her mother had never been close. She recalled cleaning alongside her mother, yet feeling very far away. Her dream was to be a housewife like her charming, fashionable mother. Even though she had learned a lot, she still felt inadequate.

Every morning Charlene got up early to cook breakfast for her father, little brother and husband and then didn't leave the kitchen until it was spotless. On weekdays she packed a lunch for her brother and made sure he got ready for school.

She jumped each time her son whimpered. *Oh, that's the baby. How am I supposed to know what he needs?* She picked up her son, Michael, and made cooing noises. *Oh, well, it can't hurt to feed him again.* She discovered that a baby demanded a lot of time. Although his naps never lasted long, she took advantage of them to accomplish as much housework as possible. No dirty dish stayed in the sink, no clutter gathered in the living room and no dust accumulated on the floors.

Washing clothes for the family took hours. She was amazed at how much the baby could mess up in one day. With boundless energy she attacked the mounds of dirty clothes, diapers and blankets. Nothing sat overnight. She washed, ironed, folded and put away everything the same day.

Jerry had had surgery two weeks before her mother's cancer surgery. Charlene made sure he had his antibiotics and pain medication. Attentive to his calls, she tried to anticipate his needs and changed his dressings each day. *I hope I'm doing this right,* she worried. *Will he stay with me if I mess up?*

From age four, she had lived with her parents in Florida, but both sides of the family lived in New England. While her father traveled to Massachusetts for the funeral, Charlene stayed in Florida caring for her younger brother, husband and baby. Jerry had recovered a month later and returned to his tool and die shop job, but then, Charlene had an unpleasant surprise.

Charlene was shopping for groceries when she realized the side of her face was numb. *What in the world is wrong? I can't feel anything on the right side.* When she poked her face with her fingers, it brought stabbing pain. *I wish I could see in the mirror. But my right leg feels funny too. I can't wait to get home.* She rushed to finish her shopping, ignoring her sweaty, trembling hands. A tingling sensation also radiated down the right side of her body. As soon as she arrived home she ran inside and screamed, "Jerry! Dad!"

"Yes?" her father asked. "Did you call me?" His voice was calm and soothing. He, rather than her mother, had always been the parent who was warm and giving. He was so perfect she thought of him as a god even though he was an agnostic.

"My face!" she said. "I can't feel anything on this side." Her finger pointed to the skin on the right side to demonstrate. "In fact, I can't feel anything on this side of my body."

"Your mom had a good neurologist," her father said with his unruffled calm. "I'll take you to see him." His eyes radiated reassurance. "Jerry can go on to work and I'll help with the baby." Her father set up an appointment while Charlene did her chores, ignoring the thumping of her heart.

"Well, she has neuralgia," the doctor said. "It is often triggered by stress." He ran tests to verify the diagnosis and gave her some medication. In a few weeks normal sensation returned.

The family grew accustomed to Charlene's frantic pace. After her mother's death, she left her childhood behind. All laughter and humor disappeared from her life. Criticizing herself all the time, she pushed herself to be perfect and buried sorrow deep inside her heart.

Am I running out of diapers? she thought when changing Michael one evening. *I can't let this happen. I must stay in charge of things.* She attacked herself for every mistake, hoping she could earn God's approval.

In June, when Michael was four months old, Charlene entered night school so she could finish her high school diploma. She had dropped out to have Michael, but was determined to graduate on time. She squeezed her studies between chores while the baby slept.

Within a few months the initial crisis ended and Charlene began to long for a home of her own. *Oh,* she sighed one day when faced with a pile of dishes. *I wish I could wash my own family's dishes. But we probably can't afford it.* In the other room, Michael began to cry. *Okay, I'm coming.* Her body was exhausted, but she paid no attention. *There is so much to do.*

In the spring, Charlene's wish became a reality. Obtaining a better job as a manager for a builder, Jerry earned more income and they could afford to move into their own home. Charlene worked hard at packing and at purchasing necessary items, such as kitchen utensils. She didn't complain about the added work involved, although she was overtaxing her strength.

The following May she gave birth to her second child, Christine. Jerry was confident that Charlene could handle the challenge of the new baby. She had managed well in the past; however, she was starting to feel overwhelmed. Whenever Jerry asked her to help him find something she began to feel resentful.

You are an adult, Charlene fumed. *I shouldn't have to baby-sit you.* Right away, she felt guilty for her inner thoughts. All her life she had attended church and religious classes. Her parents never attended church but, her father had dropped her off each week. *I shouldn't get mad. It's wrong.*

She loved being a mother, but felt drained by the constant demands of her family. *Everyone seems to need me. In fact, all the time. I'm tired.* She compared her thoughts to her father's gentle, patient personality. *Just get on with it, Charlene. Complaining isn't right. Babies are dependant.* She sighed. *I feel so alone. I wish we lived in Boston instead of Florida.* Her mind went back to her family there. *I don't fit in anywhere. But I shouldn't feel discontented. God would be angry. How can I ever earn His approval?*

Fortunately, a kind lady lived in the duplex next to her who helped out with the children at times. However, Charlene and Jerry didn't live in the duplex long and soon moved to another apartment. Charlene worked hard to get the apartment in order for her family. The strain of moving with small children added to her stress.

Why can't I keep the house clean? I need to work harder. She noticed a stray dish beside the couch. *Did Jerry leave that? Why can't he clean up after himself? I should've noticed it before. One of the children might break it and hurt themselves.*

One afternoon Jerry announced that he intended to go golfing with friends. Knowing he would brush aside her objections, Charlene held her tongue as she watched him prepare to leave. Instead, she allowed her anger to simmer and fester inside. *He just leaves whenever he wants to. I don't want him to go,* she fumed. The phone rang and she answered it. When the conversation ended, she banged the receiver down as she hung up the phone.

"Wow, that felt good," she said. Her pint-sized body had released some of her bottled up anger. She picked up the receiver and slammed it down again. "That felt *really* good," she said. Once more she picked up the receiver and whacked it down, with some of her weight behind it. Later, she felt sheepish when she realized she had disconnected the phone from the wall.

Her husband started his own construction business in 1975. *I hope he can make enough. What will we do if we run out of money?* Charlene learned the construction business has its ups and downs. She got frantic every time business slowed down. *I hope something comes along soon. These kids need food and clothes.*

In 1979 Jerry started working with a developer to build an entire subdivision. Sometimes he started houses without a buyer, but at times a client asked him to build a house with extra features.

"Charlene, you need to meet Dave and Lana," Jerry commented often. "You'd like them." While building his subdivision he met Dave, who asked for a house with a number of changes to the blueprints. Jerry found him considerate, and he decided to bring the couple home to meet his wife.

"Charlene," Jerry said smiling, "This is Dave and Lana and their little girl. Do you remember I told you about them?"

"Nice to meet you," Charlene said smiling. "Jerry keeps talking about you both." Inside she was admiring Lana. Lana was elegant, slim and had long blonde hair. *Ugh! I feel so ugly.* She glanced down at her stomach. *I look like a whale.* She was pregnant and a few days from delivering Jeannine, her third child. *She's so attractive. I never looked that good.*

In the short conversation that followed, Charlene found she liked Lana. She and Jerry began to plan outings with them, and a warm friendship grew between the two couples. Three years passed and in January of 1982, Dave started a church.

"Charlene," Jerry said, "We need to visit Dave's church. I'm curious about what they're doing. We might like it."

"No!" Charlene snapped. "They're my friends. I don't want religion to mess everything up." Dave had tried to share the gospel with them, but Charlene never allowed him to finish. "Well, how good do you have to be to please God?" She scowled. "And what about the person in Africa who never hears of the Bible? Will he go to hell?" Charlene asked before Dave had a chance to answer the first question.

"Charlene, we are going to Dave's church next Sunday," Jerry informed her one weekend in March. She argued with him, but he insisted. The church met in Dave's living room where the family had set up chairs. Dave opened his Bible and preached from Romans. Sitting with the congregation, she could not interrupt him, so she heard the gospel and struggled to understand it.

What did he say? Charlene lowered her eyebrows as she tried to catch every word. *He said–we could be sure about going to heaven? I have tried to be perfect so I could get there,* Charlene thought. *I have never felt sure, but I want to know I'll go to heaven.* Her heart began to beat faster and she felt her face grow warm. *I have tried and tried to be perfect, but I can't. I just get angry.* She felt tears sting her eyes as she tried to read the passage from a Bible that Lana had handed her when she arrived. "...in order that the promise may be certain to all the descendants..." *There is the word 'certain.' I want to be certain. That's what I've always wanted.* As she listened, she at last understood Christ's death purchased forgiveness. She'd found what she wanted. That day she put her faith in Him. *I don't have to worry now. God has forgiven me.*

Immediately, Charlene felt a sense of community with the members of Dave's church. Living a long way from her uncles, aunts and cousins, she had felt restless most of the time. However, she knew that she belonged with these other believers. Lana was kind and nurturing, while teaching Charlene how to be feminine. She taught her how to apply make-up and how to pick out flattering clothes. She also taught Charlene a lot about housekeeping and raising kids. In addition, as she heard more of Dave's Bible teaching, her heart became peaceful instead of tense and insecure.

In 1993 Charlene and Jerry moved their family to the Atlanta area. They bought a house in Marietta and settled into a church. Jerry wanted to build their own house and in November of 1999 he started constructing a house in Waleska, about thirty miles north of Marietta. However, when he completed their home in Waleska, the Marietta residence had not sold. Jeannine, their youngest daughter, was engaged to be married. Jerry and Charlene made the difficult decision to leave their daughter in their Marietta house until she married, while they moved into their new home.

"I feel as if I'm abandoning Jeannine," Charlene kept saying to her friends. "But of course, I know she is okay." One day as she took a friend from church through her new house, she revealed how she felt.

"Charlene, do you feel like your mother abandoned you when she died?" Her friend asked.

"Yes, I guess I do," Charlene said. She took a deep breath and placed her hand on her chest. "I never thought about that." She shook her head and frowned. "I was too busy to mourn when mother died." Seeking God for comfort, she spent the next few weeks recalling the sorrow she had pushed aside at sixteen. Convinced that she needed to honor her mother, Charlene visited her grave. That visit helped her to complete the grieving process and to accept God's healing.

After her decision to accept Christ, Charlene felt confident she will go to heaven. In addition, God helped her to face the sorrows of her past and accept her imperfections, control her anger, and to worry less. Her favorite verse is found in Psalms "...the Lord will accomplish what concerns me...."

Dinky's Dilemma
by Judy Becker

In the seventies when the "back to the land" craze was the rage, we bought some land in the country. We had spent a year researching about various animals and how to raise them. Having read about the efficiency of Dexter cattle on small acreages I mistakenly identified a dwarf Angus cow as such and rescued it from a slaughterhouse lot. She was solid black and only twenty-nine inches tall at the shoulders. We named her Dinky because of her size. By this time, we had been informed she was not a Dexter at all but simply a dwarf Angus.

Just beginning to build our house, we hadn't taken time to build a good fence. Dinky, as a typical herding animal, found a way into our neighbor's field with his purebred white-faced Herefords. I was anxious about her getting pregnant, but my neighbor assured me that she was too short. The bull would not be able to service her. Duh. By the time we had finished the house and added more cows to our pasture, it was evident Dinky was expecting.

As D-day drew near, I'd been careful to watch her the past week because it was evident she couldn't go much longer. Her little rear was getting puffy and her bag was unbelievable for such a wee cow, in fact, I doubt if there were more than five inches between her udders and the ground. I noticed that she hadn't come up with the rest of the cows yesterday nor again this morning as I went out to feed the new calves. Not unusual, since cows often separate themselves when they calve. I decided to see if she had had her calf.

After washing the nipple bucket, I trudged down into the woods. Near the creek at the bottom I glimpsed a black blob. I called—all our cows knew their names. She stood up and looked at me. I could tell she was not feeling well. "Oh, you are just sleeping in this morning. Well I don't blame you. I would too if I were in your condition."

Immediately I began to pray. There was a possibility that the calf would be too large for such a small cow. Deciding to leave the problem in the Lord's hands, I returned to the house to try getting some writing done; my writer's group would be meeting tomorrow. I was typing away when, right in the middle of my thoughts, the Holy Spirit began to nag me about Dinky. I could get no peace until I stopped and went to check on her.

I walked back down the hill and sure enough she had moved across the creek and there was something hanging out of her rear. Hurrying back to the house, I called Dr. Pucket. The line was busy so I drove over to the doctor's house instead. Good thing too, because he was just about to turn out of his driveway to go to a hog sale. He came home with me and looked over the situation. I explained my concern—small cow, maybe big calf.

Well, she was not as bad off as I thought. In fact she proved to be in better shape than either the doctor or me. When we got to the bottom of the hill she stood up and by this time a small bag filled with a liquid resembling blown up bubble gum was hanging out. Dinky took off running. We chased her all over the small section on the far side of the creek trying to throw a rope over her. She crossed the creek and I chased her all over the steep slope on this side of the creek. It was no use.

Finally, Dr. Pucket said, "She's not that far along. Why don't you see if you can have your children help catch her after school and I'll be through at 5:00 and come back." Then adding belatedly, "But I will only deliver the calf if you can get her up out of this narrow wooded valley."

I began to pray as I checked on Dinky periodically. At 4:00 it was evident that she was straining and in great pain. I began to pray in earnest. The kids had come home and we were just getting ready to go catch her when the doctor drove in. He had finished early. Adam and Karan and I got Dinky into our little pen. Adam managed to get a rope on her and Dr. Pucket went to work.

We could see little white toenails sticking out. Meanwhile all four of our other cows lined up on the outside of the pen to watch the show.

The doctor sprinkled his arm and his hands with disinfectant and reached down inside. He said that the head was not yet in the birth canal. He reached in to see if he could start it. He decided he would have to apply pressure. At this point he reached in with two little chains attached them to the legs of the calf. Then he said, "Which do you want to save, the calf or the cow?" How could I make that decision? I had been praying all afternoon for a safe delivery for cow *and* calf. I, being unable to make the decision, the doctor decided. The calf would have to go.

So he handed the chains to Adam and the other man and told them to pull as hard as they could after he positioned the head. They pulled and suddenly fell backward. The chain had let go. The doctor stuck his hand back in again and brought it out covered with blood. He couldn't tell if it was Dinky that was bleeding or the calf. When he grabbed the head again he decided that it was too big to come out the birth canal. So now he would have to cut our little cow open. He left to get his instruments while we started clearing out our 8' by 12' utility barn, the only out building that we had at that time. Rain was threatening, and we needed shelter for Dinky after the operation.

My husband, Harvey, drove in, and after he changed clothes he helped me get Dinky up to the front of our little storage barn at the top of the ridge. He and Adam loaded the stuff from the small barn into the truck to make room for Dinky, while Karan fed both the Holstein calves and I rushed back to the house to put on some stew.

By the time we had all finished our preparations the doctor showed up. He ordered me to get an old sheet and some towels. He gave Dinky a shot while Harvey held the rope. After she succumbed and collapsed to the ground, Harvey and the doctor tied her front legs together and then tied them to our tractor's trailer. Next they tied her back legs together and Harvey stood on that rope stretching her out tight.

Then the Doctor applied a local anesthetic to the place for the incision and shaved her side. He sprayed adhesive to the shaved area and smoothed the sheet over it. Then he cut out the sheet exposing the bare skin leaving the rest of the sheet covering her body. *What a neat way to keep the wound clean* I thought as I recognized the reason for the sheet.

With the scalpel he made a cut from above her hip to the bottom of her belly. He went through several layers of fat and muscle and lifted out some of her large intestines. He felt around for the uterus and tried to take it out before he cut it open. But it was too large. So he cut it while it while it remained in place. He reached down inside to grab the calf's leg and felt it thrash about. He exclaimed, "Well I'll be, the little devil is still alive."

Since I had started praying and committing both the cow and calf to the Lord from the time that I knew she was in labor, I let out with, "Praise God, Hallelujah!" as he pulled out the calf.

The doctor tossed the limp "goop" covered body to Karan and me and said, "I don't have time to fool with the calf, so take those towels and rub. Don't be gentle." Soon Karan and I had rubbed off most of the slime and the calf was breathing quite well. (In a normal birth the mother cow would lick the calf clean.) We put the calf aside on some hay until she could get over her grogginess.

Harvey began the task of getting some milk out of Dinky while she was still drugged. He put the milk into a calf bottle and began feeding the calf, which in the meantime had stood up. It was a long legged, white face black, which later proved to be half as tall as Dinky.

Dinky, still groggy, stood. We managed to get her and the calf into the little barn and placed a piece of plywood against the open barn doors so they would have some light. (The little barn was windowless.) As we worked, curiosity caused our other cows to line up again like a spectator's gallery.

The next morning the plywood barrier was down, the calf was alone, and Dinky was gone. Harvey could not persuade Dinky to come back. About noon she came for the calf and broke down the barricade again. Then she waddled up the hill with the little calf teetering along side. It was really cute. It was like saying "none of this barn stuff for me. I'm taking my family to the pasture just like regular cows." It was funny, since Dinky was obviously the bottom of the pecking order.

When the doctor left the night before, he gave Harvey orders to administer 20cc of penicillin to Dinky for three days. He also left him a syringe. I guess he expected us to keep Dinky in the barn. When Harvey got home that evening, it was pouring down rain. (Nothing is ever easy.) We donned our rain gear and went out to coax her up with some feed so we could give her the shot. But we couldn't get near enough. In exasperation, Harvey lunged at her and barely managed to stick the needle in her hip. The jab sent her flying furiously around the pasture with the hypo bobbing as she went. We took time out to eat supper then tried again without success. Talk about answers to prayer. That cow was not the least bit sickly.

That evening we went down to the local country filling station to get something and Harvey told several of the old men gathered there about the trouble we had had. We had told them earlier that the calf was born by caesarean section. They evidently didn't know what that meant. They began to talk about how they had helped the doctor before and asked, "Did he use his machine to jack up the cow?" Whatever that meant.

" No," Harvey told them, "He cut it out of her."

"The calf lived?" they asked in shock. They had never heard of such a thing. But in my mind I knew the reason. God did it through prayer.

But it wasn't over yet. I spent another restless and prayerful night. The next morning at the crack of dawn I donned rain gear once more and set out to assess the damage. The calf was in the barn but it looked like Dinky had not been there. I went down into the woods, but she was not there. I finally found her, grazing with the other cows on the other side of the ridge.

Meanwhile, Harvey had called the doctor to find out what to do. He said if Dinky was up and around not to worry about the needle because it would fester and fall out. Just try to feed the calf until we find out if Dinky was going to take care of her. Harvey fed Freckles from the bottle. (We named the calf Freckles because she was a white faced back with several black spots across the bridge of her nose.)

Just then, up walked Dusty, our curious six-month-old bull. While he was sniffing the new arrival, the other cows joined him, including Dinky. The calf emptied the bottle and was looking around for more. She approached Dusty thinking he must be Mama and started reaching under his legs looking for a spigot. He did several dances trying to get away while we all laughed. During the dances Dinky tried to get the calf to come to her. She finally succeeded, but the calf went round and round looking for the faucets. She was looking too high. Finally locating them she got down on her knees and emptied the bag.

This was but one of the many times the Lord aided our cattle raising, however, Freckles was the favored, most blessed cow of our nineteen years in the business. She was the tamest calf ever born on our farm. From the time she was little you could walk right up to her and pet her. I suppose that's because we were with her from the moment of birth. Later, when she grew up, she became the boss of all the cows yet so tame we could safely put grandchildren on her back. Born in 1978, she gave us many calves while living to the age of sixteen, a ripe old age for a cow. She is buried in the pasture behind our house, gone but not forgotten. Nor will we ever forget her mother, Dinky, our very first, and, probably, only, "holy" cow.

Meet Your Authors

Michael Anderson operated the award-winning New Song Christian bookstores (now Family Christian Stores) in Canton and Woodstock, GA from 1986-1999. Mike co-founded the Cherokee Christian Writers Group with Cheryl Norwood in 2000, which grew into the Christian Authors Guild, where he serves as Treasurer. Anderson has a love for writing and has published stories in the acclaimed God Allows U-Turns book series, and numerous magazines. He is a regular reviewer for Aspiring Retail magazine, the official publication of the Christian Booksellers Association. Anderson enjoys helping new Christian bookstores grow through his personal consulting ministry. He and his wife, Kathy, live in Ball Ground, Georgia, and are members of First Baptist Church Canton. The Andersons have two adult sons, both in full-time ministry.

Diana J. Baker, a graduate of the University of Southern Mississippi and the Institute of Children's Literature, is President and Historian of Christian Authors Guild. She is a Copy Editor and writer for *Christian Living Magazine*, co-author of a book for teens, and has articles published in *Focus on the Family* ministries, in *Christian Living* magazine, and in several anthology books. Diana and her husband, Larry, have been married for 36 years and have served as pastors of Prayer and Praise Christian Fellowship in Woodstock, Georgia for 25 years. Diana is an ordained minister, freelance writer, teacher, songwriter, and pianist. Her favorite hobbies are reading and collecting. Diana enjoys her collections of fast food toys, dolls, bean bag toys, kitchen antiques, old children's books, antique cameras, and children's games. Diana and Larry have three daughters, two son-in-laws, and eight grandchildren.

Farrow Beacham is a manufacturing technology consultant. Lately he is cultivating gourmet mushrooms for several restaurants in the Atlanta area. Currently he is the editor of our newsletter, The Wave, and the webmaster of our web site. He is also the newsletter editor and webmaster for the Mushroom Club of Georgia. Farrow has been the technical advisor to Ascension Monastery, in Resaca, Georgia for over 20 years, where he and his wife of 34 years, Pam, attend church. The monastery is affiliated with the Jerusalem Orthodox Church. His hobby outside of writing is collecting and promoting study of wild mushrooms with the Mushroom Club of Georgia.

Marcus Beavers was born and raised in Atlanta, Georgia. He graduated from Georgia Military Academy (now Woodward Academy) and Georgia State University. In the late 1960's, he served in the U.S. Army as an artillery officer, stationed in Germany. He was awarded the Army Commendation Medal and given Honorable Discharge from the Army while in Germany. In Europe he traveled for ten months before returning to the states. It was during this time in 1970, that he became a student at L'Abri, a study center directed by Francis A. Schaeffer in Switzerland. Since that time he has traveled to India, Bhutan and Nepal. Married for 34 years, he and his wife have three sons, and live in Canton, GA. Retired from the Dept. of Veteran Affairs, Marcus enjoys fulfilling a desire to write.

David Beck was born and raised in Atlanta, Georgia. He graduated from Georgia State University with a bachelor's degree in Political Science in 1989. During the 1990's, he played guitar in the gospel music group, *White Harvest.*

Afterwards, he earned a M.C.S.E and worked in computer support. Recently, Beck began to focus on his writing gift.

Judy Becker was born in Evanston, Illinois in 1932 while her Methodist preacher dad was in Seminary. She graduated from Marietta College, Marietta, Ohio with a BS degree in Geology in 1953.

Becker has been writing for a number of years, mostly in the Christian field. She has taught every age from kindergarten to young adults, and conducted many Ladies Bible Studies. Interest Magazine (the Plymouth Brethren official magazine), published her first article in May 1972 entitled, *The Fulfilled Woman.* It was so well received that it was reprinted in pamphlet form in English, in Spanish twice (once for Spain and once for Santo Domingo), in French (for a French Canadian magazine), and translated into Czechoslovakian, where it was smuggled in a woman's girdle into the then Communist country.

Since then, she has published two editions of a book on Revelation, currently available as *Rightly Dividing The Book Of Revelation,* finally using her Science background to explain the physical judgments.

In addition to teaching and writing on Biblical subjects, Becker is an avid gardener and has had an article, *Winter Garden* published in Back Home Magazine. For more about Judy and her books visit her web page at www.JEBecker.com. Judy is a mother of five, grandmother of sixteen, and great grandmother of nineteen, (plus three expected after this publication).

Lloyd Blackwell grew up in Alabama, graduated from the University of Alabama and eventually moved to Marietta, Georgia in 1966. Retiring in 1994 from a successful business career, he is married, has three daughters and six grandchildren. He has many interests and two great passions. His two great passions are mission involvement and world travel. Blackwell has traveled in all 50 states and in 173 countries. A CNN TV reporter called him "one of the most traveled persons on earth." Some of his adventures include expeditions to the North Pole, Antarctica and four personally organized expeditions into the Amazon Jungle in South America. He has been involved in missions in 42 states and 51 countries since 1970. As a Gideon he has distributed New Testaments in 42 countries. Mission activity included preaching in Africa and Romania in addition to his other missionary involvement. Blackwell has authored two books, *A Journey of Discovery* and *A journey of Faith*, as memoirs of these life adventures. He is a freelance writer and has taught *Writing Your Life Story* and *Creative Writing 101* for six years. Other relevant involvement includes 35 years of lay leadership at his church, 19 years with Builders For Christ and 15 years with the Noonday Baptist Association. He was inducted into *Who's Who Among Outstanding Americans in 1994.*

R.T. Byrum, Past President of the Christian Author's Guild (CAG), is the published author of three of eight completed Carver Cousins books based on his lifetime love of adventure. *The Mystery of the Shrieking Island, The Phantom Bridge,* and *Flight Into Terror,* have been selected as featured books for the 'International I Love To Write Day' events. He has published two career guidance books for Lucent Books, and has written a number of print and online magazines. Byrum is also compiler and a contributor to all three of CAG's anthologies. His resume includes: disk jockey, host of a CBC children's show, visiting professor of broadcast communications, and writer, producer, and director of commercials, specials, and news reports. Byrum has served as a lay pastor and as a volunteer chaplain. The author currently divides his time between homes in Georgia and Florida with his favorite literary critic, his wife, Karen. His books and other information may be found online at www.rtbwriter.com.

Donald Conkey was born near Caseville, Michigan in 1927, and graduated from Michigan State University. He was a professional lobbyist for many years before entering management. He has edited and written articles for numerous publications, and published his family history, gathered over 40 years, in twelve books. Since 1995, Conkey has written a weekly ed/op column for the Cherokee Tribune (Georgia) with nearly 350 columns published to date. An avid student of history, he currently publishes a weekly international e-newsletter on *Constitutional Principles and History*. Other credits include an essay entitled *Life After Suicide*, and *A Family Text Book on Government*. In 2005 he was awarded the prestigious Liberty Bell Award for his writing on government.

Cheryl Davis was born in Atlanta, grew up in the south side of the Metro area, and has lived in a log home adjacent to the property that was the model for Margaret Mitchell's Tara. It was there that she wrote her historical novel about the Revolutionary War in Georgia, *Hope Is Constant*, which won her publisher's (Treble Heart Books) Best Historical Award. A second novel, Southern Complications, will soon be published by Whiskey Creek Press. She currently lives on an unpaved, country road complete with a neglected cemetery with the graves of Civil War veterans and an abandoned railroad—the perfect atmosphere for an avid history buff.

Charlene Elder was encouraged to write by one of her elementary school teachers and continued her passion of writing through high school, college, and while raising her family. She and her husband, Jack, wrote and published a Christian-based newsletter, The Salt Shaker, for over 20 years. Together they pastored churches in Southern California and Georgia. They have a nationwide Prison Ministry that provides Bible Courses to prisoners. She earned a B.A., M.A., and Doctorate in the fields of Sociology, Psychology, and Ministry. For the past 15 years, she has worked for an environmental consulting firm in the Atlanta area. She enjoys spending her free time writing, creating crafts, hiking, and enjoying her two-year old granddaughter, Aleena. She and her husband have been married for over 31 years, live in Woodstock, Georgia, have two grown children, and will welcome their second grandchild, Dorian Robert, this summer. They are working together on a historical novel.

Jack Elder, a member of the Christian Authors Guild, is a freelance writer who enjoys writing historical fiction, as well as hiking and golf. He lives with his wife of 31 years in Woodstock, Georgia. They have four children and six grandchildren. Elder has been involved in the ministry for 30 years and is the President of Salt Mine Ministries, a prison ministry that supplies Bible Courses that he and his wife Charlene authored. Retired from IBM as a field service engineer, he presently works as a supervisor for Heidelberg, the premier printing press company. Elder has received numerous educational degrees, including doctorates in Ministry and Theology.

Robert Ellis has authored dialogue for nine Christmas pageants, a number of dramatic sketches, and *The Journey,* a three-act evangelical play. *The Journey* was performed numerous times in his church, and in a Nashville church. Ellis has been published by the National Drama Service, and has written song lyrics used in a Christmas pageant. He has also been published in the two prior books produced by CAG. He dedicates his contributions in this book to his wife, Nanci, who has enjoyed and endured the forty-one year journey with him. Robert, now retired, is the father of three, and grandfather of five, and makes his home with Nanci in Marietta, Georgia.

Jennifer Evans worked nearly 10 years, as a literacy specialist in the Philippines. She spent her spare time writing a women's Bible study entitled *Diamonds in the Rough, Jewels in the Making* which has been used throughout that country. One of her children's book, *Gaya's Gift,* was published there in diglot (English/Tagalog). She has written feature articles for one of Manila's nationally distributed newspapers, *The Philippine Star*, and any in-house technical pieces for publications of the mission organization she was serving. Evans has written curriculum for using vernacular storybooks and scripture in Filipino schools. She has been a ghost-writer for administrative correspondence and personal newsletters, and still writes promotional and motivational materials. She enjoys writing poetry and has authored several fiction short stories. Having completed six biographical stories, she continues work on her own autobiography, and recently submitted her first non-fiction book for publication. Jennifer and her husband, Gary, live in Canton, Georgia.

Visit her at: http://home.earthlink.net/~jennyevans2/

Bonnie Greenwood Grant's roots lie in Spokane, Washington. Her father, a radio operator, was recruited by the CIA when she was six years old. She grew up overseas in Nicosia, Cyprus, Frankfurt, Germany and Athens, Greece. Grant entered college at seventeen at the University of Washington. After three years of study in physical and cultural anthropology and archaeology she took a hiatus and later received an associate degree in Early Childhood Education at age thirty five, and eventually, at fifty, she graduated with a BA in Psychology from Kennesaw State University. Bonnie has been married 42 years and has four children and two fantastic granddaughters. She is an avid soccer player, health nut and wood carver specializing in large Carousel animals. She volunteers in Marietta Project Outreach, a Christian multiracial leadership training program. Bonnie has worked for various Federal Agencies including CIA, IRS, and ten years as a rural mail carrier for the U.S. Postal Service. She co-edited a postal service news letter and has completed two novels.

Robert Graves is the author of *The Gospel According to Angels* (Chosen Books/1998) and *Praying in the Spirit* (Chosen Books/1987). His writings have appeared in *Moody Monthly, Christian Parenting Today, Ministries Today, Pentecostal Evangel, Church of God Evangel, HiCall, Christ for All, Paraclete, The Pneuma Review*, and other publications. He has a master's degree in English from Georgia State University and has taught writing at Georgia State University, Kennesaw State University, and Southwestern Assemblies of God College in Waxahachie, Texas. He is the president of Robert W. Graves and Associates, a real estate firm specializing in land and easement acquisition for local governments and developers. Robert and his wife, Debbie (Hamby), originally from Marietta, Georgia, now reside in Woodstock, Georgia.

Shelley Hussey is a wife, mom, small business owner, and humor author and speaker. She has been a Faith & Values columnist for her local newspaper, contributed stories to several books and e-newsletters—including *Heartwarmers* and *Petwarmers*—and has penned a nonfiction work *titled I'm Not OK, You're Not OK, But That's OK With God.* Subtitle: *Finding the Humor and Healing in Life.* Hussey has also recorded a CD titled "Divine Secrets of the Boa," which is a compilation of her most popular "Shameless Hussey" e-columns. Information about her book, CD, and how to become a "Shameless Hussey" is at her website: www.shelleyhussey.com.

Anita C. Lee and her husband of 36 years recently moved from the Atlanta, GA, area to Albuquerque, NM., where they are closer to their grown children and grandchild. Anita's publishing credits include a weekly column for two years in Plano, TX; writing features for an Atlanta suburban paper; and children's curriculum for the United Methodist Publishing House. She is now a full-time freelance writer and speaker, and writes both fiction and non-fiction. Anita holds bachelor and master's degrees in education and has taught in the United States, Japan, and China. She presently teaches a cyberclass for Lamar University, Beaumont, TX, on writing memoirs called, *Your Life, Your Story.* She is a C.L.A.S.S. (Christian Leaders, Authors, and Speakers Services) graduate and is a Certified Personalities Trainer. Her hobbies include international travel, choral singing (including a performance at Carnegie Hall), flower gardening, and watercolor painting. Information about her writing and speaking can be found on her website at www.AltarEgos.com or www.AnitaCLee.com.

Burl McCosh has written numerous poems, typically with a theme of Christian living, and several gospel songs. His primary purpose in writing is to express ideas and to entertain in a clean and wholesome fashion. Having spent sixteen years doing technical writing in the electric power industry, he enjoys the release and freedom of non-technical writing. He has a degree and post-graduate work in biology. McCosh, his lovely wife Shelly, and three daughters reside in Canton, Georgia and are active in the ministry of their church in Kennesaw, Georgia. They enjoy taking family vacations together in different locations, the more exotic the better. Fishing is one of the author's favorite ways of relaxing.

Judy Parrott is a prolific free-lance writer, self-publishing small books of inspiration and God's miracles. She and her husband Roger who have been married almost fifty years, live in the country near Cumming, Georgia, spend winters in Florida and summers in Michigan. They have ministered many years with an outreach to bikers, the Christian Motorcyclists Association, and attend Landmark Church in Norcross. They have three sons, ten grandchildren, and four great grandchildren; all live nearby. Her website, www.mindspring.com/~dparrott, is filled with many of her stories and articles.

Jeffrey W. Reeve is a freelance designer who has contributed book cover designs for all three published works of the Christian Authors Guild. He graduated in 1994 from the University of South Carolina with a Bachelor of Arts Degree and is currently working fulltime in the printing industry. When he isn't spending time with his wife and two boys, Jeff enjoys gourmet cooking and writing short fiction.

Rose-Wade Schambach , a native of Mississippi, holds a BS in Education from the University of Southern Mississippi.

She currently teaches Developmental English, Reading, and Business Psychology at Chattahoochee Technical College in Marietta, GA. She has been previously published on numerous websites including *Heartwarmers*, *2theHeart*, and *Write2theheart*, in addition to some local publications. The author and her husband, John, have been abundantly blessed with a blended family of twelve children. They enjoy sailing, gardening, and witnessing the latest antics of their uniquely different children. They are also motivational Christian speakers who enjoy sharing their testimony of the Lord's great love and restoration in their lives.

Susan M. Schulz is a Bible teacher, writer, aerobics instructor, wife, and mother of three who lives in Woodstock, Georgia. When she is not busy writing and teaching, she is with her brood listening to someone strum a guitar, watching someone paint, or playing on the family farm in the North Georgia Mountains. Her passion to encourage the children of God to hear His magnificent voice through prayer and Bible study has birthed Listening Hearts Ministries. A listening heart for 18 years, Susan has launched an e-mail distribution of devotions excerpted from her manuscript, *The Listening Heart: Practical Ways to Discern God's Voice*

Cynthia L. Simmons, native of Chattanooga, resides in Kennesaw Georgia with her husband Ray. She has five children and has taught them at home for nineteen years. She joined Christian Authors Guild in 2003 and published three short stories in *The Desk in the Attic.* In the spring of 2005, *NATHHAN NEWS* published an article she wrote about teaching her disabled son. Since she enjoys history, she is writing a biography and compiling a book of historical fiction. In addition to writing, she arranges flowers, grows orchids, sings, plays the piano, and studies musical composition. Her website, www.clsimmons.com contains more information about her and her work.

Scarlett Smith is a 2001 Amy Foundation Award winner for her story, *The Gift of a Child*, published in the Atlanta Journal Constitution. As a member of the Christian Authors Guild, she contributed four essays in their book, *Stepping Stones,* published in 2003 and one in the 2004 book, *Desk in the Attic.* Smith teaches a class for young writers at a local YMCA. At her church, she has led writing groups to encourage seasoned and latent writers. She has also edited the Perinatal Loss Department's newsletter for Northside Hospital in Atlanta for many years. Originally, from the Midwest, Smith graduated from Iowa State University with a B.S. in Family Services.

Brenda Thompson Ward has one published novel, *Hannah's Awakening,* and is currently preparing her second novel for publication while working on her third novel. Brenda lives in Woodstock, Georgia and with her husband and is the mother of three grown children, and grandmother of five. She and her husband are actively involved in the ministry of Shiloh Hills Baptist Church in Kennesaw, Georgia where she teaches a Ladies Bible Study, enjoys singing in the choir, and her husband, John, is the administrator of Shiloh Hills Christian School.

Nancy Weber is a native of Milwaukee, Wisconsin, where she was a portrait artist and musician. While living in central Florida, she raised a family of 5. Surviving both divorce and widowhood, she enjoys a new life with her husband, Bob. They live in Marietta, GA where they are members of St. Ann's

Catholic church. Their families and 10 grandchildren fill their lives with joy. She is a retired Oncology R.N., but spent her middle years as an ordained minister. A Home Bible Study grew into an international ministry where God opened doors for her in missionary work in Africa, the Far East, and the former Soviet Union. She authored 3 books, *Tormented? God's keys to life*, *Beyond Survival*, and *Behind The Crisis; An Unseen War* (all published in several languages). She has also been a Pastoral counselor, prison minister, seminar and retreat speaker, newsletter editor, TV and radio call-in talk show guest, ACOA recovery group leader, and producer of inspirational radio shows. She enjoys golfing, swimming, biking, gardening, and is now working on her second movie documentary of God's love.

Printed in the United States
34820LVS00003B/52-510